Enid Opal Cox, DSW
Elizabeth S. Kelchner, MSW, ACSW
Rosemary Chapin, PhD, MSW
Editors

Gerontological Social Work Practice: Issues, Challenges, and Potential

Gerontological Social Work Practice: Issues, Challenges, and Potential has been co-published simultaneously as *Journal of Gerontological Social Work*, Volume 36, Numbers 3/4 2001.

Pre-publication
REVIEWS,
COMMENTARIES,
EVALUATIONS . . .

"**D**OES A GREAT JOB of helping social work professionals focus on ways to be more responsive to the increasing number of older clients. . . . Focuses on diversity, multicultural and international issues, shaping a research agenda, educational preparation, transforming social policy, and labor force and residential issues. The chapter authors, who are leaders in social work and aging, highlight the progress in these various domains, but also focus on areas where practice and policy need to develop further."

Nancy P. Kropf, PhD
Associate Professor
and Associate Dean
University of Georgia
School of Social Work

THSWPP

The Haworth Social Work Practice Press
An Imprint of The Haworth Press, Inc.

Gerontological Social Work Practice: Issues, Challenges, and Potential

Gerontological Social Work Practice: Issues, Challenges, and Potential has been co-published simultaneously as *Journal of Gerontological Social Work*, Volume 36, Numbers 3/4 2001.

The *Journal of Gerontological Social Work* Monographic "Separates"

Below is a list of "separates," which in serials librarianship means a special issue simultaneously published as a special journal issue or double-issue *and* as a "separate" hardbound monograph. (This is a format which we also call a "DocuSerial.")

"Separates" are published because specialized libraries or professionals may wish to purchase a specific thematic issue by itself in a format which can be separately cataloged and shelved, as opposed to purchasing the journal on an on-going basis. Faculty members may also more easily consider a "separate" for classroom adoption.

"Separates" are carefully classified separately with the major book jobbers so that the journal tie-in can be noted on new book order slips to avoid duplicate purchasing.

You may wish to visit Haworth's website at . . .

http://www.HaworthPress.com

. . . to search our online catalog for complete tables of contents of these separates and related publications.

You may also call 1-800-HAWORTH (outside US/Canada: 607-722-5857), or Fax 1-800-895-0582 (outside US/Canada: 607-771-0012), or e-mail at:

getinfo@haworthpressinc.com

Gerontological Social Work Practice: Issues, Challenges, and Potential, edited by Enid Opal Cox, DSW, Elizabeth S. Kelchner, MSW, ACSW, and Rosemary Chapin, PhD, MSW (Vol. 36, No. 3/4, 2001). *This book gives you an essential overview of the role, status, and potential of gerontological social work in aging societies around the world. Drawing on the expertise of leaders in the field, it identifies key policy and practice issues and suggests directions for the future. Here you'll find important perspectives on home health care, mental health, elder abuse, older workers' issues, and death and dying, as well as an examination of the policy and practice issues of utmost concern to social workers dealing with the elderly.*

Social *Work Practice with the Asian American Elderly,* edited by Namkee G. Choi, PhD (Vol. 36, No. 1/2, 2001). *"Encompasses the richness of diversity among Asian Americans by including articles on Vietnamese, Japanese, Chinese, Taiwanese, Asian Indian, and Korean Americans." (Nancy R. Hooyman, PhD, MSW, Professor and Dean Emeritus, University of Washington School of Social Work, Seattle)*

Grandparents as Carers of Children with Disabilities: Facing the Challenges, edited by Philip McCallion, PhD, ACSW, and Matthew Janicki, PhD (Vol. 33, No. 3, 2000). *Here is the first comprehensive consideration of the unique needs and experiences of grandparents caring for children with developmental disabilities. The vital information found here will assist practitioners, administrators, and policymakers to include the needs of this special population in the planning and delivery of services, and it will help grandparents in this situation to better care for themselves as well as for the children in their charge.*

Latino Elders and the Twenty-First Century: Issues and Challenges for Culturally Competent Research and Practice, edited by Melvin Delgado, PhD (Vol. 30, No. 1/2, 1998). *Explores the challenges that gerontological social work will encounter as it attempts to meet the needs of the growing number of Latino elders utilizing culturally competent principles.*

Dignity and Old Age, edited by Rose Dobrof, DSW, and Harry R. Moody, PhD (Vol. 29, No. 2/3, 1998). *"Challenges us to uphold the right to age with dignity, which is embedded in the heart and soul of every man and woman." (H. James Towey, President, Commission on Aging with Dignity, Tallahassee, FL)*

Intergenerational Approaches in Aging: Implications for Education, Policy and Practice, edited by Kevin Brabazon, MPA, and Robert Disch, MA (Vol. 28, No. 1/2/3, 1997). *"Provides a wealth of concrete examples of areas in which intergenerational perspectives and knowledge are needed." (Robert C. Atchley, PhD, Director, Scribbs Gerontology Center, Miami University)*

Social Work Response to the White House Conference on Aging: From Issues to Actions, edited by Constance Corley Saltz, PhD, LCSW (Vol. 27, No. 3, 1997). *"Provides a framework for the discussion of issues relevant to social work values and practice, including productive aging, quality of life, the psychological needs of older persons, and family issues." (Jordan I. Kosberg, PhD, Professor and PhD Program Coordinator, School of Social Work, Florida International University, North Miami, FL)*

Special Aging Populations and Systems Linkages, edited by M. Joanna Mellor, DSW (Vol. 25, No. 1/2, 1996). *"An invaluable tool for anyone working with older persons with special needs." (Irene Gutheil, DSW, Associate Professor, Graduate School of Social Service, Fordham University)*

New Developments in Home Care Services for the Elderly: Innovations in Policy, Program, and Practice, edited by Lenard W. Kaye, DSW (Vol. 24, No. 3/4, 1995). *"An excellent compilation. . . . Especially pertinent to the functions of administrators, supervisors, and case managers in home care. . . . Highly recommended for every home care agency and a must for administrators and middle managers." (Geriatric Nursing Book Review)*

Geriatric Social Work Education, edited by M. Joanna Mellor, DSW, and Renee Solomon, DSW (Vol. 18, No. 3/4, 1992). *"Serves as a foundation upon which educators and fieldwork instructors can build courses that incorporate more aging content." (SciTech Book News)*

Vision and Aging: Issues in Social Work Practice, edited by Nancy D. Weber, MSW (Vol. 17, No. 3/4, 1992). *"For those involved in vision rehabilitation programs, the book provides practical information and should stimulate readers to revise their present programs of care." (Journal of Vision Rehabilitation)*

Health Care of the Aged: Needs, Policies, and Services, edited by Abraham Monk, PhD (Vol. 15, No. 3/4, 1990). *"The chapters reflect firsthand experience and are competent and informative. Readers . . . will find the book rewarding and useful. The text is timely, appropriate, and well-presented." (Health & Social Work)*

Twenty-Five Years of the Life Review: Theoretical and Practical Considerations, edited by Robert Disch, MA (Vol. 12, No. 3/4, 1989). *This practical and thought-provoking book examines the history and concept of the life review.*

Gerontological Social Work: International Perspectives, edited by Merl C. Hokenstad, Jr., PhD, and Katherine A. Kendall, PhD (Vol. 12, No. 1/2, 1988). *"Makes a very useful contribution in examining the changing role of the social work profession in serving the elderly." (Journal of the International Federation on Ageing)*

Gerontological Social Work Practice with Families: A Guide to Practice Issues and Service Delivery, edited by Rose Dobrof, DSW (Vol. 10, No. 1/2, 1987). *An in-depth examination of the importance of family relationships within the context of social work practice with the elderly.*

Ethnicity and Gerontological Social Work, edited by Rose Dobrof, DSW (Vol. 9, No. 4, 1987). *"Addresses the issues of ethnicity with great sensitivity. Most of the topics addressed here are rarely addressed in other literature." (Dr. Milada Disman, Department of Behavioral Science, University of Toronto)*

Social Work and Alzheimer's Disease, edited by Rose Dobrof, DSW (Vol. 9, No. 2, 1986). *"New and innovative social work roles with Alzheimer's victims and their families in both hospital and non-hospital settings." (Continuing Education Update)*

Gerontological Social Work Practice in the Community, edited by George S. Getzel, DSW and M. Joanna Mellor, DSW (Vol. 8, No. 3/4, 1985). *"A wealth of information for all practitioners who deal with the elderly. An excellent reference for faculty, administrators, clinicians, and graduate students in nursing and other service professions who work with the elderly." (American Journal of Care for the Aging)*

Gerontological Social Work in Home Health Care, edited by Rose Dobrof, DSW (Vol. 7, No. 4, 1984). *"A useful window onto the home health care scene in terms of current forms of service provided to the elderly and the direction of social work practice in this field today." (PRIDE Institute Journal)*

The Uses of Reminiscence: New Ways of Working with Older Adults, edited by Marc Kaminsky (Vol. 7, No. 1/2, 1984). *"Rich in ideas for anyone working with life review groups." (Guidepost)*

A Healthy Old Age: A Sourcebook for Health Promotion with Older Adults, edited by Stephanie FallCreek, MSW, and Molly K. Mettler, MSW (Vol. 6, No. 2/3, 1984). *"An outstanding text on the 'how-tos' of health promotion for elderly persons." (Physical Therapy)*

Gerontological Social Work Practice in Long-Term Care, edited by George S. Getzel, DSW, and M. Joanna Mellor, DSW (Vol. 5, No. 1/2, 1983). *"Veteran practitioners and graduate social work students will find the book insightful and a valuable prescriptive guide to the dos and don'ts of practice in their daily work." (The Gerontologist)*

Gerontological Social Work Practice: Issues, Challenges, and Potential

Enid Opal Cox, DSW
Elizabeth S. Kelchner, MSW, ACSW
Rosemary Chapin, PhD, MSW
Editors

Gerontological Social Work Practice: Issues, Challenges, and Potential has been co-published simultaneously as *Journal of Gerontological Social Work*, Volume 36, Numbers 3/4 2001.

The Haworth Social Work Practice Press
An Imprint of
The Haworth Press, Inc.
New York • London • Oxford

Published by

The Haworth Social Work Practice Press, 10 Alice Street, Binghamton, NY 13904-1580 USA

The Haworth Social Work Practice Press is an imprint of The Haworth Press, Inc., 10 Alice Street, Binghamton, NY 13904-1580 USA.

Gerontological Social Work Practice: Issues, Challenges, and Potential has been co-published simultaneously as *Journal of Gerontological Social Work*, Volume 36, Numbers 3/4 2001.

Cover design by Thomas J. Mayshock Jr.

Library of Congress Cataloging-in-Publication Data

Gerontological Social Work Practice / Enid Opal Cox, Elizabeth S. Kelchner, Rosemary Chapin, editors.
    p. cm.
    "Published also as Journal of Gerontological Social Work, volume 36, numbers 3/4 2001."
    Includes bibliographical references and index.
    ISBN 0-7890-1940-X (hard : alk. paper)–ISBN 0-7890-1941-8 (pbk: alk. paper)
    1. Social work with the aged–United States. I. Cox, Enid Opal, 1941- II. Kelchner, Elizabeth S. III. Chapin, Rosemary Kennedy.
HV1461 .G477 2001
362.6–dc21
                                        2002005629

Indexing, Abstracting & Website/Internet Coverage

This section provides you with a list of major indexing & abstracting services. That is to say, each service began covering this periodical during the year noted in the right column. Most Websites which are listed below have indicated that they will either post, disseminate, compile, archive, cite or alert their own Website users with research-based content from this work. (This list is as current as the copyright date of this publication.)

Abstracting, Website/Indexing Coverage . . . . Year When Coverage Began

- *Abstracts in Social Gerontology: Current Literature on Aging* **1989**

- *Academic Abstracts/CD-ROM* **1993**

- *Academic Search: data base of 2,000 selected academic serials, updated monthly: EBSCO Publishing* **1995**

- *Academic Search Elite (EBSCO)* **1995**

- *AgeInfo CD-Rom* **1995**

- *AgeLine Database* **1993**

- *Alzheimer's Disease Education & Referral Center (ADEAR)* **1994**

- *Applied Social Sciences Index & Abstracts (ASSIA) (Online: ASSI via Data-Star) (CDRom: ASSIA Plus) <www.csa.com>* **1987**

- *Behavioral Medicine Abstracts* **1992**

- *Biosciences Information Service of Biological Abstracts (BIOSIS) a centralized source of life science information. <www.biosis.org>* . . **1993**

- *caredata CD: the social & community care database <www.scie.org.uk>* **1994**

(continued)

(continued)

*Special Bibliographic Notes related to special journal issues
(separates) and indexing/abstracting:*

- indexing/abstracting services in this list will also cover material in any "separate" that is co-published simultaneously with Haworth's special thematic journal issue or DocuSerial. Indexing/abstracting usually covers material at the article/chapter level.
- monographic co-editions are intended for either non-subscribers or libraries which intend to purchase a second copy for their circulating collections.
- monographic co-editions are reported to all jobbers/wholesalers/approval plans. The source journal is listed as the "series" to assist the prevention of duplicate purchasing in the same manner utilized for books-in-series.
- to facilitate user/access services all indexing/abstracting services are encouraged to utilize the co-indexing entry note indicated at the bottom of the first page of each article/chapter/contribution.
- this is intended to assist a library user of any reference tool (whether print, electronic, online, or CD-ROM) to locate the monographic version if the library has purchased this version but not a subscription to the source journal.
- individual articles/chapters in any Haworth publication are also available through the Haworth Document Delivery Service (HDDS).

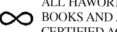

Gerontological Social Work Practice: Issues, Challenges, and Potential

CONTENTS

ABOUT THE EDITORS

Enid Opal Cox, DSW, is Director of the Institute of Gerontology, Professor of Social Work, and Director of the Doctoral Program at the University of Denver Graduate School of Social Work. Dr. Cox has extensive experience in gerontology, including program development and administration as well as teaching and research. She has special expertise and has published extensively on the development of empowerment-oriented practice with the elderly and issues of elder care receivers. She teaches in the area of aging policy and service delivery. Dr. Cox's current research focuses on intervention research for elder care receivers and other issues related to aging.

Elizabeth S. Kelchner, MSW, ACSW, is a doctoral student and adjunct faculty member at the Graduate School of Social Work, University of Denver. Her research interests include health care, intergenerational concerns, the integration of research and practice, issues related to forming and being a community, and issues concerning women. As Assistant Administrator of a long-term care facility in upstate New York, she was the principal investigator of a New York State Dementia Grant. She has over twenty-five years of social work experience, including direct and community practice. She is the author of an article on ageism published in the *Journal of Gerontological Social Work*. Her doctoral research concerns health care communications between physicians and older adults.

Rosemary Chapin, PhD, MSW, is Associate Professor at the University of Kansas School of Social Welfare. An award-winning teacher and scholar, she has extensive teaching, research, policy and program development experience in the long-term care arena. After receiving her PhD in Social Work at the University of Minnesota, she worked for the Minnesota Department of Human Services as a Research/Policy Analyst where she was involved in crafting numerous long-term care reform initiatives. Dr. Chapin joined the faculty of the University of Kansas School of Social Welfare in 1989. She currently teaches Social

Work and Aging and Social Policy in the KU MSW and PhD program. She also directs the Office of Aging and Long Term Care. Dr. Chapin was the 2001 recipient of the Budig Award for Excellence in Teaching. She has published numerous articles and book chapters in the area of long-term care policy and strengths-based practice with elders. She is currently developing interdisciplinary Web based education modules for gerontological professionals. She also recently coauthored a handbook on strengths-based care management for older adults.

Preface

This special edition was developed to stimulate the ongoing dialogue regarding the role, status, and potential of gerontological social work in an aging society. The consequences of rapid social change including internationalization and economic, demographic, and political/socio-cultural change for social policy, social services, and intervention approaches, as well as societal attitudes about aging and the elderly, are dramatic and require ongoing critical analysis. Beyond analysis gerontological social workers must develop multilevel strategies and act!

As a veteran of the past forty years of development of gerontological social work, I have witnessed the often-gallant efforts of social workers to meet the needs of older Americans. The mid-1960s and the 1970s allowed social workers through the auspices of community action programs (EOA sponsored), departments of social service, and the senior centers movement (often sponsored by OAA funds) to develop a variety of community-based intervention strategies. These strategies were community-based not only as services provided in the community, but rather as services directed toward developing community resiliency, mutual support, and strengthening self-help efforts. Both preventative and problem-solving interventions were often focused on education, fostering volunteerism, and based in the assumption of client and community strengths and potential. Social casework that was advocacy focused and the rudiments of empowerment and strengths-based models were well on their way. By the mid-1970s the medicalization of services and programs for older adults was gaining strength, and social work was drawn into this focus as funding for social models declined. The community mental health movement of the era also provided limited opportunity to focus on issues of older adults. This period supported the development of more sophisticated psychologically oriented models of gerontological social work. The growth of attention to program evalua-

[Haworth co-indexing entry note]: "Preface." Cox, Enid Opal. Co-published simultaneously in *Journal of Gerontological Social Work* (The Haworth Social Work Practice Press, an imprint of The Haworth Press, Inc.) Vol. 36, No. (3/4), 2001, pp. xxi-xxiii; and: *Gerontological Social Work Practice: Issues, Challenges, and Potential* (ed: Enid Opal Cox, Elizabeth S. Kelchner, and Rosemary Chapin) The Haworth Social Work Practice Press, an imprint of The Haworth Press, Inc., 2001, pp. xv-xvii. Single or multiple copies of this article are available for a fee from The Haworth Document Delivery Service [1-800-HAWORTH, 9:00 a.m. - 5:00 p.m. (EST). E-mail address: getinfo@haworthpressinc.com].

tion in the early 1970s and the beginning attention of academic social work research in aging received more emphasis in the 1980s and 1990s. Today more sophisticated research methods and measurement tools provide the opportunity for better documentation of intervention outcomes. However, this ongoing struggle within social work to both increase attention of the profession to aging issues and sustain development of effective practice interventions, has often been waged in reaction to larger environmental forces, through the isolated work of individuals and small groups, and without much attention and support from the profession of social work as a whole.

The increased recognition of the reality of aging in and of societies around the world and increased communication capacity may well afford both the attention and opportunity for a more organized gerontological social work response. Gerontological social work has the opportunity to capture the best in both community-oriented and individually-oriented interventions, document their effectiveness, and at the same time develop more effective political skills. In sum, social work has much to offer societal efforts to address changes related to aging populations and to the quality of life for elders and their families. We must, however, assess our potential contribution and find new ways to assure this contribution is realized. Authors in this volume challenge us to this end and suggest possible directions.

Jeanette C. Takamura, Fernando Torres-Gil, and Karra Bikson Moga present a provocative overview of the national and international context relative to aging. Both suggest the absolute necessity that social workers focus on the larger economic, political, and social issues and that we must find our way to the tables of national and international decision-making if we are to realize our ability to be of service to the elder population.

Morrow-Howell and Burnette provide us with an insightful overview regarding the status of current research and need for future research. The critical challenge of gerontological social work education is addressed by Rosen and Zlotnik. A brief overview of the state of gerontological social work in Canada and Japan including key policy directions is provided by Wells and Taylor and Inaba. These contextuating articles provide a comprehensive look at the challenges facing gerontological social workers.

The following articles address selected areas of gerontological social work practice. While space limitations did not allow presentations of a number of key areas of practice such as work in senior centers or work with volunteer programs, many issues and challenges are raised and potential strategies are suggested. Kaskie and Estes raise significant issues related to aging and mental health, an arena in which social work plays a significant role and overlaps in many areas of gerontological service. Kelchner focuses on the growing challenges in provision of adequate services to meet the needs of older residents of health related settings, while Hobart focuses specifically on concerns and social work interventions related to death and dying. St. James critically reviews isuues related to elder mistreatment and suggests specific challenges and directions for the profession. Ford and Hatchett provide an overview of issues and interventions as they relate specifically to older African American adults. Chapin and Cox, coming from different perspectives (strengths-based versus empowerment-oriented) social work practice with elders collaborate to suggest common grounds of the two approaches as well as differences. Dooley calls attention to the needs and potential social work contribution to the issue of older workers. The question for gerontological social workers is how do we find ways to carry on the dialogue and action necessary to address these challenges in a more collective and organized manner in the coming decades. How can we keep a strong linkage between those whom are developing and testing practice interventions and those who are skilled political advocates?

Enid Opal Cox, DSW

I wish to acknowledge the consultation and assistance I received from Dr. Barbara Silverstone and the late Dr. Rosalie Wolf in the development of this special edition.

Towards a New Era in Aging and Social Work

Jeanette C. Takamura, PhD, MSW

SUMMARY. Population aging presents an increasingly global community with one of the greatest social and health policy challenges in the emergent century. Despite this, the social work profession has been slow to demonstrate discernible interest in addressing the needs of growing numbers of older Americans and their families. If social work can embrace the opportunity which aging and other converging forces present, as have a cadre of social work educators, the profession may be able to position itself for leadership in the decades ahead. *[Article copies available for a fee from The Haworth Document Delivery Service: 1-800-HAWORTH. E-mail address: <getinfo@haworthpressinc.com> Website: <http://www.HaworthPress.com> © 2001 by The Haworth Press, Inc. All rights reserved.]*

KEYWORDS. Leadership, future of aging and social work, international aging and social work

Among the most complex issues to engage policy makers in the United States in this and in coming decades will be approaches to con-

Jeanette C. Takamura is Former Assistant Secretary for Aging, U.S. Department of Health and Human Services and Edward R. Roybal Endowed Chair for Gerontology and Public Service, California State University at Los Angeles, 5151 State University Drive, Los Angeles, CA 90032.

[Haworth co-indexing entry note]: "Towards a New Era in Aging and Social Work." Takamura, Jeanette C. Co-published simultaneously in *Journal of Gerontological Social Work* (The Haworth Social Work Practice Press, an imprint of The Haworth Press, Inc.) Vol. 36, No. (3/4), 2001, pp. 1-11; and: *Gerontological Social Work Practice: Issues, Challenges, and Potential* (ed: Enid Opal Cox, Elizabeth S. Kelchner, and Rosemary Chapin) The Haworth Social Work Practice Press, an imprint of The Haworth Press, Inc., 2001, pp. 1-11. Single or multiple copies of this article are available for a fee from The Haworth Document Delivery Service [1-800-HAWORTH, 9:00 a.m. - 5:00 p.m. (EST). E-mail address: getinfo@haworthpressinc.com].

tinue to assure the economic security of an aging population, to secure and sustain affordable access to health care including prescription drugs, and to assist families with the costs and care requirements entailed in providing long term care, whether informally or through formal service programs and institutions. Because of their economic scope and social implications, these are issues that will broadly impact the quality of life of all Americans, irrespective of age. They are among a growing number of thorny issues raised by population aging that are being examined and deliberated by multiple sectors–from finance to defense and health–of the international community. The influence of global perspectives and discussions of these much broader, multi-sectoral issues upon how health and social policy issues and feasible options are defined cannot be underestimated. This article is intended to provide a cursory introduction to some of the complex issues that are inevitable as aging concerns are further defined as among one of the broadest-reaching international challenges for the 21st century. It briefly notes other converging forces that have already begun to shape health and social policies, programs, and services within the United States, although less perceptibly than might be expected in the future, and it asserts that these can offer the social work profession the opportunity to strengthen its practice and relevance. Most importantly, it argues that the social work profession must come to terms with population aging as a reality and determine whether it has the interest and the will to be a visible, evidence-driven player in circles that will establish and articulate the policy agenda and alternatives which will inevitably affect social work practice.

THE GLOBAL DIMENSIONS OF POPULATION AGING

Aging issues were catapulted onto the world stage during the closing years of the 20th century. In 1997, at the urging of Japan, the G-8 Summit in Denver, Colorado, included on its policy agenda a discussion of aging as a global concern, focusing particularly upon the eight participant nations' labor force and pension, health, and long term care challenges. For Japan and many of the European nations in the developed world, the longevity revolution has long been underway. Currently at 17.1%, 16.4%, and 15.9% respectively of Japan's, Germany's, and France's populations, persons 65 years of age and older will comprise 26.2%, 21.6%, and 20.2% respectively of each country's population in 2020 (Anderson & Hussey, 2000). With replacement rates below 2.1 in the G8 community, it is not surprising that the eight heads of state from Canada, France, Germany, Great Britain, Italy, Japan, Russia, and the United States declared:

> One of the most important challenges we face is responding to the economic, financial, and social implications of the changing demographics in our aging societies. It could significantly affect our pension and health care costs and influence our public budgets; reduce public and private savings; and affect global flows of capital. We therefore pledge to undertake structural reforms that will address these issues. We have asked our Finance and Economic Ministers to examine, in conjunction with other competent national authorities, the economic and fiscal implications of aging . . . (G8, 1997)

Rather than casting population aging as a negative phenomenon and challenge, they also agreed to promote an "active aging" framework through which many of the longevity-related issues facing the developed world can be examined and programs and policies can be crafted. The intent in deliberately adopting this theme was to abandon "old stereotypes of seniors as dependent," "to advance structural reforms in the areas of health and social welfare," and to capitalize upon the ability and the desire of many older persons to remain engaged in economically and socially productive activities, recognizing freedom of choice as a fundamental principle (G8, 1997).

The demographic revolution occurring in industrialized nations will not by-pass the developing nations of the world. In fact, the developing nations will have to contend with two populations that typically face more than the usual share of risks: younger children and older adults (Kiyak & Hooyman, 1999). While the older adult population 60 years of age and older is expected to grow from 580 million persons currently to 1.2 billion worldwide, almost 75% of the elderly population will be citizens of developing countries (Suzuki, 1999). Projections for developing nations over the next two decades indicate that increasing life expectancy, declining fertility rates, immigration, and other factors are resulting in population aging at rates faster than has been the case in the industrialized countries. Shrestha (2000) notes, to illustrate:

> In Belgium . . . it took more than 100 years for the share of the population over age sixty to double from 9 percent to 18 percent. In

China the same transition will take thirty-four years; in Venezuela, only twenty-two years.

China's transition deserves comment, as the number of Chinese elders at mid-century will exceed the total population of persons of all ages in the United States. Like the developed nations that have large gray populations, China will also be compelled to determine how best to care long term for frail elders and to offer reliable economic sustenance to an enormous number of older persons. There are many who could now plausibly argue that the one child policy adopted by China in the 1970s may have succeeded too well.

There is good reason to believe that the strongest impetus for refocusing the international policy agenda to give heightened and timely attention to aging as a social and economic issue of significant resonance will continue to come from outside of the United States. Compared to Japan, Germany, France, Canada, Australia, New Zealand, and the United Kingdom, the U.S. population is aging at a slower rate. The United Nations reports that between 2000 and 2020, the anticipated percentage of growth of the 80+ population is an astonishing 106.5% for Japan, 75.6% for Germany, 45.3% for France, 42% for Canada. For the United States, the 80+ population is expected to grow by 13.7% (Anderson & Hussey, 1999). However, U.S. rates will not exempt policymakers from having to secure the Medicare and the Social Security programs for future generations.

While the G8 Summit brought aging to the global roundtable, its call for further work by the Organization for Economic Cooperation and Development (OECD) and other international and national organizations promises to advance the development of substantive policy proposals. Ongoing research by the European Council (EC), the International Labor Organization (ILO), the World Health Organization (WHO), and activities by the Center on Strategic and International Studies (CSIS), and an increasing number of other international organizations which predated and followed the Denver Summit have provided more detailed examinations of a range of aging-related issues. Among the foci of these studies have been the specific comparative ramifications of population aging for developed and developing nations, international economy and its markets, the balance of economic power, and the resource implications for the defense community in its role in maintaining international security. As mentioned previously, there is an abiding concern about rising dependency ratios and, consequently, the costs and benefits of removing disincentives to labor force participation by older persons, the net outcomes of potential adjustments to immigration policies aimed at enhancing the supply of workers, the possible necessity of pronatalist policies to reverse dramatic declines in fertility, pay-as-you-go vs. market-based financing of pension systems, likely saving and investment trends, and options for addressing long-term care needs.

The activities that are mounting in the international sphere at ever-higher levels of influence and involving more and more sectors were inevitable and are welcome, as the longevity revolution will most certainly reverberate far beyond the realms of health and human services policy and service delivery. In the United States alone, the number of Baby Boomers who are soon to be older Americans is nearly double the number of older persons in the United States today. Although more serious discussions about Medicare and Social Security reform are ongoing, there is no consensus about how the eventual fiscal costs and the care and economic security needs of the Boomers will be addressed. With an eye to the global community, the Center for Strategic and International Studies recently noted that the fiscal challenge of an aging society "could make it difficult for nations to afford other important spending priorities, including infrastructure, defense, and education" (Center for Strategic and International Studies, 2001). It is not unreasonable to expect that population aging will alter our economy in the 21st century. Nor is it unimaginable that the demographic shifts that are occurring will require that other societal issues be redefined and reordered, including the reformulation or modification of social contracts with differing segments, as is being discussed not just in the United States, but in many nations in our global community.

In such an emerging context, can the social work profession afford to be ill prepared? Kiyak and Hooyman have said it well: the economy and [societal] values about aging will determine how we will deal with the graying of our nation. What roles will social work choose to play in the discussions that are designing our collective future, as it is shaped by population aging?

OTHER FACTORS

If globalization is a 21st century reality, then so too are continuing advances in the domain of science and technology, in particular in the biomedical sciences and in electronic information and assistive technologies. Described by former President William J. Clinton as "the scientific breakthrough of the century–perhaps of all time" (Clinton, 2000), the completion of the sequencing of the human genome code during the first year of this century has already begun to open a universe of possibilities for understanding human biology and effectively preventing, treating, and curing a full range of illnesses and disease conditions, ethical issues notwithstanding. Genetic research and research on the brain are also shedding new light on the patterns of human behaviors and emotions. Meanwhile stem cell research is offering new hope in the treatment of certain cancers, Parkinson's, and other diseases.

Many social workers will remember that nearly thirty years ago, dysfunctional mother-child relationships, "double bind" interactions, and other causal explanations were widely accepted in the treatment of schizophrenics. Since then, scientific research has dispelled these myths, new medications have been developed to help with the management of the disease, and the national Joint Genome Project has been in pursuit of the DNA sequences for three chromosomes whose genes are tied to schizophrenia and to more than 150 diseases.

The implications of breakthroughs in the biomedical sciences for developing more efficacious social work interventions and achieving more reliable outcomes are immense. They will give social work the potential ability to better define the problems of persons with troubling behavioral and health conditions and to more precisely target and work with their concerns. Breakthroughs are entirely reasonable to expect, given the record of achievement to date of the National Institutes of Health and the dramatically higher levels of funding support that are being appropriated by the U.S. Congress to it and other federal agencies involved in health-related research and development activities. These activities bear a rich promise of improvements to the human condition and of opportunities to fuel the nation's economic engine via technology transfers.

At least three other developments will shape the unfolding future. They are: advancements in technology, the demand for greater measures of accountability, and the increasing diversity of our population. Of these, perhaps the least needs to be said about technological advancements.

One set of illustrations can quickly make the case. In 1991, the worldwide web was released by its developer. By 1993, there were 600 worldwide web sites. Four years later, there were more than a million sites. The rapidity of development and growth in the information technologies has been remarkable, but numerous examples of technological advancements in other areas can be cited. The laser, magnetic resonance imaging (MRIs), computerized axial tomography (CAT) scans, and nanotechnology are but a sample. For older persons with functional limitations, initiatives such as the Personal Robotic Assistants for the Elderly Project are designing robots that can help with daily life activities. The Personal Robotic Assistants Project is also exploring how it might build a capacity for social interaction into the mobile personal service robots that it calls "nursebots" (Mann, 2000).

During the past decade, the United Way and local and state governments have expected service delivery organizations to account for outcomes generated with funds allocated for health, human services, and education purposes. The U.S. General Accounting Office (GAO) is straightforward in explaining the purpose of the Government Performance and Results Act of 1993 (GPRA) that underpins the federal mandate for performance measurement. The GAO has stated that GPRA "forces a shift in the focus of federal agencies . . . toward a single overriding issue: results" (U.S. General Accounting Office, 1997). Because of this, professionals in communities across the nation are at various stages of establishing systems, identifying indicators, and testing methods for the measurement of outcomes against performance objectives. In the case of the provision of services to older Americans and their families, Applebaum (2000) describes this as an opportunity to measure quality of care and client or customer satisfaction through the use of quality standards, evaluation, and quality assurance mechanisms.

The increasing diversity of the U.S. population is altering everything from the attention given by private industry to various market segments to the dominant languages used by the media and also to grassroots organizing of ethnic communities by political and advocacy groups. Although the majority of older Americans will be white in 2030, the number of minority elders will grow rapidly. White older Americans will increase by 81% from 1999 to 2030. More than 25 percent of all older Americans will be members of minority ethnic or racial groups as compared to 16.1 percent in 1999, and they will have an overall growth rate of 219 percent. Within this, some minority groups will grow at significantly faster rates than others over the same time frame. It appears that elderly Hispanic Americans will increase in number by 328%, Asian and Pacific Islander Americans by 285%, American Indians, Eskimos, and Aleuts by 147%, and African Americans by 131% by 2030. With larger numbers of ethnic minority elders, culturally appropriate services will be in even greater demand than ever before. And with a larger minority population of all ages in the United States, it is inevitable that American culture will be enriched with lifestyles, values, norms, and beliefs brought by a citizenry drawn from around the world.

POPULATION AGING AND SOCIAL WORK

Pioneers such as Bernice Neugarten, Matilda Riley, Ethel Shanas, Robert Butler, and Jacob Brody were among those who undertook seminal work on aging in the social sciences and in medicine. In social work, Louis Lowy, Elaine Brody, Rose Dobrof, Myrna Lewis, Rosalie Kane, Robert Morris, and other early educators and researchers played instrumental roles, describing client populations and their concerns, practice issues, developing methods, and identifying policy and program opportunities to improve the quality of life of older Americans and their families through improvements to health and social service delivery systems.

Because social workers serve older adults in a wide range of settings, they have intimate familiarity with the policy and program gaps, inadequacies, and constraints that too often leave older persons and their families with no recourse but to impoverish themselves and to then be institutionalized. They know persons who sacrifice either some of the necessities of daily living or costly prescription drugs, are untreated even when caught by overwhelming depression, and who must find ways to stretch further their limited retirement incomes in order to raise grandchildren who have no other reliable kin. Along with health professionals, they have forewarned their fellow citizens of the need to be prepared for the huge wave of 76 million baby boomers who will begin to reach 60 years of age in 2005. Whether in the area of health or long term care, it is anticipated that the rise in the sheer number of older persons will require a skilled workforce of social workers, geriatric nurses, and geriatricians, despite evidence of steady declines in the rate of chronic illness within the elderly population (Manton et al., 1997; Federal Interagency Forum on Aging-Related Statistics, 2000).

Recently, the Council on Social Work Education–Hartford Foundation Strengthening Aging and Gerontology Education for Social Work (SAGE–SW) Project completed a comprehensive review and analysis of the challenges facing the social work profession in an aging society. The Council and its Advisory Panel did not shy from offering their assessment of the profession's failure to be prepared for the aging of the population. Reasons for the failure cited in the Project's recently published report, *Strengthening the Impact of Social Work to Improve the Quality of Life for Older Adults and Their Families: A Blueprint for the New Millennium,* included ageism and:

. . . a lack of leadership on a national level by social work practice, education, and research organizations . . . focused on changing the culture of social work in order to strengthen the profession's response to a growing aging population. (CSWE, 2001)

Ironically, an often-cited National Association of Social Workers (NASW) survey found that 62% of all social work respondents expressed felt need for aging knowledge (Peterson and Wendt, 1990).

Obviously, the potential number of consumers seeking gerontology content through social work education and continuing education is larger than the needs of the existing pool of professionals. According to the Council, an estimated 60,000 to 70,000 social workers with the requisite knowledge and skill set will be required to work with the older adult population that will begin to burgeon when the Baby Boomers come of age in 2011. These estimates are more than double the number of social workers who were working on a full or part-time basis with older Americans in 1987 (CSWE, 2001).

It would appear that a nearly monumental effort will be required in order to address all of the critical issues and to complete all of the recommended actions laid out in the Blueprint. It will not be an easy matter to provide the educational content and requisite experiences to a sufficient number of social work students to enable them to demonstrate professional competence as a critical mass as they serve an age group characterized by ethnic and generational diversity. Hence, the CSWE–Hartford SAGE–SW Project could not be more timely, if the profession truly aims to meet the service needs and assume a leadership role in policy and program development for a rapidly aging U.S. population.

In the second phase of its work, the SAGE–SW Project will concentrate its efforts upon training a critical mass of social work educators who can begin to infuse social work curricula with gerontological content. The Council and the Project staff deserve to be fully and widely acknowledged for this critically needed initiative. However, hard questions must be posed about the measurable depth and breadth of substantive knowledge and skill building that can be achieved–of the competencies that professional social work education will be accountable for producing–within the constraints of the existing two-years masters program with all of its requisites. Both the graduate and undergraduate social work degree programs are already crammed full of educational aspirations and requirements that cannot be altogether consistently achieved, except perhaps in rare instances.

WHICH WAY TO WHICH FUTURE?

It may be pertinent to ask: what is "essential content" for a social worker to be prepared for competent practice and leadership in a changing world–in a century in which globalization, biomedical and technological advances, the measurement of program outcomes, diversity, and population aging will be part of everyday life? Would not familiarity with macro and microeconomics, alternative economic security models, the dynamics of the labor market, and other content be of value to social work professionals? Ironically, it may be necessary for social work, a profession that emphasizes the importance of understanding and working with "the person-in-environment" (Karls & Wandrei, 1993) in serving individuals and families, to look beyond itself and design its future fully cognizant of the expanse and the critical touchstones of the current and emergent ecosystems within which it will be expected to practice. It may need to look at the profession through the lens of a global environment and its impact upon individuals, families, and communities.

One all-important question that the profession must answer is: Is there not an urgent need to develop a modernized capacity to engage as discussants and thought-leaders at the macro level, where policies from which the parameters for health and human services systems, financing, and ultimately services are determined? Without this, the profession in effect will cede opportunities to shape humankind's global future, even as it comes to the celebration of the victory that longevity represents.

REFERENCES

Anderson, G. F., & P. S. Hussey. (2000). Population aging: A comparison among industrialized countries. *Health affairs, 19* (3),191-203.

Applebaum, R. (2000). The what and how of outcomes measurement. *Building the network on aging toolkit.* The Administration on Aging Symposium. Washington, D.C.: U.S. Administration on Aging, 2-3 to 2-5.

Federal Interagency Forum on Aging-Related Statistics. (August, 2000). *Older Americans 2000: Key indicators of well-being.* Washington, DC: U.S. Government Printing Office.

Center for Strategic and International Studies. (2001). *Report to world leaders: Findings and recommendations to the Commission on Global Aging.* Washington, DC: CSIS.

Council on Social Work Education. (2001). *A blueprint for the new millennium.* Alexandria, Virginia.

G8. (1997). *Chair's conclusion.* Kobe Jobs Conference. Kobe, Japan.

G8. (1999). *Compliance with G8 commitments: From Birmingham 1998 to Köln 1999.*

G8. (1997). *Confronting global economic and financial challenges: Denver Summit statement by seven.*

G8 Research Group. (1997). *Draft communiqué: Denver Summit of the Eight–I.* Economic and social issues.

Karls, J., & K. Wandrei (Eds.). (1993). *Person-in-environment system.* Washington, D.C.: NASW Press.

Kiyak, H.A., & N.R. Hooyman. (1999). Aging in the Twenty-First Century. *Hallym international journal of aging.* Seoul, Korea. 55-66.

Mann, W. (2000). *The continuum of independent living: A service delivery model for the at-risk elderly. Building the network on aging toolkit.* The U.S. Administration on Aging Symposium. Washington, D.C., 7-3 to 7-6.

Manton, K.G., Corder, L., & Stallard, E. (1997). Chronic disability trends in elderly United States populations, 1981-1994. *Proceedings of the National Academy of Science, 94,* 2593-2598.

Peterson, D. A., & Wendt, P. F. (1990). Employment in the field of aging: A survey of professionals in four fields. *The Gerontologist, 30,* 679-684.

Shrestha, L. B. (2000). Population aging in developing countries. *Health affairs, 19* (3), 204-212.

Suzuki, Y. (1999). Assuring that global aging is active aging. *Coming of age: Federal agencies and the longevity revolution.* Washington, D.C.: U.S. Department of Health and Human Services.

U.S. Administration on Aging. (2000). *Building the network on aging toolkit: Summary report.* U.S. Administration on Aging Symposium. Washington, DC: U.S. Administration on Aging.

U.S. Administration on Aging. (2000). *Profile of older Americans 2000.* Washington, DC: U.S. Administration on Aging.

U.S'General Accounting Office. (1997) *Agencies' strategic plans under GPRA: Key questions to facilitate congressional review.* Washington, D.C.

White House. (March 14, 2000). President Clinton's remarks at the medal of science and technology awards. Washington, D.C.

Multiculturalism, Social Policy and the New Aging

Fernando Torres-Gil, PhD
Karra Bikson Moga, MSW, MA

SUMMARY. This paper examines the nature of multiculturalism, demographics and social policy. In an aging society, we will see a nexus between aging and diversity, accompanied by changing views about gerontology and social policy. Growth of minority populations, continued immigration, increases in longevity, the aging of the baby boomer and public policy responses to these trends will affect the design and provision of human services to older persons, caregivers and providers. The article provides a conceptual framework for understanding the complex intersection of these trends, suggests that social work move beyond narrow parameters of race, assimilation and accul-

Fernando Torres-Gil is Professor of Social Welfare and Policy Studies at the UCLA School of Public Policy and Social Research and Director of the UCLA Center for Policy Research on Aging.

Karra Bikson Moga is a doctoral student and teaching fellow in Social Welfare at UCLA's School of Public Policy and Social Research. She earned an MA in Gerontology from San Francisco State University and an MSW from UCLA. In addition to her academic work, Karra is a clinical social worker for Trinity Care Hospice in Los Angeles County.

Acknowledgements and appreciation are given to Ms. Karra Bikson Moga, co-author and doctoral candidate at UCLA's Department of Social Welfare and to Dr. Barbara Branstetter for her invaluable assistance in the preparation of this paper.

[Haworth co-indexing entry note]: "Multiculturalism, Social Policy and the New Aging." Torres-Gil, Fernando, and Karra Bikson Moga. Co-published simultaneously in *Journal of Gerontological Social Work* (The Haworth Social Work Practice Press, an imprint of The Haworth Press, Inc.) Vol. 36, No. (3/4), 2001, pp. 13-32; and: *Gerontological Social Work Practice: Issues, Challenges, and Potential* (ed: Enid Opal Cox, Elizabeth S. Kelchner, and Rosemary Chapin) The Haworth Social Work Practice Press, an imprint of The Haworth Press, Inc., 2001, pp. 13-32. Single or multiple copies of this article are available for a fee from The Haworth Document Delivery Service [1-800-HAWORTH, 9:00 a.m. - 5:00 p.m. (EST). E-mail address: getinfo@haworthpressinc.com].

13

turation, and raises implications for social policy and social work practice. *[Article copies available for a fee from The Haworth Document Delivery Service: 1-800-HAWORTH. E-mail address: <getinfo@haworthpressinc.com> Website:
<http://www.HaworthPress.com> © 2001 by The Haworth Press, Inc. All rights re-
served.]*

KEYWORDS. Aging, diversity, demographics, social policy, social
work practice

This paper examines the nature of multiculturalism, demographics
and social policy. In an aging society, we will see a nexus between aging and diversity, accompanied by changing views about gerontology
and social policy. Growth of minority populations, continued immigration, increases in longevity, the aging of the Baby Boomers, and public
policy responses to these trends will affect the design and provision of
human services to older persons, caregivers and providers. These factors will require social work to rethink issues of diversity, to move beyond generalized notions of race, and to have a greater understanding of
population aging and its long-term consequences. This article provides
a conceptual framework for understanding the complex intersection of
these trends and suggests implications for social policy and social work.

SETTING THE STAGE

By 2050, just 50 years from now, the United States will see the
merging of two inexorable trends: aging and diversity. The Census
Bureau projects that, by that time, the U.S. population will have grown
by 50 percent. Forty percent of that growth will be equally composed
of older persons and Hispanics (Day, 1996; *U.S. News and World Report*, 1986). Hispanics, of course, are not the only group that will add
to the nation's diversity. Between the doubling of the retiree population and dramatic increases among Asians and Pacific Islanders, Hispanics and other immigrant groups, as well as African Americans and
Native Americans, a substantial portion of the U.S. population will be
composed of older persons and members of diverse populations. What
does this mean for U.S. society? What are the implications for the
helping professions? How should social policy and social work prepare for and respond to its inevitable demographic destiny? Many implications arise from this nexus, but one overriding concern is for
those involved in gerontological social work to adopt a longer-term

perspective in assessing and preparing for these trends. By doing so, there emerges a need to use the next few years as a window of opportunity to influence public policy, alter professional practice and the delivery of services, and redefine how we view the issues of race, ethnicity and diversity.

Why is that necessary? The social welfare of the nation will be heavily affected by the aging of the population and its growing diversification. Social work is more responsive than most disciplines, yet, if it is to be in a leadership role, social work should examine the complex aspects of this nexus and push the field to look at aging and diversity, not as two separate and categorical areas of research, policy and practice, but as two intertwined phenomena that can inform gerontological social work. By beginning this process, the field of social work and the arena of social policy can well use the next few years to prepare the profession and influence the nation as the year 2050 approaches.

THE DEMOGRAPHIC IMPERATIVE

The United States is aging, this much is well known. The 2000 Census Bureau data reinforce public recognition that, as a society and as individuals, there will be more older persons, and longevity will increase. The median age increased from 32.9 years in 1990 to 35.3 years in 2000 and is expected to increase to 39 years or older by 2030 (U.S. Census, 1990, 1996, 2000). Since 1900, life expectancy has increased by 31 years for women (from 48 to 79) and by 28 years for men (from 46 to 74). In the last century, while the total U.S. population tripled (including those under 65 years of age), the elderly population increased 11-fold (U.S. Census, 1996). The elderly population is expected to grow substantially from 2010 to 2030 (U.S. Census, 1996). While Census 2000 found that 12.4 percent of the population was over 65, the percentage is expected to increase to 15.7 percent by 2020 and to 21 percent by 2040 (U.S. Census, 1996, 2000; Day, 1993).

Population and individual aging are reshaping the American demographic landscape. While Census 2000 data indicate a leveling off in the growth rate of older persons (due to the lower fertility rates of the 1930s and 1940s), that will change shortly, when the Baby Boomers begin to reach 65 years of age, and the projected doubling of the retiree population becomes a reality. Yet, as the society ages, the United States is witnessing a unique phenomenon: the diversification of its population.

Census 2000 data make this point more vivid than ever before. Nearly one in every three Americans is a member of a minority group, reflecting the immigration surge of the 1990s (Rosenblatt, 2001). Not since the early 1900s have we seen such a dramatic growth of immigrants and minority groups. From 1990 to 2000, the nation's non-Latino white population dropped from 75.6 percent to 69.1 percent (U.S. Census, 1990, 2000). Latinos are now roughly equal to African-Americans as two of the nation's largest minorities groups. Latinos accounted for nine percent of the U.S. population in 1990 (22.4 million) and increased to 12.5 percent (35.3 million) in 2000. African Americans showed a more modest increase, from 12.1 percent (30 million) to 12.3 percent (34.6 million). In the same period, the population of Asians and Pacific Islanders increased from 2.9 percent to 3.7 percent. There is greater diversity in the United States today than at any time in its history. About 10 percent (more than 25 million) of Americans today are foreign-born–less than the highest share this century (15 percent in 1910, or less than 15 million), but double the lowest share (five percent in 1970, or less than 10 million) (U.S. Bureau of the Census, 2001a).

These two trends–aging and diversity–have heretofore been viewed separately and parallel to each other, as if they coexisted but did not connect. As Figure 1 illustrates, those trends are about to converge, and as they do so, they raise important questions: How will social policy respond? How should we conceptualize an approach to policy, practice and research that incorporates these two trends? What are the implications for gerontological social work? As we explore those questions, it is useful and perhaps necessary to clarify certain concepts and terms that arise whenever issues of diversity and immigration are discussed.

CONCEPTS AND TERMS

In rethinking the nature of aging and diversity and responding to the nexus of these two trends, conceptual frameworks and the clarification of certain terms allow for a more enlightened discussion about future implications and consequences. The following terms are often used in these types of discussions: multiculturalism, ethnicity and diversity. The term multiculturalism, as used in social work, appears to reference the value and even desirability of encouraging racial and ethnic groups to maintain their group self-identities. Diversity is an overarching term for the proliferation of many racial, ethnic and minority groups. Ethnicity focuses on the particular customs, traditions and languages of each

FIGURE 1. Nexus of Aging & Diversity: 2000-2010

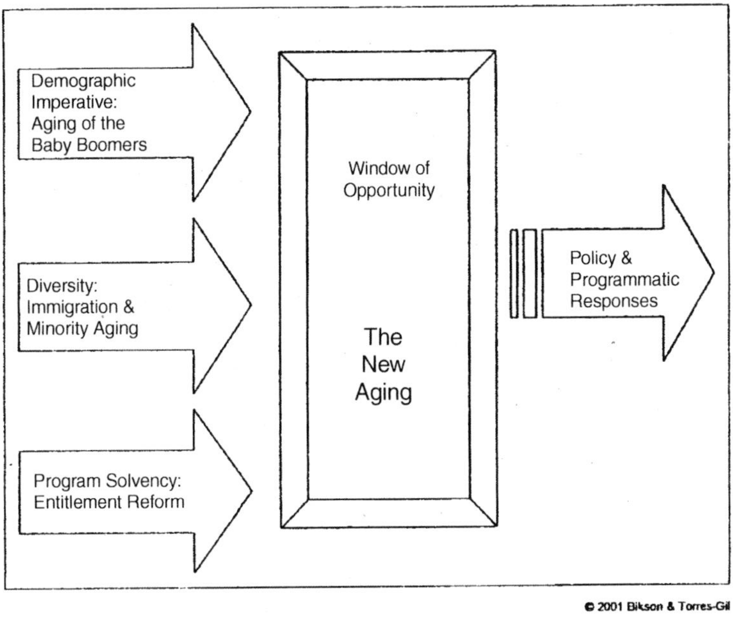

© 2001 Bikson & Torres-Gil

racial and ethnic group. One premise of this article is to question the usefulness of those terms as they are used to influence and prescribe political and public policy goals. Advocacy and social action appear to applaud the growth of diversity, the heightened presence of ethnicity and the promotion of multiculturalism as virtues and wholly positive benefits to the nation. In other words, greater numbers of ethnic and minority groups and the retention of self-identity are fully beneficent. In fact, the reality of a nation becoming more diverse is that it creates complexities and conflicts as well as opportunities. Allocating finite public resources and addressing the economic and linguistic needs of minority and racial groups become problematic as their numbers and diversity increase. Reaction from native-born Americans (of all races and ethnicities) becomes more sensitive, as witnessed by debates over bilingual education and affirmative action. Thus, using these concepts and terms requires that we have an objective analysis of the costs, conflicts and opportunities that a more diverse population engenders.

Central to this mandate is another reality: The proliferation of ethnic, racial and immigrant groups is not a status-quo or steady-state process. With few exceptions, each group is influenced by its stay in this country. Assimilation and acculturation invariably change the individual and group identity. Assimilation (adopting a host country's language, values and customs) and acculturation (becoming more adept at competing and functioning in the host nation) are basic American norms that have caused ethnic and immigrants groups (with the possible exception of African Americans and Native Americans) to become more "Americanized." Proponents of multiculturalism may view assimilation and acculturation as dated and undesirable, but the fact is that, by their second and third generation in the United States, minorities and immigrants improve their social and economic conditions, intermarry, and ascribe to basic American democratic and civic values. In our view, this is positive and to be encouraged, lest the balkanization of a more varied and diverse U.S. population leads to nationalistic and separatist behavior.

Thus, this article's assessment of aging and diversity is based on a fundamental premise: As we become more diverse and as we age, the unique American effort toward a cohesive polity drawing on the virtues and talents of each ethnic and immigrant group ought to be fostered. Utilizing a cohort approach to aging brings out the long-term consequences and benefits of this goal. The term cohort refers to generations born at the same historical point and influenced by similar historical experiences. Figure 2 is a chart reflecting a 150-year period, 1900 to 2050, that provides a framework for examining the aging of five cohorts: the New Deal Generation, the Silent Generation, Baby Boomers, Generation X and the Baby Boomlet (Generation Y). Each cohort, as indicated by the model, has certain group characteristics and was influenced by specific historical events. What we draw from this model is that society is constantly influenced by the aging of these groups which are themselves evolving in their interests and views about themselves and government. In a society becoming older and more diverse, these cohorts will influence and shape the demographic landscape.

What does that mean for gerontological social work? As the country becomes older and more diverse, there will be far greater heterogeneity among and within groups, based on race, language, age, socio-economic circumstances, region, education, assimilation and acculturation levels, and historical circumstances. Thus, social work and gerontology must become more adept at analysis that accounts for these greater differences while seeking common reference points that lessen separation,

FIGURE 2. 20th and 21st Century Time Line

1900	1920	1940	1960	1980	2000	2020	2040	2060

(New Deal Generation   33 Million)

    (Silent Generation   32 Million)

      (Baby Boomers   75 Million) →

        (Generation X   44 Million) →

         (Generation Y   65 Million) →

          (All Cohorts Exist   )

Political Mood For Policy Change

Period of
Greatest
(Immigration)
Respite
Window of
Opportunity
Generational
(Tensions)
Baby Boomers:
(Senior Lobby)
Entitlement Crisis
Demand for
(Political Action)
Deficits come due. Full
Impact of Social
Trends. A New Diversity
Economic Restructuring,
(Technological Applications)
Longevity. The
(Young Become Old)

Cohort Analysis: Politics of Aging

Cohorts	Historical Events	Attitudes/Mood
New Deal Generation 1900-1929	Depression, WWII, Welfare State Social Contract	Traditional Values Socially Conservative Politically Liberal
Silent Generation (Depression and WWII Babies) 1930-1945	Cold War Prosperity, Economic Opportunity, Stability, Golden Years	Conformity Socially and Politically Conservative
Baby Boomers 1946-1964	Civil Rights, Kennedy, Vietnam, Watergate	Socially Tolerant, Antipathy to Big Government, Big Labor, Big Business, Peter Pan Generation
Generation X 1965-1976	Ronald Reagan, Budget Deficit, Persian Gulf War	Materialism, 1950s Values Cynical, Self-Reliant, Antipathy to Baby Boomers
Baby Boomlet Generation Y 1977-1994	Clinton Challenger Explosion	Diverse College and High School Students Suburban Values

segregation and disunity. This requires a longer term perspective that looks ahead to the year 2050, when the nexus of America's diversity and aging will be at its fullest, but also understanding the historical evolution occurring in the politics of aging since 1900.

THE NEW AGING

Over the last 100 years, we have seen the development of a unique political event–the rise of older persons as a political force. This politics of aging refers to older persons and their organized interest groups shaping public policy and influencing the political agenda. The history of the politics of aging can be viewed in three time periods: the Young Aging (pre-1930), the Modern Aging (1930-1990) and the New Aging (1990-2050) (Torres-Gil, 1992). The Young Aging refers to the world's historic proclivity of reverence toward old age and filial responsibility. Admittedly, there are many exceptions to this rule, but in general, most societies, including the United States, assumed that families and communities were responsible for the care of older persons. Old age was generally respected and commanded authority. Much of this was due to relatively low life expectancy throughout human history. This changed dramatically, at least in the United States, by 1930, when the Great Depression put older persons in a precarious situation with many losing their homes and retirement security. Blatant poverty among the elderly (and among much of the general population) led to organizing by older persons for some measure of pension and financial support from the government (witness the Ham and Eggs movement of the 1930s). This agitation prompted President Franklin D. Roosevelt to support the passage of the Social Security Act of 1935. Subsequently, increased recognition of the vulnerabilities faced by older persons and their families, and the proliferation of senior citizen groups (e.g., American Association of Retired Persons, National Committee to Protect Social Security and Medicare, Gray Panthers) led to the passage of old-age entitlement programs such as Medicare, Medicaid, the Older Americans Act, Supplemental Security Income, and a host of publicly financed benefits and volunteer programs for older adults. The sanctity of this social compact–that the U.S. government would take care of its elders if they paid their taxes and were good citizens (and not change the rules)–began to erode by 1990. This New Aging period raised serious questions about the legitimacy and obligation of government to provide an extensive safety net based on age, particularly since poverty rates for persons 65 and over had dropped from as high as 75 percent during the Great Depression to 13 percent by the 1990s. Correspondingly, poverty rates for children had increased to 20 percent (Torres-Gil, 1992).

By 2000, concerns about longevity, federal deficits (and then federal surpluses), generational conflicts and competing national priorities had lessened the clout of organized senior citizen advocacy groups and led to serious efforts at revamping entitlement programs for the elderly. Today, the U.S. median age is the highest ever, and life expectancy is at 74 for men and 79 for women (U.S. Census, 2001b). Federal deficits, and now federal surpluses, have led to debates about tax cuts versus expenditures for children, families and education, rather than expanding benefits for the elderly. Groups supporting less government, more support for kids, and fewer taxes have argued that too much was being done for older persons. The high costs of entitlement programs and fears about the pending aging of Baby Boomers (and hence doubling of the older population) have led to proposals for structural changes in Social Security and Medicare. These arguments and the public perception that all older persons were doing just fine compared with the equally inaccurate perception during the Modern Aging that all elderly were poor, led to decreased political influence by senior citizen advocates. Where might these political developments lead in the future? How might they influence the nature of social policy and diversity as we move toward 2050?

The cohort analysis of the politics of aging in Figure 2 provides a 150-year historical context that suggests key milestones and developments likely to occur. Beginning with the year 1900, we see the birth and aging of the New Deal Generation leading to the life cycles of the Silent Generation, Baby Boomers, Generation X and the Baby Boomlet. Between 2000 and 2010, all five cohorts will co-exist. This is a unique moment in American history and helps to explain why multigenerational households and communities will be common, with households consisting of great grandparents, grandparents, parents, children and grandchildren. This will be a time when generational tensions will be evident. But it will also be a window of opportunity to plan for the subsequent aging of younger cohorts. Between 2010 and 2020, we will see an entitlement crisis in which our inability to make structural changes to programs for the elderly will make the programs untenable and unaffordable. Our lack of preparation for aging (e.g., limited savings and retirement coverage, lack of long-term care and medical coverage) will put a large portion of older persons at risk for poverty and poor health. This rather dire forecast need not come true if we use the window of opportunity to plan and take the political actions necessary to address the demographic inevitability. However, at this point, there is little political stomach for the hard decisions necessary to prepare for the aging of the Baby Boomers. Between 2020 and 2050, we will see the full flowering of current social trends, (e.g., fewer traditional nuclear households, more women living alone, fewer children), the full diversity of the United States, economic restructuring, and technological applications. By 2050, the Baby Boomer cohort will have largely passed on, today's younger cohorts will be old, and the current diversity in the younger populations will be reflected in the older population.

MINORITY AGING AND YOUTHFUL IMMIGRATION

By the year 2050, the full nexus of aging and diversity will be seen. Yet, aging among and within minority and ethnic populations will contain two key elements: minorities who are now old and minority and immigrant populations who are currently young. These elements influence the politics of aging and a society becoming older and more diverse in different ways.

ELDERLY MINORITIES

Older members of U.S. minority groups face multiple jeopardies and are at a disadvantage, compared with the non-Hispanic white elderly. Hispanics, African Americans, Native Americans and Asian/Pacific Islander elderly generally have higher poverty rates. For example, while African American elderly account for only eight percent of the population 65 and over, they represent 36 percent of the low-income elderly (Kiyak and Hooyman, 1994). Among Hispanic American elderly, 27 percent are poor. Three out of every five dollars of retirement income comes from Social Security or Supplemental Security Income for Hispanic elderly, compared with two out of every five dollars for the white elderly. High poverty rates persist for Pacific and Asian elderly such as the Vietnamese, Hmong, Filipino and Chinese. The overall rate of education is lower for minority older persons than for white elderly, and minorities are less likely to have private pensions and retirement plans and rely more heavily on Social Security and SSI than whites. Chronic diseases and greater limitations in activities of daily living are higher for minority older persons (Kiyak and Hooyman, 1994). Overall, with some exceptions, today's older cohort in minority groups is more disadvantaged than older whites. The reason in part reflects the fact that these groups were first-generation immigrants or came of age before the advent of civil rights protections, affirmative action and the opportunities now available for younger minorities. These cohorts have experienced the full effects of racism, nativism, poverty and discrimination.

Yet, lest their situation seem dire, minority elders today also possess strengths and resiliencies not often seen among young, native-born minorities. Minority elders oftentimes are the bedrock of their communities–leaders in their church, role models and advocates. They have survived a legacy of troubled times and retain a sense of pride and self-worth reflected in their struggles and perseverance. They retain the customs, language, traditions and values of their countries of origin and ethnicity. Whether survivors of the overt racism of the South or of the hostility faced as new immigrants to this country, minority elders are the proud legacy of a group's survival and progress. Their importance to their families and communities is sadly seen in the rising phenomenon of grandparents raising grandchildren–when their own offspring succumb to drugs, gangs and social ills–often at a physical, emotional and financial cost (*Generations,* Spring 1996, Grandparenting at Century's End, Paula Dressel, guest editor; Emick & Hayslip, 1996; Watson & Koblinsky, 1997).

YOUNG GROWING OLD

However, for young minority members, opportunities abound in ways that were not available for their elders. Progress in social advancement and civil rights means that young minority and immigrant persons have greater opportunities for education, careers, retirement plans and acculturation. But in many ethnic communities, there is a growing generational divide between elders living with the old customs and children and grandchildren unable to speak the language or less interested in preserving the values of their ethnic cultures. Individual aging among minority and immigrant groups is replete with tensions around assimilation, acculturation and the changing roles of the elders. Yet, when we look at population aging, we see another implication of an aging society becoming more diverse. Simply put, minorities are becoming a greater share of the work force, while white elderly dominate the old-age category.

Non-Hispanic whites, for example, accounted for 71 percent of the total U.S. population in 1999, but the proportion varied with age: they accounted for 68 percent of the population under age 55 and 82 percent of those 55 and over. Among the older population, the proportion was

79 percent in the 55-to-64 age group, 82 percent in the 65-to-74 age group, and 86 percent in the 75-to-84 age group (Smith & Tillipman, 1999). At the same time, as noted earlier, minorities and immigrants are rapidly increasing their share of the U.S. population, but they are generally concentrated among the young. The white population has a higher proportion of elderly than any other racial group–13 percent, compared with five percent of Hispanics, six percent of Asians/Pacific Islanders and eight percent of blacks (U.S. Census, 1996). Thus, what we have presently is an age-race stratified society, where older cohorts are primarily white and English speaking, and younger groups are increasingly minority, immigrant and non-English speaking. By 2050, minorities will account for a greater proportion of the elderly. Hispanic and Asian/Pacific Islander elders will increase by nine percent, compared with only a seven percent increase for whites (U.S. Census, 1996). What does this mean for a society becoming older and more diverse?

The central issue for the period of 2000 to 2020 may well revolve around political and public policy debates over the education, training and well-being of a younger, more diverse population. These groups will be the work force and the taxpayers from whom the financial solvency of programs for the elderly will derive. In places like California, for example, minorities account for the fastest growing percentage of the work force, while the non-Hispanic whites' share of the labor force is decreasing. During this decade, the Hispanic and Asian labor forces are projected to increase faster than other groups–by 37 percent and 40 percent, respectively, due to high immigration and higher than average fertility (Bureau of Labor Statistics, 1999). The black labor force is expected to grow by 20 percent–twice as fast as the white labor force (Bureau of Labor Statistics, 1999). In short, it is upon immigrants and minority youth that older persons will depend for a prosperous economy and generous public benefits (Torres-Gil, 1999). This trend can be seen in the replacement ratio–a measure of a society's demographic health. For a country to ensure adequate replacement and maintain its population, each childbearing woman must have 2.1 children to replace those individuals who pass away. The white replacement ratio is currently at 1.8, yet the overall replacement rate for the U.S. population has averaged 2.0 for the past 20 years (U.S. Census Bureau, 2001c). The difference is based on the higher fertility levels of minorities and immigrants, primarily the Hispanic population, whose replacement ratio is 2.4. It is 2.1 for both Asians and blacks (U.S. Census Bureau, 2001c).

Thus, in the unfolding politics of aging in the early part of this century we see two elements at work: minority elderly facing multiple jeopardies and younger minority populations growing as a segment of the work force. What this may mean in the public policy debates of a society becoming older and more diverse can be gleaned in the current political debates over entitlement reform.

ENTITLEMENT REFORM:
THE INTERSECTION OF AGE, RACE, AND DIVERSITY

The politics of aging in the year 2000 have led to an interesting and important debate over the future of Social Security, the bedrock of the New Deal era. This program has become the basic income security for persons over 65 years of age. Social Security is especially crucial to low-income older persons, particularly minority elderly. Yet it faces fundamental changes that reflect generational tensions, concerns over the aging of the Baby Boomer cohort, and the use of race and diversity as political tools.

The Social Security Act of 1935 established the basic federal old-age benefits program and a federal-state system of unemployment insurance (Torres-Gil and Villa, 2000). Social Security includes Old Age and Survivors Insurance, Disability Insurance, survivors' benefits and Supplemental Security Income. The money collected from payroll taxes ($450 billion by 2001) goes to pay monthly benefits to more than 45.4 million beneficiaries, including 28.5 million retired workers, 3.3 million dependents or retirees, 6.7 million disabled workers and their dependents, and seven million survivors of workers (Social Security Administration, 2001a). Social Security has come to symbolize a social contract and an expectation by all Americans that they will have a measure of protection from the vicissitudes of old age. However, Social Security is facing its greatest test in proposals to privatize and alter its basic eligibility structure.

Privatization, as currently presented, would allow taxpayers to carve out of their payroll tax an individual security account. This would allow workers to use a portion of their Social Security contributions for investments in the private market. Currently, Social Security is a social insurance program whereby workers pay a portion of their payroll taxes. In 2001, the tax rate was 7.65 percent for workers and for employers on salaries up to $80,400 (Social Security Administration, 2001b). Each worker has a general account and their contributions go into a Social Security trust fund, which in turn is used to cover current beneficiaries and to pay for administrative costs. Any surplus funds are invested in federal treasury notes. Privatization would erode the social insurance nature of this system by allowing workers to control some of those contributions and thus divert some of the payroll taxes away from current beneficiaries. Proponents of this plan argue that individuals should have the freedom to choose how their payroll taxes are invested and that the rate of return in the private market (e.g., the stock market) is historically higher than the low treasury interest rates, which are between three and seven percent. Opponents argue that Social Security is not an investment seeking rates of return but a civic commitment to provide a measure of protection to all workers, regardless of how much an individual may pay or receive. Furthermore, they argue that the transition costs for creating individual retirement accounts would add up to a trillion dollars to cover the reduction in funds going to current beneficiaries.

The fuel for these burning debates hinges on the aging of the Baby Boomer cohort and the reality that, while Social Security is running big surpluses today and can cover the 45 million disabled and retired persons now living in the United States, the surpluses will disappear and turn into annual deficits after 2038, when the Baby Boomers will have retired (Rich, 2001). Those future deficits, as well as funds drained out of Social Security through private accounts, could require cutbacks in benefits, increases in payroll taxes, a raising of the eligibility age or all of the above. Along with the demographic pressures are concerns that the diminishing program dependency ratio will mean fewer workers supporting more retirees. That ratio has dropped from 5/1 in 1960, to 3.3/1 today and could reach 2/1 by 2040 (American Society on Aging, 1998[1]).

In the midst of this debate, proponents of privatization, including groups such as the Heritage Foundation, insurance companies and financial planners, have focused on potentially influential allies: Hispanics, African Americans and immigrants. The interest groups opposing privatization are the old liberal coalition of labor unions, senior citizen advocacy groups, progressives and civil rights organizations. However, proponents have raised an argument with potentially great appeal to minorities and immigrants: As relatively young groups, they have the most to gain with the purported higher rates of return in private accounts. In recent years, conservative groups have courted the Congressional Black Caucus, the Congressional Hispanic Caucus and leaders of minority and immigrant groups and pointed out that, as relatively young groups accounting for an increasingly larger share of the work force, and with increasing life expectancy, they should have the right to invest their funds as they wish (Torres-Gil & Bikson, unpublished manuscript). With this argument comes the subtle implication that minorities should not have to shoulder the burden of supporting an older white retiree population. And for the most ideologically-minded minority advocates, white retirees represent the source of past discrimination and injustices. This argument has crucial weaknesses: It does not account for the crucial safety nets that Social Security represents, including DI, SSI, and survivors' benefits, nor for the fact that minority elderly depend on Social Security (and OASI) to a greater extent than older whites. In a longer-term perspective, privatization ignores the fact that younger minorities, especially those most at risk, will need the full benefits and protections of the Social Security system. Regardless, privatization has potentially enormous appeal for younger members of minority groups, who are concerned more with the immediate needs of survival, jobs, families and their children. The regressive nature of the payroll tax means that lower income persons pay a greater share of their income than higher income individuals, because of the cap on income subject to withholding. Thus, the politics of privatization have engendered new ingredients: race, minority status and diversity.

The outcome of these debates is unclear. President Bush has created a commission to study Social Security reform with a mandate to give workers optional personal savings accounts invested in stocks and bonds. Democrats and their allies will oppose this plan, but public opinion polls indicate that a large majority of the American public, particularly younger workers, are open to some form of privatization. Minority and immigrant groups can expect to be courted by both sides. However this unfolds, in a society becoming more diverse and with an increasingly diverse work force where the retiree population is still largely white and English speaking, we can expect that the politics of aging will be more affected by diversity. And therein lie lessons for social policy, multiculturalism and the New Aging.

IMPLICATIONS AND CHALLENGES

This article has attempted to bring together seemingly disparate themes: the nexus of aging and diversity, the use of concepts and terms in assessing the implications of the politics of aging, the dual elements of minority aging and age/race stratification, and Social Security as a case study of the New Aging. The use of cohort analysis provides a conceptual framework for understanding the historical and generational contexts of these issues. What might all of this mean for gerontological social work? Several implications and challenges come to mind.

1. The need to rethink multiculturalism. The New Aging will require that we come up with different definitions and terms for assessing and discussing the demographic, social and political changes facing a society becoming older and more diverse. For example, a paradigm that sees race as simply the issue of blacks and whites confronting racism will not suffice in a society with myriad racial, ethnic and immigrant groups. The advent of Hispanic demographics and political influence cannot assume that Hispanics will be the new "power" group when many other ethnic and immigrant groups are also vying for respect and influence. Ethnic separatism and cultural nationalism, both of which encourage narrow self-identify at the cost of national unity and civic norms (e.g., becoming a U.S. citizen, voting, adhering to U.S. constitutional values and traditions), will not work for a country experiencing extraordinary immigration from throughout the world.

2. The need for a longer-term perspective and acceptance of constant change. As the cohort analysis chart demonstrates, there will be constant change and evolution over the next 50 years, as there has been over the past 100 years. The aging of various cohorts and the ongoing process of assimilation and acculturation will mean constant change and will require ongoing analyses and understanding of this process.

3. Interest-group politics and shifting alliances. Advocacy around gerontology and social work must accommodate the reality of shifting alliances. Advocacy today tends to follow group allegiances; that is, Hispanics advocate for all Hispanics, African Americans for all blacks, and senior citizens for all older persons. While this is admittedly an overgeneralization, there are limited instances of coalitions among these groups. In the New Aging, however, alliances and coalitions will need to be more sophisticated. For example, we already see tremendous economic progress by some Hispanic, African American and immigrant groups. These upper-income individuals will have more in common with affluent whites, and as they age, will more likely focus on preserving their retirement and health insurance plans, home equity and tax shelters than they will advocate for publicly funded programs benefiting low-income persons. Thus, we may see poor blacks, Hispanics, and immigrants working with low-income elderly whites for the expansion or preservation of Medicare, Medicaid and universal health care.

4. The adjustment of services and programs for new cohorts of diverse older persons. The programs and intervention approaches of the Modern Aging will not be adequate in the New Aging. Future cohorts of older persons will be quite unlike the current elderly. For example, congregate meal sites for the elderly are finding that clientele tend to be the

old-old (those in their 80s or above), and that the young-old (those in their 60s and 70s) are more active, less willing to go to senior citizen centers, and seek more opportunities for leisure, education and recreation. Minority elders in the future may seek opportunities as the affluent and white young-old do today. The presence of poor and disadvantaged minority and immigrant elders will still exist, as will their need for publicly funded programs, but there will be greater variations among those populations.

5. A requirement that the New Aging move beyond over-generalizations, rethinking quotas, targeting and affirmative action. Today, for example, Older Americans Act programs give preference to Hispanic, Black, Asian/Pacific Islander, and Native American minority elderly groups. Each group has a separate senior center, for example. This will become increasingly difficult to maintain as diversity leads to an increase in ethnic and immigrant groups, as well as to the growing number of biracial and multiracial elders who do not necessarily identify with 20th Century definitions of ethnicity. Moreover, we cannot assume that all are poor and "oppressed." Many more will be affluent, conservative and advantaged, while the lower-income elders of all backgrounds may be at risk. Functional limitations may become a better predictor of who is most at risk and in need of services and programs than traditional age or race eligibility criteria.

6. The importance of education and training in gerontological social work as we prepare for the aging of our society. The John A. Hartford Foundation and the Gerontological Society of America are responding to this challenge with grants for master's and doctoral degrees, as well as for faculty development in education, training and scholarship, which are part of a major initiative to improve the well being of older adults by strengthening geriatric social work. Less than five percent of master's-level students and only seven percent of doctoral-level students specialize in aging, even though most of the 600,000 practicing social workers in the United States report that gerontological knowledge is needed in their jobs. These Hartford Geriatric Social Work initiatives are important steps toward cultivating professionals and scholars to fill this critical service and knowledge gap. More efforts and incentives of this kind are needed.

7. A mandate to include minority aging in research, such as education and training. Too often, we look at aging as a white issue and neglect diversity, while those interested in multicultural social work focus on youth. Moving beyond our contemporary notions of aging and diversity, research must attempt to meet the challenge of understanding people in

their environment–in all their heterogeneity and complexity. This is a challenge for social work and calls for rigorous, theory-driven research.

At the beginning of the 21st Century, we have a great opportunity to plan for the aging and growing diversity of American society. Social workers, including practitioners, educators and scholars, must prepare to meet these challenges. Not only must we meet these challenges by stretching our understanding of the aging and the diverse nation in which we live, but we must expand our reach beyond academies and communities to public leadership and policymaking roles. We must be prepared to inform and influence policy debates with the kind of specialized knowledge and advocacy that will serve and improve the lives of vulnerable members of our society.

NOTE

1. The dependency ratio of retirees to workers is shrinking because of increased longevity and the aging of the Baby Boomers. However, in 1960, the United States had the greatest non-working population because, at that time, the majority of the Baby Boomers was either in its infancy or in school. If we consider a consumer-to-worker ratio, i.e., comparing all non-workers to workers, there was a 2.56-to-1 ratio in 1960. Today, there is a 2.03-to-1 ratio, and in 2040, there will be a 2.15-to-1 ratio (American Society on Aging, 1998).

REFERENCES

American Society on Aging. (1998). Understanding income security: Between policy and politics [Electronic version]. *Aging Today, March/April*. Retrieved July 13, 2001, from <http://www.asaging.org/at/at-192/incomesec.html>.

Bureau of Labor Statistics. (1999). *BLS Releases New 1998-2008 Employment Projection*. Retrieved July 9, 2001, from http://stats.bls.gov/news.release/ecopro.nr0.htm

Day, J. C. (1996). *Population projections of the United States by age, sex, race, and HispanicoOrigin: 1995 to 2050*. U.S. Bureau of the Census, Current Population Reports, pp. 25-1130. Washington, DC: U.S. Government Printing Office.

Day, J. C. (1993). *Population projections of the United States by age, sex, race, and Hispanic origin: 1993 to 2050*. U.S. Bureau of the Census, Current Population Reports, pp. 25-1104. Washington, DC: U.S. Government Printing Office.

Dressel, P. (1996). Grandparenting at century's end. *Generations, Spring*.

Emick, M. A., & Hayslip, B. (1996). Custodial grandparenting: New roles for middle-aged and older adults. *International Journal of Aging & Human Development, 43(2)*, 135-154.

Kiyak, H. A., & Hooyman, N. R. (1994). Minority and socioeconomic status: Impact on quality of life in aging. In R. P. Abeles & H. C. Gift (Eds.), *Aging and Quality of Life* (pp. 295-315). NY: Springer Publishing Co.

Rich, S. (2001, April 25). A tiny middle ground in the Social Security privatization debate. *National Journal*, p.33.

Rosenblatt, R. (2001, March 13). Census illustrates diversity from sea to shining sea. *The Los Angeles Times*, p. A1-16.

Smith, D., & Tillipman, H. (1999). *The Older Population in the United States*. U.S. Bureau of the Census, Current Population Reports, pp. 20-532. Washington, DC: U.S. Government Printing Office. Retrieved July 9, 2001, from <http://www.census.gov/prod/2000pubs/p20-532.pdf>.

Social Security Administration (2001a). *Fast Facts and Figures about Social Security*. Office of Policy, Social Security Administration, June 2001. Retrieved July 16, 2001 from, <http://www.ssa.gov/statistics/fast_facts/2001/ff2001.pdf>.

Social Security Administration (2001b). *2001 Social Security Changes*. Retrieved July 9, 2001 from, <http://www.ssa.gov/cola/cola2001.htm>.

Torres-Gil, F. (1992). *The New Aging: Politics and Change in America*. Westport, CT: Auburn House.

Torres-Gil, F. (1999, November 21). The aging and Latinization of California. *The San Francisco Chronicle*.

Torres-Gil, F. & Bikson, K. (unpublished manuscript). Redefining a political agenda: Social Security, ethnic politics and the Congressional Hispanic Caucus. In B.J. Nelson, & M.T. Maki (Eds.), *Leadership for the Twenty-first Century: Inclusion and Change*.

Torres-Gil, F., & Villa, V. (2000). Social policy and the elderly. In J. Midgley, M. Tracy, & M. Livermore (Eds.), *The Handbook of Social Policy*, (pp. 209-220). Thousand Oaks, CA: Sage Publications.

U.S. Bureau of the Census (1990). Table DP-1. Profile of General Demographic Characteristics for the United States: 1990.

U.S. Bureau of the Census (1996). *65+ in the United States*. Current Population Reports, Special Studies, pp.23-190. Washington, DC: U.S. Government Printing Office. Retrieved July 9, 2001 from, <http://www.census.gov/prod/1/pop/ p23-190/p23-190. html>.

U.S. Bureau of the Census (2000). Census 2000. Table DP-1. Profile of General Demographic Characteristics for the United States. Retrieved from, <http://www.census.gov/Press-release/www/2001/tables/dp_us_2000.PDF>.

U.S. Bureau of the Census (2001a). Adding diversity from abroad: The foreign-born population, 1999. *Population Profile of the United States 1999: America at the Close of the 20th Century*, pp. 67-69. Current Population Reports, Special Studies, Series pp. 23-205. Washington, DC: U.S. Government Printing Office. Retrieved July 9, 2001 from, <http://www.census.gov/population/pop-profile/1999/chap17. pdf>.

U.S. Bureau of the Census (2001b). Keeping up with older adults: Older adults, 1999. *Population Profile of the United States 1999: America at the Close of the 20th Century*, 70-71. Current Population Reports, Special Studies, Series pp. 23-205. Washington, DC: U.S. Government Printing Office. Retrieved July 9, 2001 from, <http://www.census.gov/population/pop-profile/1999/chap18.pdf>.

U.S. Bureau of the Census (2001c). Motherhood: The fertility of American women, 1998. *Population Profile of the United States 1999: America at the Close of the 20th Century*, pp. 16-17. Current Population Reports, Special Studies, Series pp. 23-205. Washington, DC: U.S. Government Printing Office. Retrieved July 9, 2001 from, <http://www.census.gov/population/pop-profile/1999/chap04.pdf>.

Profile of tomorrow's new U.S. (1986, November 24). *US News and World Report, 32.*

Watson, J. A., & Koblinsky, S. A. (1997). Strengths and needs of working-class African-American and Anglo-American grandparents. *International Journal of Aging & Human Development, 44* (2), 149-165.

Gerontological Social Work Practice: A Canadian Perspective

Lilian M. Wells, MSW, DASW
Laura E. Taylor, PhD, MSW

SUMMARY. Canadian social work practice is set in the context of a growing older population, valued universal health care undergoing restructuring and cutbacks, comprehensive income security yet pockets of poverty, pressures of globalization. Research has documented social and economic costs of piecemeal, medicalized service. Ageism is a factor even within the profession and the skills required in Gerontological so-

Lilian M. Wells is Professor Emerita and Associate Dean at the Faculty of Social Work, University of Toronto. She is particularly interested in the quality of life of older people; especially those affected by frailty and disability. She has researched reciprocity in relationships of older people and been involved in action research to enhance standards of long-term institutional and home-based care. Her interests in resiliency and empowerment have also led to collaborative projects with parents who have HIV and with Aboriginal organizations.

Laura E. Taylor is Associate Professor, Faculty of Social Work, University of Manitoba, Winnipeg, MB, Canada. She teaches in the areas of gerontology, mental health, addictions, social work practice, social welfare and the history of social work. Her research interests include re-settlement, resiliency, and homesickness, the process of adjusting and integrating into a new country and culture for older and younger people.

Address correspondence to: Lilian M. Wells, Faculty of Social Work, University of Toronto, 246 Bloor Street West, Toronto, ON, Canada M5S 1A1 (E-mail: Lilian. Wells@utoronto.ca).

The authors thank our colleagues across the country who contributed their expertise to our understanding of practice issues. We take responsibility for any errors or omissions.

[Haworth co-indexing entry note]: "Gerontological Social Work Practice: A Canadian Perspective." Wells, Lilian M., and Laura E. Taylor. Co-published simultaneously in *Journal of Gerontological Social Work* (The Haworth Social Work Practice Press, an imprint of The Haworth Press, Inc.) Vol. 36, No. (3/4), 2001, pp. 33-50; and: *Gerontological Social Work Practice: Issues, Challenges, and Potential* (ed: Enid Opal Cox, Elizabeth S. Kelchner, and Rosemary Chapin) The Haworth Social Work Practice Press, an imprint of The Haworth Press, Inc., 2001, pp. 33-50. Single or multiple copies of this article are available for a fee from The Haworth Document Delivery Service [1-800-HAWORTH, 9:00 a.m. - 5:00 p.m. (EST). E-mail address: getinfo@haworthpressinc.com].

cial work are not fully appreciated. Developments are being made in several areas including, models of practice in abuse, in work with families, in understanding resilience and strengths. The challenge lies in putting our knowledge into action. *[Article copies available for a fee from The Haworth Document Delivery Service: 1-800-HAWORTH. E-mail address: <getinfo@haworthpressinc.com> Website: <http://www.HaworthPress.com> © 2001 by The Haworth Press, Inc. All rights reserved.]*

KEYWORDS. Interdependence, caregiving, costs, best practices

This article examines the framework for the practice of gerontological social work in Canada and offers an overview of major practice issues. Many such issues are similar to those in other industrialized countries (Cox & Parsons, 1994; Payne, 1997; Rosen, 2000; Scharlach, Damron-Rodriguez, Robinson, & Feldman, 2000). We emphasize Canadian literature, set practice in the context of social, economic and political factors and highlight some practice developments.

GROWING OLDER IN CANADA

As elsewhere, the Canadian population is aging. People 65 and over are now 12% of the population, by 2021 this is expected to be 18%. The fastest growth is in older age groups with the number of people 75 to 84 almost doubling in the past two decades; while one in ten seniors is 85 or older (Statistics Canada, 1999).

Relatively large proportions (27%) of seniors are immigrants but 85% of these have been in Canada over twenty years. Most immigrants (71%) are of European background and only about 6% identify themselves as being of a visible minority (primarily Chinese, South Asian or Black).

Seniors are integral and vital participants in society. In general they are closely connected to family and the community in reciprocal relationships (Statistics Canada, 1999). Interdependence, that is, both giving and receiving practical aid, resources, information and emotional support is the normal pattern.

Most seniors (78%) are in good health (Statistics Canada, 1999). While 2% have dementia, 5% are taking educational programs and 13% have computers. TV favorites are news and public affairs. Ninety-three percent have a religious affiliation with 37% participating weekly. At the same time just over a quarter have some limitations in their activities due to health-related problems, and similar percentages report chronic pain or forgetfulness.

While most seniors live with family, a substantial number, 29% live alone. Women are more likely to live alone (58% of those 85 and over, 49% of those 75 to 84). The oldest women are also more apt to be living with extended family (22% of those 85 and over, 12% of those 75-84). While on average only 7% of seniors reside in institutions this increases to 34% of those 85 and over (Statistics Canada, 1999).

Seniors are active volunteers, almost one quarter formally contribute to organizations giving more hours per year (202) than any other age group (Chappell, 1999). Even greater numbers (58%) participate in informal volunteer activities outside their own home. Awareness is growing that the well being of individuals and communities depends greatly on the "social capital" to which seniors are major contributors (National Advisory Council on Aging, 2000).

The overall economic well being of seniors has improved over the last twenty years although the average income is lower than most younger age groups. However, pockets of poverty remain: unattached women over 65 have a poverty rate of 49%, one of the largest of any group: for unattached men it is 28.9% (National Council of Welfare, 2000).

In 1996 the national General Social Survey (GSS) documented "informal caregiving," all assistance provided and received in household tasks, errands or personal care. Similar proportions of seniors and non-seniors received assistance indicating that seniors are not the disproportionately high recipients of assistance that is often assumed (Keating, Fast, Frederick, Cranswick & Perrier, 1999).

Keating's et al. (1999) analysis of informal caregiving and its consequences gives insights that are important for designing and providing services. A wide diversity of Canadians are involved in caregiving. The young care for extended family members, the middle-aged for parents, and the oldest for spouses and friends (Keating et al., 1999, p. 53). While the main group of caregivers is adult children as expected, the relatively large number providing care to extended kin and friends was not. Women predominate (61%), yet men represent a larger segment of the caregiving population (39%) than was previously understood. Most caregivers have been involved two or more years with the hours spent increasing over time. Elderly spouses carry high caregiving loads (on average 15 hours per week). They are the least likely to ask for assistance and they may even under-report the care they do provide.

Only three GSS questions addressed the benefits of caregiving, however, respondents found it rewarding because it allowed them to reciprocate for their own good fortune and to strengthen personal relationships (Keating et al., 1999). There was more information on negative aspects including. While spouses spent the most time providing care, people caring for parents reported the greatest consequences. Overall, the most common was guilt. Nearly 25% of caregivers experienced serious socio-economic impact. Sons experience higher levels of social and psychological consequences, while daughters experience more socio-economic, job adjustments, postponed opportunities, and burden. While there are differences in the patterns of factors that predict serious consequences, greater the number of hours spent and the provision of personal care were important. Keating et al. (1999) point out that personal care is demanding and unremitting. Needs are immediate and cannot be put off to a more convenient time: those providing this care are more likely to have to change their own plans, incur extra expenses, and disrupt sleep (p. 94).

Organization of Health and Social Services

Services to seniors in Canada are part of a complex social and health services network at three levels of government (local, provincial, and national) and a mixture of public and private auspices (Neysmith, 1988). A universal old-age pension is available for all Canadians at 65 with a supplement for those whose income is below a national standard. In addition, there is a universal contributory pension for those retired from the labor force.

Health care and social services are provincial responsibilities. By the early 1970s all provinces had negotiated cost-sharing agreements with the federal government for universal hospital and physician services, the main sites of health care at the time. The Canada Health Act ensures universal coverage with no user fees. Cost-sharing agreements by the federal government also facilitated the development of social services.

In 1995, in response to budget deficits, demands for more control by provincial governments and neo-conservative trends in social thought, the federal government changed its cost-sharing arrangements with the provinces. It introduced a new block-funded program, the Canada Health and Social Transfer to provide federal contributions to health care, post-secondary education, social assistance and social services. While standards of the Canada Health Act were maintained, the rather loose federal standards for welfare and social services were dropped and the new formula led to major funding cuts to the provinces. This meant that health and social services throughout Canada faced down-sizing and re-structuring. Regional differences also increased.

While each province has home care programs there are not universal standards and home care is not guaranteed. With more early hospital discharge, home care resources are stretched and services capped. It is generally the chronic needs of older people that have borne the brunt of cutbacks.

A joint federal-provincial National Framework on Aging aims to guide a more coordinated approach to policy. Proposals for a National Home Care Program have been raised recently and it is generally recognized that, with the move to community care plus a wider range of service providers, change is required, but a vision and political will to undertake this has not yet emerged. A newly established Royal Commission on Health Care may provide new directions.

The drift away from equity in social policy and the move to a market-based society has lead to a deterioration of the social safety net that is now sparking increased public debate. There are some interesting proposals being brought forward, for example, in 2001 the Clair Commission in Quebec proposed an Autonomy Insurance that people would contribute to during their work-life and receive benefits from when needed.

A major policy body is the National Advisory Council on Aging (NACA) composed primarily of older people to provide advice to policy makers and information to the public so that people can act in their communities and with elected representatives to bring about necessary change. Independent advocacy groups, such as Pensioners Concerned, also press for change. However, government funding bodies are withdrawing from support of advocacy organizations. This reduces the power of citizen groups, and has particularly detrimental impact on seniors who may not have the resources or energy for sustained action.

Issues in Social Work Practice

The current practice of social work is set in the context of major cutbacks in government spending in response to economic slow-down, deficits and concern about tax rates. Funding for community programs, seniors' independence projects, action research, public transportation for frail and disabled people has been drastically cut across Canada over the past five years. Moreover, the profession itself tends to underestimate the knowledge and skills required, the diversity of older people, and the complexity of providing services.

Social Work Education in Gerontology

In Canada the BSW is the primary degree for generalist practice (offered in all but two of the thirty-four schools). At the graduate level, over half include a gerontology emphasis or option (ECAH, 1993). However, the recent study of Canadian social work found that while gerontological studies had increased, the number of students remains very small (Stephenson, Rondeau, Michaud and Fiddler, 2000). A striking feature was that employers were least satisfied with the knowledge and skills of social workers in gerontology. They reported only 50% of workers "meet or exceed expectations" in contrast to other areas of practice where 75% met this criterion. Overall, employers reported that they look for ability to work in teams yet be autonomous, good communication, maturity and good judgement, openness to diversity, commitment, comfortable with the grieving process and one's own mortality, ability to learn quickly and under pressure, administrative skills and understanding of the policy environment.

A number of current issues such as the three outlined below have direct implications for social work education.

Addressing Aboriginal Practice Issues

Attention to an Aboriginal perspective has long been neglected in social work education and practice contributing to racism and inappropriate services. It has now become a priority with required content in curricula. Unlike conventional social work organized around a problem-solving process, "an Aboriginal approach centres around the abstract goal of pimatasiwin–a good life and the lifelong journey. The emphasis on this journey is on wholeness, balance, connectedness/relationships, and harmony. Like the Strengths approach . . . (it) emphasizes people's vitality and capacities. . . . People need to solve their own problems, and as the journey toward pimatasiwin continues, problem-solving capacity increases and improves" (Hart, 2001, p. 253). The role of seniors in Aboriginal culture is of particular importance. Hart (2001) notes that "significantly Elders are often seen as people who have learned from life and are able to transmit culture . . . a key aspect of the healing process for Aboriginal people. . . . Elders also provide counseling, offer spiritual guidance and conduct ceremonies . . . (p. 247). Increasingly, Aboriginal communities are providing their own network of social services. Many seniors are just beginning to confront the trauma and abuse that is the legacy of the residential school system. It is therefore important to understand where individual seniors are in the process of re-claiming their Aboriginal culture following the experience of cultural genocide. Sensitivity to their wishes and needs around Aboriginal cultural practices and their journey is critical, as this is an area of serious post-trauma stress within the Aboriginal community.

Spirituality

This area is only beginning to be addressed systematically in social work schools. The domain of spirituality is now often included in assessments and viewed as an aspect of resiliency. Kivick (1991) offers an excellent way to introduce this topic as part of a larger over-all "meaning of life" discussion. It is interesting that this area is strengthened by the Aboriginal teachings around the Sacred Tree, the symbols, and the Medicine Wheel that offer ways of reflecting upon cultural values around spirituality.

Rural Practice Realities

Most textbooks prepare practitioners for an urban-based practice. The reality is that there is a substantial rural, northern, isolated and cadre of social workers. Their issues offer a unique perspective. Where many of the citizens are long-time friends or relatives there is the advantage of knowing the family history of the client and having considerable insight into the reasons for the presenting problem. However workers have the increased challenge of maintaining confidentiality and being aware of their own biases developed over years in the community. Many specialized services are located in urban centers which means flying seniors away from family, familiar surroundings, and known caregivers to the more impersonal and less culturally sensitive urban health care centers.

Paternalism, Ageism and Legal Rights

While ageism is a continuing problem, there is growing recognition of legal rights and of the importance of the older person being an active participant in decisions affecting his or her life. It affirms that the individual has the right to explicit information from professionals involved in his or her care regarding the likely risks and benefits of options.

NACA (1995) emphasizes that for consent to be free the person must be able to choose without undue pressure from formal care providers or family and if the individual's decision does not coincide with theirs, he or she should not feel abandoned or rejected. Any value judgments made by a professional in assessing benefits and risks should be clearly communicated to the individual (e.g., the professional's assumptions about 'acceptable' quality of life). Advanced directives enable choice to be extended to situations where the person is no longer competent.

Best Practices

A number of initiatives are defining models of practice and standards. The following are three examples.

Quality of Life, Personhood, Autonomy, Empowerment

A multi-disciplinary group of nurses and social workers has developed educational programs that highlights how to identify the personhood and the strengths of people in long term care (Buzzell, Meredith, Monna, Ritchie, & Sergeant, 1993) and to foster autonomy (Sergeant, Whittaker and Black, 1996). Guidelines for helping institutions change from a medical or custodial model to an empowering quality of life model are available (Wells, Singer, & Polgar, 1992).

End-of-Life Care

An interdisciplinary group has developed a consolidation of "best practices" to improve end-of-life care for seniors and facilitate increased autonomy and independence in decisions. The Guidelines (Fisher, Ross, & MacLean, 2000) state that "end-of-life care is sensitive to personal, cultural and spiritual values, beliefs and practices and encompasses support for families and friends up to and including bereavement" (p. 9). The relevance of "physical and emotional comfort, resolution and growth in personal relationships, and issues of spiritual meaning or peace" is heightened (p. 11).

Elder Abuse

This area has received considerable attention in research and practice. It was recognized that older people who are abused are often treated differently than people of other ages. The characteristics of a person who has been mistreated tend to involve depression, confusion, forgetfulness, and indecision that, in an older adult, are often interpreted as incompetence (McKenzie, Tod and Yellen, 1995).

The risk is of neglect and abuse in long-term care is higher when economic restraints lead to a reduction in number and experience of staff at the same time that the care needs of residents are greater. Preventive programs, such as educating staff about causes and ways of coping with violent behavior in people with Alzheimer's disease, can be implemented but issues of detection and intervention are more difficult. Clear rules about acceptable staff behavior and residents' rights are inadequate without resources for caregivers and the provision of a healthy work atmosphere.

Adult protection legislation, modeled on child welfare legislation was instituted in four eastern provinces in the late 1980s. Such legislation has been criticized because of its intrusiveness, ageism, paternalism and lack of due process. A domestic violence model may be more appropriate as it does not violate human rights nor discriminate on the basis of age. Mistreatment of older people can be best handled by the expansion, modification and coordination of existing health, social and legal services (McDonald, Hornick, Robertson, and Wallace, 1991).

Reis and Nahmiash (1995a,b, Reis, 1999) have developed a research-based model of intervention based on principles of prevention, empowerment and protection. Prevention involves sensitizing and informing the public plus raising the awareness of caregivers and receivers as to what constitutes abuse, personal and legal rights, and the consequences of abusive behavior. Teaching new skills such as stress management and reduction, how to deal with undesirable behavior, how to address feelings of frustration guilt and anger is important (p. 9). Empowerment involves increased feelings of control and efficacy, ways to manage power struggles and violence, how to use the criminal justice system and other resources (p. 10). Protection is necessary where people are unable to protect themselves due to physical or cognitive disability.

Reis and Nahmiash describe seven elements to their intervention model (1995a, p. 5).

- Tools for screening and documenting intervention strategies.
- An Intervention Team screens, assesses and intervenes with the aid of a multidisciplinary group of experienced social workers, nurses and other care providers.

- Expert Consultants (psycho geriatrician, lawyer, police, bank manager, and representative of the human rights commission) provide specialized service and advice.
- Trained Volunteer Buddies are available to listen, encourage, assist and cut isolation.
- An Empowerment Group for abused seniors addresses problems, strengths and solutions to improve self-esteem and the ability to respond effectively. Learning and practicing skills of constructive criticism proved particularly important.
- Abusive caregivers receive practical aid, help with emotional problems and education through a Caregiver Support Group. They also often need individual or specialized help, especially if they have a history of personal or emotional problems or substance abuse.
- An independent volunteer Community Senior Abuse Committee advocates and arranges programs and publications to educate and sensitize the community.

The practice model was developed in the context of a home care program and the guidelines describe the roles of various staff (Reis & Nahmiash (1995a, p. 30). The social worker plays critical, leadership roles in all elements, developing a relationship with the client, assessing, crisis intervention, devising an intervention plan, and maintaining contact and being alert to future abuse. (Where there is conflict of interest, the person abused and the abuser may each need their own social worker.) The worker is the coordinator and facilitates communication amongst family members, formal and informal helpers. With the abused person, the social worker discusses the consequences of the abuse, precautions and means to protect oneself, alternative steps to take (for example, direct deposits to banks). Empowerment strategies also include emphasis of client's areas of competence, validation of the experience and ensuring that the client does not feel responsible for the abuse. The worker also can reduce isolation and dependency on the abuser by creating alliances in the client's natural network and with volunteers, and by obtaining additional services. In working with an abusive caregiver, the social worker addresses areas of stress, better understanding of the care-receiver's disabilities and needs, understanding of abuse and its consequences, the caregiver's confidence and feelings of self-control, respite and other resources, treatment and support groups. Social workers are also involved in the training and supervision of volunteer "buddies" and in the leadership of groups. Participation in support groups was associated with abusers and abused lobbying for improved services (Nahmiash, 1999).

Gravel, Lithwick and Beaulieu (1998, also cited in Lithwick, 1999) found that spousal abuse was associated with psychological dependence of the abuser or the person abused, a caregiver overwhelmed by stress, longstanding conjugal violence or poor marital relationships and a physically dependent abuser. The history of marital problems was not evident when abuse involved people with dementia. One quarter of spouses with cognitive impairment were the abusers and in almost half the situations there was mutual abuse. Caregivers often did not understand the impact of the impairment on the behavior.

Interventions by the home care agencies were most effective in areas where the staff had experience, that is, placement or responding to concerns about caregiving or loss of autonomy Lithwick (1999). They were also successful in 65% of the situations where abuse was committed by non-family, most was financial and intervention led to protective guardianship. The team was less successful with marital discord and dealing directly with abuse.

Podnieks (1995) also identified a hardiness in older adults who had been abused she stressed that use of the passive term "victim" undervalues the person's strength and dignity. This highlights the importance of "tapping the inner strength of the older person" that Quinn and Tomata (1997) discuss as an important intervention strategy.

Complexity of Family Dynamics and Family Caregiving

Research on caregiving highlights difficulties and satisfactions that caregivers face. Globerman's (1994) study of family systems has identified the importance of in-depth understanding of the family's development, member's development and family's negotiation patterns. In the crises imposed by Alzheimer's, members may retreat to past known and safe roles and inflexible relationships. She suggests proactive intervention over the course of the illness with family, not just temporal work with the designated caregivers.

O'Connor (1999) addressed the complexity of caregiving in a spousal relationship and the implications for practice. She stressed, in developing relationships of respect and mutuality, the necessity of acknowledging the expertise of the spouse and reinforcing competence. O'Connor found that while this was accepted in principle, service providers tended to discount the special knowledge of the impaired person's preferences, values, needs and life history that contextualize their behaviors and maintain their humanity, and left the well spouse feeling patronized. It is also important to recognize the impaired partner's power and develop new ways of working with them. She highlighted how social work can provide one context in which the well spouse can reconstitute his or her identity and, through community building, find ways to break the intense isolation.

Social workers need a range of sophisticated skills in family practice. There is also increasing interest in modifying mediation models to meet the needs of older people and their families (Irving, personal communication 2001; Lee, 1996).

Themes

We consulted a number of colleagues across the country, asking them to identify areas of strength and challenge in practice. Common themes were:

- Uncertainty, demoralization and pressure related to restructuring and cutbacks;
- Medicalization of services to older people;
- Codified assessments which may push overburdened staff to focus on a yes/no format of questions to complete a form;
- The need for attention to the needs of rural elderly and how this is neglected in the urban focus of educational programs;
- The decrease in interagency cooperation in areas where they now bid competitively for service contracts;
- Progress in understanding and responding to abuse: older people are now more willingly to raise these issues and workers are more able to initiate discussion;
- Pride in the impact of their work including programs of transition counseling, skills of congregate living, bereavement work, group work;
- Social workers take on innovative responsibilities including resources for the public (Silin's (2001) work is one example).

Some expressed discouragement and despair, others, who tended to be those closer to practice than academia, saw the current situation as an opportunity.

Features of Practice

Direct social work practice is located in a wide-range of primary settings such as family service and multi-service seniors' centers. The provision of transportation and home visits are critical factors. Marital counseling is characterized by the greater commitment to the marriage by the couple and the focus on communication problems. Many long-standing clients have mental health issues, but have not necessarily been connected with psychiatric service at a younger age.

Social work in health care has been an important context for development of gerontological practice with individuals, groups and families. Social workers are involved throughout hospitals, in long term care facilities, geriatric assessment units and day programs. As elsewhere in North America, program management is having a significant impact on social work (Fort Cowles, 2000; Globerman, McDonald, & White, 2000). While discharge planning is still a major focus, shorter hospital stays can limit working through individual and family concerns and puts more responsibility on workers in long-term care settings.

The first comprehensive, province-wide, universal home care program began in 1974 in Manitoba. A range of services are provided to people whose function is likely to deteriorate, and who without supports are not able to remain in the home. Home care and roles of social work vary by province. In Manitoba, social workers are partnered with nurses and their functions include eligibility assessment, planning care and securing services, managing institutional placement when required. They are responsible for liaison to ensure collaborative, coordinated delivery of services, quality assurance and evaluation, quality improvement that critiques existing practice and makes plans for the future (Manitoba Health, 2001).

To illustrate the importance of a range of social work services for older people we outline two programs that specifically address health determinants, well being and quality of life.

Language Programs as a Source of Empowerment and Well-Being

Lack of competence in the language of the dominant culture is isolating, disempowering, dependency creating, and a multiple risk factor for health, integration and acquisition of basic needs. Framed within the resiliency and well-being knowledge, language competency is a significant protective factor. Winnipeg's English as a Second Language (ESL) Program for Seniors has been developed to increase language confidence and competency, to foster integration and to promote health and well being. It has proved successful because, in addition to classes, it identified and overcame barriers that discourage learning.

The program showed limited growth until barriers, identified by a need assessment were removed. Classes moved from high schools to senior's centers where seniors felt safe, transportation and child-care are now provided if needed; feelings of alienation were addressed by providing a teacher or aid who speaks participants' language and community outreach workers who maintain contact with the senior throughout the program. A major goal has been to foster integration of the ESL seniors into the senior's centers (which are not cultural-specific) and into the community. Many activities take place in real-life situations such as trips to the bank, using the bus system, cooking, and shopping. Non-ESL seniors are recruited as mentors both to help in using English and to forge a link to seniors' activities. A cross-generational/cross-cultural partnership of seniors with grade 7 students was initiated in which seniors identify their interests and the students find books that match these interests and visit them monthly to read together.

The resulting dynamic program has grown from 90 participants to over 300 serving fifteen different languages. Participants evaluate it highly and emphasize their new skills: being able to communicate with grandchildren, greet neighbours, use the telephone, take the bus, go shopping and communicate health-care needs. As one senior said "This proves you can teach an old parrot new tricks."

The Senior Friendly Program

Older people are leaders in an initiative designed to facilitate community services in understanding and meeting the needs of seniors more appropriately. The program was developed by Alberta's Council of Aging with federal funding and is now moving across the country. It takes an educative approach that includes the following: increasing self-awareness, assertiveness and skills of social change in older people; a framework for assessing the senior friendly qualities of local businesses, health and social services; seniors provide leadership in training management and staff; and certification of implementation of senior friendly standards.

Trends and Challenges

There is a body of knowledge based on practice wisdom and research in social work and other disciplines and evidence of the range and depth of knowledge and skills required. The tension lies in being able to put this knowledge into practice.

In some ways Canada has moved away from social models of care and issues of quality of life that characterized the emphasis of developments in the 1980s. In an atmosphere of fiscal constraint, case management can be a set of procedures for dehumanizing "cases" and rationing services rather than a creative process of working with the older person and family members to develop and implement a program of care responsive to their individual and joint needs. Within the dominant rhetoric of managed care social workers and others are pressed to focus on the immediate, the practical and the surface (Chambon, 1994). The use of the term empowerment can mask dumping services on the family or leaving isolated older people without meaningful support. As Aronson (1999, p. 61) states, ironically, the rhetorical invocation of 'community' care is often bereft of community connection and means, rather, that older people simple survive in private households with 'consumer of service' as the only identity available to them.

She (1999) discusses how older people come to home care and service providers from a position of subordination in a culture that devalues age and bodily frailty (p. 56). Her research with older women showed some were able to continue 'to manage' in an active self-directed way in contrast to 'being managed.' She cites examples of women who were able to persuade their homemakers to assist them with in particular ways, for example, to forgo a sanctioned grocery shopping on occasion in order to use the time for a home permanent. This ability to maintain control and personalize their service is not available to all. Success hinges on the woman's capacity (cognitively, socially) to establish positive relationships with their care providers who, simultaneously, have the capacity to personalize their work and extend themselves (Aronson, 1999, p. 56).

Marshall (1989 cited in Aronson, 1999) states "the need to stand alongside the old person against the forces of ageism, and insist they deserve and must have at least as much as other people. A simmering anger characterizes the best social workers in the field" (p. 117).

A component of ageism is the belief that services are unproductive. Herbert (1997) found that nearly one-third of older people experiencing functional decline recover their lost abilities. He states this invalidates the traditional defeatist attitude and justifies assessment treatment and rehabilitation (p. 1044). Services should encompass resocialization and reintegration as a full participant in normal life as possible.

Devolution of social services from direct government provision to third party delivery has accelerated rapidly in the last decade (Stephenson et al., 2000). Moreover most health service restructuring currently focuses on downsizing institutional care and the devolution of services to the home. Vulnerable older people are often invisible.

There is growing public concern about adverse impacts of cutbacks and research is documenting the importance of health and social services and their economic advantages. Browne and her colleagues (1999) have found that comprehensive care costs no more. Their studies over ten years have shown that a piecemeal approach to helping vulnerable populations can not only be expensive, but also miss the causes of the problems. People who rely heavily on the health system use fewer or less expensive health and social services when all their needs are met appropriately. Savings may also occur as family members are able to return to employment. Browne (1999) states that this research suggests that the most successful strategies are those that are:

- cooperative and cross-sectional, linking physical, mental, social and other services;
- comprehensive and holistic, treating the whole person or whole family in context;
- proactive, reaching out to those who are unlikely to be able to find help they need on their own.

A recent study (Hollander cited in Picard, 2001) has shown even cutbacks of cleaning service can be counterproductive. Over a three-year period people whose service was eliminated had increased health care costs, increased institutionalization and increased mortality.

Drover (1998) stated that every decade has required social work action in the area of social reform. He concludes, "like those social workers who preceded us, we need . . . to have confidence in ourselves, to build on our roots, to profess what we believe, to engage in practice of the highest ethical standards we can attain, and to struggle with others in creating a better society" (p. 89).

REFERENCES

Aronson, J. (1999). Conflicting images of older people receiving care: Challenges for reflexive practice and research. In S. M. Neysmith (Ed.), *Critical Issues for Future Social Work Practice with Aging Persons*, (pp. 47-70). New York: Columbia.

Browne, G., Roberts, J., Gafni, A., Byrne, C., Weir, R., Majumdar, B., & Watt, S. (1999). Economic evaluations of community-based care: Lessons from twelve studies in Ontario. *Journal of Evaluation in Clinical Practice, 5*, 367-385.

Buzzell, M., Meredith, S., Monna, K., Ritchie, L., & Sergeant, D. (1993). *Personhood: A teaching package*. Hamilton: Education Centre for Aging and Health, McMaster University.

Chambon, A. S. (1994). Postmodernity and social work discourses. In A. S. Chambon & A. Irving (Eds), *Essays on Postmodernism and Social Work* (pp. 63-72). Toronto: Canadian Scholar's Press.

Chappell, N. L. (1999). *Volunteering and Healthy Aging: What We Know*. Ottawa: Volunteer Canada.

Cox, E. O., & Parsons, R. J. (1994). *Empowerment-Oriented Social Work Practice with the Elderly*. Pacific Grove, CA: Brooks-Cole.

Drover, G. (1998). Social work–our roots, our future. *The Social Worker, 66*, 79-92.

ECAH. (1993). *Educational Development and Curriculum Content in Aging and Health*. Ontario University Coalition for Education in Health Care of the Elderly. Hamilton: Educational Centre for Aging and Health, McMaster University.

Fisher, R., Ross, M., & MacLean, M. J. (2000). *A Guide to End-of-Life Care for Seniors*. Toronto, ON: University of Toronto, Division of Geriatrics.

Fort Cowles, L. A. (2000). *Social Work in the Health Field: A Care Perspective*. NY: The Haworth Press, Inc.

Globerman, J. (1994). Balancing tensions in families with Alzheimer's disease: The self and the family. *Journal of Aging Studies, 8*, 211-232.

Gravel, S., Lithwick, M., & Beaulieu, M. (1998). *Les Dynamiques des mauvais traitment envers les personnages agees: Connaissance theorique et enjeux pratique*. Final research report. CLSC Rene-Cassin, University Institute of Social Gerontology of Quebec.

Hart, M. (2001). An Aboriginal approach to social work practice. In T. Heinonen & L. Spearman (Eds.), *Social Work Practice Problem Solving and Beyond* (pp. 231-256). Toronto: Irwin.

Herbert, R. (1997). Functional decline in old age. *Canadian Medical Association Journal, 157*, 1037-1045.

Keating, N., Fast, J., Frederick, J., Cranswick, K., & Perrier, C. (1999). *Eldercare in Canada: Context, Content and Consequences*. Ottawa: Statistics Canada, Housing, Family and Social Statistics Division.

Kivick, H. Q. (1991). *Living with Care, Caring for Life: The Inventory of Life Strengths, Assessing Psychosocial Strengths in Long-term Care Clients*. Minneapolis, MN: University of Minnesota Long-Term Care Resource Center.

Lee, W. (1996). *The Efficiency and Effectiveness of Hospital Discharge Planning with the Use of Mediation Principles*. Toronto: University of Toronto School of Social Work.

Lithwick, M. (1999). The dynamics of elder abuse and the options for intervention. In J. Pritchard (Ed.), *Elder Abuse Work: Best practice in Britain and Canada* (pp. 354-376). London: Jessica Kingsley.

Manitoba Health. (2001). *Manitoba Home Care Program*. Winnipeg, MB: Author.

McDonald, P. M., Hornick, J. P., Robertson, G. B., & Wallace, J. E. (1991). *Elder Abuse and Neglect in Canada*. Toronto: Butterworths.

McKenzie, P., Tod, L., & Yellen, P. (1995). Community-based intervention strategies for cases of abuse and neglect of seniors: A comparison of models, philosophies and practice issues. In M. J. MacLean (Ed.), *Abuse and Neglect of Older Canadians: Strategies for Change*. Toronto: Thompson.

Nahmiash, D. (1999). From powerlessness to empowerment. In J. Pritchard (Ed.), *Elder Abuse Work: Best Practice in Britain and Canada* (pp. 294-319). London: Jessica Kingsley.

National Advisory Council on Aging, (1995). *The NACA Position on Determining Priorities in Health Care: The Senior's Perspective*. Ottawa: Minister of Supply and Services Canada.

National Advisory Council on Aging. (2000). *Expression*, *13*, 4, 1-10.

National Council of Welfare. (2000). *Poverty Profile 1998*. Ottawa: National Council of Welfare.

Neysmith, S. (1988). Canadian social services and social work practice in the field of aging. *Gerontological Social Work*, 41-60.

O'Connor, D. (1999). Constructing community care: (Re) storying support. In S. M. Neysmith (Ed.), *Critical issues for future social work practice with aging persons* (pp. 71-96). New York: Columbia.

Paine, M. (1997). *Modern Social Work Theory*. Chicago: Lyceum.

Picard, A. (2001, May 26). Cutting "frills" to seniors' care costs thousands. *Globe and Mail*, pp. A1, A8.

Pittaway, J. (1995). Risk factors for abuse and neglect among older adults. *Canadian Journal on Aging*, *14*, supplement, 21-44.

Podnieks, E. (1995). *A New Perspective on Elder Abuse: Hardiness in Victims*. Unpublished doctoral dissertation, University of Toronto, Toronto.

Quinn, M. J. & Tomita, S. K. (1997). *Elder Abuse and Neglect: Causes, diagnosis and intervention strategies*. New York: Springer.

Reis, M. (1999). Innovative interventions when seniors are abused. In J. Pritchard (Ed.), *Elder Abuse Work: Best practice in Britain and Canada* (pp.378-407). London: Jessica Kingsley.

Reis, M., & Nahmiash, D. (1995a). *When Seniors Are Abused: A Guide to Intervention*. Toronto: Captus Press.

Reis, M., & Nahmiash, D. (1995b). When Seniors Are Abused: An Intervention Model. *Gerontologist*, *35*, 5, 666-671.

Rosen, A. (2000). *CSWE/SAGE-SW Social Work Gerontological Competencies*. Alexandria, VA: Council on Social Work Education.

Scharlach, A., Damron-Rodriguez, J., Robinson, B., & Feldman, R. (2000). Educating social workers for an aging society: A vision for the 21st century. *Journal of Social Work Education*, *36*, 521-538.

Sergeant, D., Whittaker, S., & Black, M. (1996). *Autonomy: A teaching package*. Hamilton: Education Centre for Aging and Health, McMaster University.

Silin, P. (2001). *Nursing Homes: A Family's Journey*. Baltimore, MD: Johns Hopkins.

Statistics Canada. (1999). *A Portrait of Seniors in Canada* (3rd ed.). Ottawa: Statistics Canada.

Stephenson, M., Rondeau, G., Michaud, J. C., & Fiddler, S. (2000). *In Critical Demand: Social Work in Canada, Final Report*. Ottawa: Canadian Association of Schools of Social Work.

Wells, L. M., Singer, C., & Polgar, A. T. (1992). *To Enhance Quality of Life in Institutions: An Empowerment Model in Long Term Care*. Toronto, ON: Canadian Scholar's Press.

Challenges and Issues
Under Long-Term Care Insurance
for the Elderly in Japan

Miyuki Inaba, PhD

SUMMARY. This article examines the Long-Term Care Insurance (LTCI) program for the elderly in Japan. LTCI is presented as Japan's policy approach to the growing need for care for the elderly. The paper describes the context around which the policy was developed, describes details about the policy, and the implementation issues of the policy. The paper traces the role of social work as a profession in Japan as it relates to the issues of implementing LTCI. Suggestions are made in this paper for possible integration of social work professional roles in effective implementation of LTCI. *[Article copies available for a fee from The Haworth Document Delivery Service: 1-800-HAWORTH. E-mail address: <getinfo@haworthpressinc.com> Website: <http://www.HaworthPress.com> © 2001 by The Haworth Press, Inc. All rights reserved.]*

KEYWORDS. Long-Term care insurance, gerontology, social work in Japan, elderly care, elderly policy

INTRODUCTION

This article offers an overview of major social policies for the elderly in Japan and examines the current status of social work with particular

---

Miyuki Inaba is Assistant Professor at the Department of Social Welfare at Fukuoka Prefectural University, 4395 Ita, Tagawa-shi, Fukuoka 825-8585, Japan.

[Haworth co-indexing entry note]: "Challenges and Issues Under Long-Term Care Insurance for the Elderly in Japan." Inaba, Miyuki. Co-published simultaneously in *Journal of Gerontological Social Work* (The Haworth Social Work Practice Press, an imprint of The Haworth Press, Inc.) Vol. 36, No. (3/4), 2001, pp. 51-61; and: *Gerontological Social Work Practice: Issues, Challenges, and Potential* (ed: Enid Opal Cox, Elizabeth S. Kelchner, and Rosemary Chapin) The Haworth Social Work Practice Press, an imprint of The Haworth Press, Inc., 2001, pp. 51-61. Single or multiple copies of this article are available for a fee from The Haworth Document Delivery Service [1-800-HAWORTH, 9:00 a.m. - 5:00 p.m. (EST). E-mail address: getinfo@haworth pressinc.com].

51

reference to Long-Term Care Insurance (LTCI) that has been under implementation since April 2000. A brief review of the status of the social work profession and the challenges and issues of social work within the framework of LTCI are also suggested.

The Demographics: Population Age 65 and Older

Japan is the most rapidly aging society in the world. In October 1999, the number of those aged 65 and over reached 21.2 million, making up 16.7%, a 0.5% increase from the previous year, of the whole population. The percentage of the population over age 65 is projected to be 26.2% in 2020, roughly comparable to a U.S. forecast for the same age group (Anderson & Hussey, 2000; Office of the Prime Minister, 2000). By 2015, one-fourth of Japan's population will be over age 65 (Crowell & Murakami, 1998). This trend is expected to continue for another century and also implies an increase of the elderly in need of long-term care due to physical and/or mental disabilities. The number of elderly needing long-term care is expected to increase from 2.8 million in 2000 to 5.2 million in 2025 (Usui & Palley, 1997). The average life expectancy in 1999 was 83.9 years for women and 77.1 years for men (Health and Welfare Statistics Association (HWSA), 2000), both the highest life expectancy in the world. The percentage of the population age 80 and older will grow more rapidly in Japan (from 3.7 % in 2000 to 7.5% in 2020, a 107% increase), while it will grow from 3.3% in 2000 to 3.7% in 2020 in the United States.

In contrast, the declining birth rate particularly since the 1980s is another contributing factor to Japan's rapidly aging society. In 1997, a woman gave birth on average to only 1.38 children in Japan (HWSA, 2000), which is one of the lowest worldwide, while it was approximately 2.03 in the United States (Ministry of Health and Welfare (MHW), 2000). Given the context of an ever-increasing population of the elderly coupled with a steadily decreasing population of children, care systems for the elderly in Japan are under increasing strain.

Weakening Family Care for Elderly

With regard to informal care for frail elderly in Japan, co-resident family members are the most dependable source of social support (Koyano, Hashimoto, Fukawa, Shibata, & Gunji, 1994). These are elderly populations living with their children and grandchildren in some cases. The Ministry of Health and Welfare (MHW) survey in 1995 (MHW, 1997) found that 84% of caregivers for bed bound people of 65 years and over were females and only 16% were males. In addition, those female care-givers themselves are often over 60 (Crowell & Murakami, 1998; Maeda, 1983). According to the survey conducted by the Metropolitan Tokyo Government in 1995, co-resident family members cared for 88.4% of the disabled elderly, 31.5% of principal caregivers were wives, 23.0% were daughters, and 22.1% were daughters-in-law (Metropolitan Tokyo, 1996). It can be said the high percentage of co-resident families has sustained a key role in providing care for the frail elderly in Japan.

However, this system of family care for the elderly is being eroded in Japan today. There are many factors affecting this change in Japanese family support: (1) low birth rate, (2) more mobility, (3) changing atti-tudes of elderly people preferring more independent living, (4) more nuclear families, and (5) urbanization and industrialization (Kaplan & Thang, 1997; Kono, 2000).

Although the proportion of elderly aged 65 and over living in three-generation households is still high compared to other countries, the rate declined from 50.1% in 1980 to 27.3% in 1999 (MHW, 2000). The percentage of Japanese elderly living with their children has also declined from 81.4% in 1960, 69.0% in 1980, to 54.3% in 1995 (Kono, 2000). Hence, there are an increasing number of elderly living alone and elderly couples living by themselves. In 1999, 18.2% of elderly over 65 were living alone (MHW, 2000). Elderly couple households also increased to 27.7% by 1999 (HWSA, 2000). Many of them have problems in the areas of finance, housing, health, nutrition, and social network (Shimizu, Asano, & Miyazaki, 1994). More than half of those over 65 have some health problems (Hashimoto & Takahashi, 1995).

Another factor that contributed to the decreased capability of fami-lies to care for the elderly is a growing number of working women. Women who have more education and marketable skills than in the past are not as readily available to assume the family caregiving roles and are more critical of traditional styles of family care.

For the reasons stated above, providing informal family care for frail elderly is now more difficult. While it is true that the Confucian ethic of "filial piety," which has been the basis for family support for the el-derly, is still ingrained in Japanese society, caregiving commitment re-lated to filial piety is expected to weaken in the future.

SOCIAL POLICIES FOR THE ELDERLY

Faced with rapid demographic changes, Japan has embarked on a va-riety of programs and initiatives to meet the needs of the elderly population. In 1989, Japan announced a comprehensive national plan for the future entitled a Ten-Year Strategy to Promote Health Care and Welfare for the Aged, known as the "Gold Plan." The plan was revised in 1994, and requires strong local involvement.

The Gold Plan especially addressed the needs of the growing number of bedridden or senile old people (Campbell, 1992). The seven major goals of the plan are: (1) urgent development of in-home services for the aged in municipalities, (2) reduction of bedridden aged people to zero, (3) establishment of a "Longevity Social Welfare Fund," (4) urgent development of institutional facilities for the aged, (5) promotion of measures to enhance productive aging, (6) promotion of gerontological research, and (7) development of comprehensive welfare institutions for the aged that includes a huge increase in the number of in-home helpers, short-stay beds in institutions, day-service centers, and in-home care support centers (Hashimoto & Takahashi, 1995). Three home services play a vital role in this plan: home help, short-stay in residential care service, and day-service centers. The major change the Gold Plan represents is a shift from institution-based services to home-care services. This plan is also significant because this was the first time that care for frail elderly had been acknowledged through national policy. The 1994 revisions placed stronger emphasis on increasing the number of home helpers, increasing long-term facilities for skilled nursing home care, and short-stay institutions beds. However, the primary focus of the revised Gold Plan was on providing manpower and services for in-home care for the elderly.

Long-Term-Care Insurance (2000)

In April 2000, Japan instigated a mandatory Long-Term Care Insurance (LTCI) program. LTCI replaced the long-term care portion of medical service for the elderly and departs drastically from traditional services to the long-term-care of the frail elderly in Japan. According to Campbell and Ikegami (2000), there are five objectives under this new program: (1) shift a major responsibility for caregiving from the family to the state; (2) integrate medical care and social services via unified financing; (3) enhance consumer choice and competition by allowing free choice of providers, including even for-profit companies; (4) require older persons themselves to share the costs via insurance premiums as well as copayments; and (5) expand local government autonomy and management capacity in social policy.

Under this program, the insurer is the municipalities and the insured are all residents aged 40 and over. Premiums come from two categories: those aged 65 and over (Category 1) deducted from their public pensions and those aged between 40 and 64 (Category 2) who pay a supplemental to their health insurance premium. LTCI covers long-term care services irrespective of the cause of disability for Category 1. However, for Category 2, services are only covered if one's disability is caused by "geriatric disorders" such as cerebrovascular stroke or Alzheimer's disease (Koyano, 1999). Eligibility is exclusively defined based on age and physical and mental condition regardless of income and family situation: that is one of the major differences from traditional welfare services. Municipalities have the formal responsibility to determine how much they will spend on LTCI statutory benefits for their eligible residents.

The insured (individual or family) must apply to the insurer (municipality) for assessment of eligibility with regard to applicant's physical and mental status. Assessment data will be analyzed by a government computer program that will classify eligible applicants into six levels. After review by an expert committee at the municipal level, the applicants will be informed of their eligibility and can purchase required services by paying 10% of the cost. For each level, recipients can receive an explicitly defined monetary amount of services ranging from $535 to $3,115 per month. At their own expense, recipients can purchase additional services. Eligibility is reevaluated every six months.

A new type of certified professional called care manager plays a key role in implementing LTCI. One of their major responsibilities is to formulate a weekly care plan that specifies the contents of care services in consultation with the recipients. The services covered under this insurance include both institutional and community-based care. There are numerous health and social service professionals who can become care managers, these include nurses, occupational therapists, medical doctors, pharmacists, certified social workers, certified care workers, massage therapists, acupuncturists, and home helpers who have more than five years of work experience in elderly care. They have to pass the exam and participate in a brief training. The first exam took place in 1998. Out of 230,000 applicants, 90,000 passed the exam.

Social Work Profession

Social workers in Japan are employed at all levels in the services for elderly including the care manager position under LTCI. However, the profession of social work is still in the process of becoming established in Japan and social workers' identity is still obscure. The quest for professional status by social workers is in process in Japan and the struggle for increased acceptance of social work credentials continues. There are a number of practitioners who work as social workers but do not necessarily identify themselves as social workers; instead they identify themselves as, for instance, counselors, welfare workers, and employment supervisors. Due to having different fields of specialization and working in a wide variety of institutions, it is currently difficult for many to identity themselves as social workers. The following section will briefly describe the main manpower for social welfare in Japan (Kyogoku, 1997; HWSA, 2000).

1. Social Welfare Officer (*Shakaifukushi-shuji*) established by the Law of Social Welfare Works of 1951: In order to become Shakaifukushi-shuji, there are generally several paths to take: studying three social science courses out of sociology, economics, psychology, law, etc., at a college/university; obtaining a B.A. degree from social welfare college/university; graduating from welfare-related technical school with work experience; and working in welfare-related institutions over so many years. They are usually employed in the public sector and transferred to various positions every three to five years.

2. Certified Social Worker (*Shakaifukushi-shi*) established in 1987 by The Law of Certified Social Workers and Care Workers: They must pass a national examination. Those who are graduates of a social work four-year university program are eligible to take an exam upon completing requirements (course work and field placement) while graduates of a two-year social welfare-related college program must have two years of working experience. Graduates of four-year universities with any majors can be eligible to take the exam if they have one-year work experience. Certified Social Workers' responsibilities include providing advice, counseling and supervision as a professional with special knowledge and skills with regard to the welfare of the physically and mentally handicapped.

3. Certified Care Worker (*Kaigofukushi-shi*) established in 1987 by The Law of Certified Social Workers and Care Workers: They must also pass a national examination. Their work includes providing care and advice on the care to the physically and mentally handicapped and their families. In most cases, they will be home-helpers

in private homes and caretakers in assisted living and nursing home facilities.

4. Certified Psychiatric Social Worker (*Seishin Shakaifukushi-shi*) established in 1997 by the Law of Psychiatric Social Workers: They must also pass a national examination, which started in 1999. Their responsibilities include counseling and supervision as a professional with special knowledge and skills to assist people with mental health problems with daily living and help them making a transition to independent living in communities.

5. Social worker without certification: Since the certification of social workers was only established in 1987, there are still many human services practitioners who are working as social workers with no certification.

Roles for Certified Social Workers in Long-Term Care Insurance

This article focuses on the possible role of Certified Social Workers (CSW), working as care managers in the Long-Term Care Insurance system. As new services develop and are being implemented under LTCI, roles and functions of human services practitioners including Certified Social Workers who are working with frail elderly need to be reconsidered in the areas of direct practice, access services, staff development, policy analysis and advocacy, and research. Most important, LTCI presents both challenges and opportunities for the social work profession to enhance the professional's status and credentials.

Direct Practice

Under the LTCI, as mentioned above, the care manager plays a key role in assessing applicants' needs and formulating a weekly care plan in consultation with them. Care managers' responsibilities also include locating suitable services within or outside of LTCI, linking recipients to resources, and assisting recipients to remain at home as long as possible. This requires extensive knowledge of community resources including informal networks as well as skill in making effective referrals to community-based services. Referrals to other community resources seem to be entirely up to individual care managers. Many critics state that care managers seem to simply be acting as matchmakers among available care services and the maximum monetary limit of services within the framework of LTCI (*Asahi,* April 1, 2001; Ikegami, 2000; Watanabe, 2000). In other words, care managers could easily overlook the recipients' psychosocial conditions and the type of interventions needed for independent living, thereby not making a holistic assessment of the recipients. Given large caseload sizes (national caseload is 50 per month) and limited preparation time under LTCI, many care managers have been implementing the program under much uncertainty. However, this is the area in which certified social workers CSW could take a leadership role as care managers since social workers are well prepared to conduct a thorough psychosocial assessment and trained in case management and community work.

Access Services

Under LTCI, the eligible elderly have a choice with regard to the contents of care services. Providing accurate and timely information in terms of available services, upper limit of monetary amount of services, the 10% copayment, and anything else to new LTCI recipients is an important direct service. Recipients of LTCI services may be newly classified as frail elderly. These individuals and/or family members have had prior contact with service providers, and stigma may be an issue.

Case advocacy may also play an important role in protecting recipients' rights for fair and timely services. According to *Asahi's* survey of community-base-care, many municipalities reported that service use was much less than expected (*Asahi,* March 8, 2001). The process of complaints about services or access is not yet well established. In addition, almost all care managers are employees of service providers. Therefore, there might be a tendency to favor one's employer (provider) whatever the recipients' interests/needs. Attention must be taken to ensure that recipients are treated fairly and receiving the services agreed to in the contract.

Staff Development

Long-Term Care Insurance created a drastic change in the long-term care of frail elderly in Japan. All human service practitioners require in-service training or continuing education regarding this new system. Since its inception in April 2000 many issues seem to be emerging; for example, initial assessment of eligibility does not appear to be uniform among care managers (*Asahi,* October 3, 2000). Under LTCI, care managers will need extensive training in many areas, including family functioning, economic background, cultural awareness and sensitivity, knowledge of community resources, skills for advocacy, and basic counseling skills. Without such training, care managers will not be able to serve recipients responsibly. Social workers are trained in these areas and can contribute to the development of training programs.

Policy Analysis and Advocacy

Almost all care services under the previous welfare services were publicly funded and users usually did not have to pay; if they did, it was a very small amount. The old system also took into account the socio-economic condition of applicants. The issue of copayment has emerged as a problem particularly for low-income recipients.

Social work's policy analysis and advocacy roles are needed as LTCI is implemented. Social work must point out the financial burden that has been heavily placed on elderly with low income. Both at the national and prefectural levels, the profession's values and commitment to disadvantaged people, frail elderly in this case, should frame the profession's advocacy role. Advocacy efforts will be necessary for poor elderly in terms of LTCI copayment system when LTCI is reviewed and evaluated. At the local level, social workers can advocate for developing a sufficient base of community services that will fulfill the needs of elderly they serve.

Involvement of social workers in advocacy is still not well developed in Japan. There is a need for social workers to get more actively involved in case and class advocacy roles. Involvement as a care manager under LTCI might provide an opportunity to do so.

Research

Researchers in all human service areas including social work have a critical role to play as LTCI moves forward. Researchers in the human services, particularly social work may be well positioned to consider two major areas. First, research needs to be done on the effects of LTCI on the lives of elderly recipients and their families. LTCI has been under implementation for over a year and many issues have been emerging. How many qualified elderly are actually using services under LTCI? What factors are hindering and interfering with service use? Are elderly recipients receiving quality care and services? Second, as LTCI moves forward, it will be important for social work researchers and advocates to conduct studies on experiences and opinions of care managers as well as their roles and functions. According to a survey conducted by *Asahi* (April 1, 2001), more than 60% of 2000 care managers thought about quitting the job due to overwork. Some stated that they are not in a position to formulate care plans based on recipients' needs and interests.

CONCLUSION

Japan's social work profession is in the process of establishment. At the same time, social work is challenged to define and establish its role in services and programs for the Japanese aging population. Rapid development in the field of gerontology such as Long-Term Care Insurance presents new opportunities and challenges to social workers. By making a contribution to the development of more responsive services and social policies for frail elderly, social workers can increase the professional status and recognition of social work in Japan.

Challenges such as identifying the role of social workers vis-à-vis other professions, exclusion of psychosocial factors in assessment and intervention; increasing the status of social work in advocacy and policy decisions as gerontological social work grows in Japan appears to be similar to challenges faced by social workers in the United States. Even though social work is a long-established profession in the United States, the entry of many disciplines and lay workers into the policy dialogue and the provision of social services to the elderly raise common cross-national concerns. Specifically the need to clearly articulate social work's real and potential contributions, to create and develop new effective interventions, and to be proactive in policy and program development are issues that are common to gerontological social work in both countries.

REFERENCES

Anderson, G. F., & Hussey, P. S. (2000). Population aging: A comparison among industrialized countries. *Health Affairs, 19* (3), 191-203.

Campbell. J. (1992). How policies change. *The Japanese Government and the aging society.* Princeton, NJ: Princeton University Press.

Campbell, J. & Ikegami, N. (2000). Long-Term Care Insurance Comes to Japan, *Health Affairs, 19* (3), 26-39.

Care Manager: 60% thought about quitting. (2001, April 1). *Asahi Newspaper,* pp.1 & 3.

Crowell, T., & Murakami, M. (1998, July 24). Japan faces the challenges of a fast-aging population. *Asiaweek,* 46-51.

Hashimoto, R., & Takahashi, M. (1995). Between family obligation and social care–the significance of institutional care for the elderly in Japan. *Journal of Sociology & Social Welfare, 22*(4), 47-67.

Health and Welfare Statistics Association. (2000). *Journal of Health and Welfare Statistics*. Tokyo: Author.

Ikegami, N. (2000). The Launch of Long-Term Care Insurance. *Japan Echo, 27* (3), 28-33.

Kaigo hoken hantoshi: [aratana futan] wareru taiou [Long-term Care Insurance after 6 months: divided responses to new burden]. (2000, October 3). *Asahi Newspaper*, p. 13.

Kaplan, M., & Thang, L. L. (1997). Intergenerational programs in Japan: Symbolic extensions of family unity. *Journal of Aging and Identity, 2* (4), 295-315.

Kono, M. (2000). The impact of modernization and social policy on family care for older people in Japan. *Journal of Social Policy, 29* (2), 11-203.

Koyano, W. (1999). Population aging, changed in living arrangement, and the new long-term care system in Japan. *Journal of Sociology & Social Welfare, 226* (19), 155-167.

Koyano, W., Hashimoto, M., Fukawa, T., Shibata, H. & Gunji, A. (1994). The social support system of the Japanese elderly. *Journal of Cross-Cultural Gerontology, 9*, 323-333.

Kyogoku, T. (1997). Evaluation and Issues for Professionalization of social welfare workers after 10 years–Licensing of social worker. *Social Welfare Studies, 69*, 42-49.

Maeda, D. (1983). Family care in Japan. *The Gerontologist, 23* (6), 579-583.

Metropolitan Tokyo. (1996). *Living conditions of the elderly: Report of the 1995 basic survey on social services*. Tokyo: Metropolitan Tokyo (written in Japanese).

Ministry of Health and Welfare. (1997). *White Paper on Health and Welfare*. Tokyo: Author.

Ministry of Health and Welfare. (2000). *White Paper on Health and Welfare*. Tokyo: Author.

Office of the Prime Minister. (2000). *Kourei Hakusyo (White Paper on the Aged)*. Tokyo: Ministry of Finance Printing Bureau.

Shimizu, Y., Asano, J., & Miyazaki, A. (1994). (Eds.). *Social welfare services for the elderly: Concepts and methods in policy and practice (3rd ed.)*. Tokyo: Kaisei sha.

Teichaku ye kaizen no yochi. [Room for improvement with LTCI establishment]. (2001, March 8). *Asahi Newspaper*, p. 13.

Usui, C., & Palley, H. A. (1997). The development of social policy for the elderly in Japan. *Social Service Review, 71* (3), 360-381.

Watanabe, R. (2000). Care manager ka Kaigo Hoken Kyufu Kanrisya ka? Care manager or eligibility administrator of LTCI? *Care Manager*, 2000 October, 15-16.

Gerontological Social Work Research: Current Status and Future Directions

Nancy Morrow-Howell, PhD, MSW
Denise Burnette, PhD, MSSW

SUMMARY. This article assesses the current state of gerontological social work research and suggests future directions for the field. We review data that suggest social workers are contributing to the multidisciplinary knowledge base in aging, although their contributions to this literature are incommensurate with their involvement in interdisciplinary practice. Social workers are not adequately represented among researchers supported by public and private funds. We offer some strategies to augment initiatives already in place to increase the production of gerontological social work research. *[Article copies available for a fee from The Haworth Document Delivery Service: 1-800-HAWORTH. E-mail address: <getinfo@haworthpressinc.com> Website: <http://www.HaworthPress.com> © 2001 by The Haworth Press, Inc. All rights reserved.]*

KEYWORDS. Social work research, gerontological research, social work profession, social work research agenda

Nancy Morrow-Howell is Associate Professor, George Warren Brown School of Social Work, Washington University, Campus Box 1196, St. Louis, MI 63130.

Denise Burnette is Associate Professor, School of Social Work, Columbia University, 622 West 113th Street, New York, NY 10025.

[Haworth co-indexing entry note]: "Gerontological Social Work Research: Current Status and Future Directions." Morrow-Howell, Nancy, and Denise Burnette. Co-published simultaneously in *Journal of Gerontological Social Work* (The Haworth Social Work Practice Press, an imprint of The Haworth Press, Inc.) Vol. 36, No. (3/4), 2001, pp. 63-79; and: *Gerontological Social Work Practice: Issues, Challenges, and Potential* (ed: Enid Opal Cox, Elizabeth S. Kelchner, and Rosemary Chapin) The Haworth Social Work Practice Press, an imprint of The Haworth Press, Inc., 2001, pp. 63-79. Single or multiple copies of this article are available for a fee from The Haworth Document Delivery Service [1-800-HAWORTH, 9:00 a.m. - 5:00 p.m. (EST). E-mail address: getinfo@haworthpressinc.com].

There has much discussion during the past decade about preparing health and social service systems for the aging population. Although progress has at times seemed slow, there is renewed energy in the social work profession to rectify the shortage of gerontological social workers, social work educators, and social work researchers. This energy emanates from myriad sources, including a new Aging Section in the National Association of Social Workers (NASW), growing membership in the Association for Gerontology Education in Social Work (AGE-SW), and a substantial investment in the profession's advancement by the John A. Hartford Foundation of New York City. Any attempt to assess progress toward expanding and enhancing gerontological social work requires consideration of these and other efforts.

The purpose of this paper is to take stock of where we are in gerontological social work research. There have been repeated calls to increase the number of well-trained and productive social work researchers who can advance knowledge for practice and policy in aging (Lubben, 2001; Scharlach, Damron-Rodriguez, Robinson, & Feldman, 2000). As several major initiatives aimed at increasing this type of scholarship are now underway, it is timely to assess the current state of research in the field and to consider how best to consolidate and advance our gains. Such an accounting can also serve as a baseline for future evaluations of progress as the initiatives now underway have their intended impact.

Specifically, this article aims to: (1) assess the current state of gerontological social work research; (2) review current initiatives aimed at enhancing research; and (3) suggest future directions for the field. We accomplish the first aim by examining four questions: Are social work faculty identifying research interests in gerontology? Are social work researchers contributing to the multidisciplinary knowledge base of gerontology? What topics are gerontological social workers investigating? Are social workers being funded for their research? We accomplish the second aim by describing current initiatives to enhance gerontological social work research. Specifically, we consider efforts to build individual research capacity; promote gerontology within national organizations; and identify and prioritize gerontological social work research topics. Finally, we identify several potential strategies for future development.

CURRENT STATE OF GERONTOLOGICAL SOCIAL WORK RESEARCH

Are Social Work Faculty Identifying Research Interests in Gerontology?

We were unable to identify a database to answer this question. The 1999 Council on Social Work Education (CSWE) annual survey of BSW and MSW programs reports a total of 6,943 faculty (Lennon, 2001). This source does not systematically obtain data on areas of expertise, but the number of faculty interested in gerontological social work can be estimated from two sources. In 2000, membership in the Association for Gerontology Education in Social Work (AGE-SW), the national association for gerontology faculty, was at least 108. The CSWE *Strengthening Aging and Gerontology Education for Social Work* (SAGE)[1] database lists 271 full-time, adjunct, and administrative social work faculty interested in aging. The overlap between the CSWE/SAGE-SW list and AGE-SW membership is 83 people (Anita Rosen, personal communication, June, 2001). We thus estimate that about 296 social work faculty have an expressed interest in aging by virtue of their membership in AGE-SW or on the SAGE-SW interest list. This figure represents 4% of all social work faculty enumerated by CSWE. It is important to note, for the purpose of this manuscript, that not all individuals identified thusly are actively engaged in research.

Using Austin's (1998) *Report on Progress in the Development of Research Resources in Social Work,* we can also compare the number of gerontology faculty with those interested other social work domains. According to Austin, the domains in this report were derived through, "reports of on-going research in social work education programs, including research centers and institutes and the activities of individual funded researchers" (p. 19). About 60 social work researchers in this pool identified aging as a research interest. This number compares with over 300 researchers who identified families/children/adolescents/child welfare as their main area of research interest, and approximately 100 in mental health, 100 in health, 60 in poverty/income maintenance, 60 in women issues, and 40 in substance abuse. Austin also reports on an e-mail survey of members of the Society for Social Work and Research regarding their main areas of research interest. Gerontology ranked fourth as a domain of current or future research interest in this survey, after children, mental health, and health respectively.

The aforementioned effort by CSWE/SAGE-SW to identify social work faculty interested in aging also queried respondents about areas of interest and expertise. Respondents could list multiple interests, and the 129 faculty members who answered the question identified a total of 343 topics (Angela Curl, personal communication, May, 2001). About 40% of the responses were in five broad areas: education (including field education and certificate programs) (10%); clinical practice (9%); health and wellness (9%); caregiving and kinship care (6%), and mental health (6%). Other categories that registered at least 10 responses (3% response rate) were elder abuse, administration/organizations, end-of-life care and bereavement, family/intergenerational issues, long-term care, minority aging and cultural competence, income and health policy, and the status and needs of special populations of older adults.

Likewise, the AGE-SW membership database reports on areas of interest and expertise. Here again, multiple categories may be listed. In 2000, the 108 members listed 198 responses that represented 32 categories. Almost one quarter of responses were in the areas of family caregiving, including grandparent caregiving (13%) and long-term care, including nursing home and community care (11%). Professional education (7%), mental health (7%), death, dying, and bereavement (6%) and ethnic diversity issues (5%) accounted for another quarter of responses.

Data from these sources thus suggest that a relatively small proportion of the nation's social work faculty is interested in gerontology, particularly when compared to other substantive domains. A necessary but not sufficient initial step to enhancing the field is thus to increase the number of social work faculty who are interested in aging; the next step is to increase the subset of these faculty who are engaged in research.

Are Social Workers Contributing to Multidisciplinary Knowledge in Gerontology?

We assessed social workers' contributions as lead or co-authors to articles published in *The Gerontologist* from 1995. We selected this journal because it is a widely read peer-review journal, it has rigorous publication standards, and it focuses on applied, multidisciplinary research. We reviewed articles published in the main body of the journal and in Practice Concepts from 1995 (volume 35, #1) through 2001 (volume 40, #1). We dropped seven articles for which we failed to determine the authors' disciplines. Social workers were lead authors of 12% (n = 50) of the 415 articles reviewed, and co-authors of another 8% (n =

38). There was thus social work involvement in 20% of articles in *The Gerontologist* during this period.

What Topics Are Gerontological Social Workers Investigating?

We reviewed the topics of social work-authored articles in *The Gerontologist* and in the *Journal of Gerontological Social Work* in recent years. We selected the former because it is the premier multidisciplinary journal in the field, and the latter because it is the specialty journal most exclusively devoted to gerontological social work.

As noted above, we identified 50 articles in *The Gerontologist* from 1995 to the present in which the lead author was a social worker. Based on the title (and abstract when necessary) of each article, two raters (one of the authors and a graduate student) worked together to categorize each article into a unique category. Fifteen categories emerged. The largest category was caregiving. Nearly one third (32%; n = 16) of articles focused on issues of caregiving, e.g., gains and burdens in the caregiving experience; psychiatric co-morbidity; impact of caregiver-care receiver relationship; caregiver transitions; caregivers of disabled adult children; grandparent caregiving; and caregiving-work conflicts.

Fourteen percent of articles (n = 7) focused on ethnicity. Specific topics in this category included ethnicity and disability, ethnic elders' participation in research protocols and Alzheimer's Disease centers, and the influence of ethnicity on grandparenting, post-acute care, depressive symptoms, and morbidity and co-morbidity. Another 12% of articles addressed formal service use. These papers compared users and non-users and examined high users, extended users, and formal and informal care mixes. Smaller categories included four articles on nursing homes and three on interventions (a model for abused elders with dementia; a seminar group for early stage Alzheimer's Disease, and a support group for gay and lesbian elders).

The same two raters also reviewed all volumes of the *Journal of Gerontological Social Work* published from volume 23, #1 and #2, 1994 through volume 34, #1 and #2, 2001 We eliminated five special volumes of solicited articles not representative of work being submitted for peer-review. The topics of these special volumes are informative, however, as they address high-priority areas for the editors. The topics were Latino elders; intergenerational approaches to education, policy, and practice; special aging populations and system linkages; developments in home care; and a social work response to the 1995 White House Conference on Aging.

Again, we reviewed the titles (and abstracts when necessary) of all 143 articles published during this period to classify topics. We identified 34 categories, most of which included only a few articles. About 17% focused on caregiving, i.e., grandparent, spousal, daughter, older, and employed caregivers. Only two caregiving articles evaluated service effectiveness. About 10% of articles reviewed addressed ethnic diversity, mostly describing the needs of sub-groups of ethnic elders, and a few focused on service use and ethnic-sensitive practice. Another 7% examined international aging, including aging issues in China, Hong Kong, Israel, Sweden, Britain, Canada, Japan, and Puerto Rico.

About one quarter of articles (6% each) addressed four broad topics–adjustment to new settings or situations; volunteerism and work; professional gerontological social work training; and changing families. Approximately 5% addressed development and testing of psychosocial interventions, including solution-focused treatment for problem behaviors, a personal advocacy model, strengths-based approaches, and a model of community-based mental health services. Examples of topics that received only minimal attention in these issues of the *Journal of Gerontological Social Work* were formal service use and delivery, income and insurance, elder maltreatment, end-of-life care, mental health, and interdisciplinary practice. Social workers may, of course, be publishing on these topics in interdisciplinary or more specialized journals.

This review suggests that social work researchers are investigating a broad range of critical issues in aging. Yet, nearly 40% of the articles reviewed in *The Gerontologist* and 30% in the *Journal of Gerontological Social Work* focused on family caregiving or ethnic diversity. Although these are certainly key issues for professional social work, a number of other important topics appear to be neglected. Very little attention is being paid to developing and testing interventions to directly inform practice and policy.

Are Social Workers Being Funded for Their Research?

We also sought information on the number of gerontological social worker researchers supported by external funding. These data would show funding trends within social work and comparisons of social workers' success in obtaining competitive funding with that of other disciplines. Unfortunately, reliable estimates of these counts are not readily available, so we offer tentative findings on this question.

Austin noted in 1998 that social work had yet to establish strong ties with its chief federal funding body, the National Institute on Aging

(NIA). We found little evidence of progress on this front. Using the National Institutes on Health's CRISP system (computer retrieval of information on scientific projects), we ran a query of all RO1 research projects funded by the NIA in 2001. We reviewed the 808 unique Principal Investigators (PIs) listed and identified only 7 social workers[2]. Our inquiries with two NIA program officers who are most familiar with social science research confirm our finding that few social workers are currently funded as PIs by the NIA. We acknowledge that our calculations are just estimates, but we nevertheless conclude that social workers are grossly under-represented among NIA-funded investigators.

We also assessed how gerontological social work researchers are faring with private funders. We reviewed research grants at the AARP Andrus Foundation and the Retirement Research Foundation, two major funders of social, behavioral, and economic research on aging. We searched a list of current research grants posted by the AARP Andrus Foundation on April 2, 2001 (www.andrus.org). Based on these data and a search of university websites, we identified the disciplines of all PIs. Almost 20% (5 of 26 grants posted) were social workers. Projects examined topics of consumer satisfaction with continuing care, retirement income, home care for persons with Alzheimer's Disease, sensory impairment, and long term care insurance.

We reviewed projects funded by the Retirement Research Foundation (RRF) between 1996 and 2000. Of the 48 grants classified as research, four investigators (8%) were social workers. Their projects addressed safety versus autonomy in long term care, Medicare vouchers for in-home care, end-of-life care, and long term care insurance. RRF staff cautioned that excluding demonstration projects from our analysis would result in underestimating social work investigators. However, we conclude that social workers are under-represented among PIs of research projects funded by RRF.

CURRENT INITIATIVES TO ENHANCE RESEARCH

Developing Research Capacity of Social Work Faculty

The John A. Hartford Foundation of New York City is currently funding a major national initiative on *Strengthening Geriatric Social Work* to improve the health and well being of older Americans and their families through enhanced social work knowledge and services. Recognizing the key role of social work in the development and application of geriatric knowledge and services, a major component of this multi-pronged effort aims to rectify the shortage of geriatric social work faculty by building research capacity in the field. Two programs, the Hartford Geriatric Social Work Faculty Scholars Program and the Hartford Geriatric Social Work Doctoral Fellows Program, address this objective.

Administered by the Gerontological Society of America, the Faculty Scholars and Doctoral Fellows programs are designed to: increase visibility and desirability of geriatric social work as a field of practice, teaching and research; develop new knowledge about social work's contributions to improving the lives of older adults and their families; and, establish a close cadre of gerontological social work scholars who will engage in ongoing network development and collaboration in the interest of expanding and improving the field of geriatric social work (Berkman, Silverstone, Simmons, Volland, & Howe, 2000; Lubben, 2001).

The goal of the Faculty Scholars Program is to augment the individual research capacity of forty national faculty scholars and to enhance their scholarship, teaching, and academic careers. These scholars, in turn, are expected to develop individual and institutional research capacity by functioning as academic leaders, role models, and mentors for future generations of geriatric social work scholars. Major components of the Faculty Scholars Program include financial support of a research project; the sponsoring of faculty development workshops and training institutes; and the provision of a national mentor.

The Hartford Geriatric Social Work Doctoral Fellows Program complements and extends the Faculty Scholars program by cultivating the next upcoming generation of geriatric social work faculty. The Fellows program is expected to enhance the scholarship, teaching, and academic careers of twenty-four Geriatric Social Work Fellows (three waves of eight fellows). In addition to financial support of the dissertation phase of their doctoral work, fellows receive career coaching and participate in cohort-building and professional development events.

Together, the Hartford Faculty Scholars and Doctoral Fellows programs constitute an unprecedented long-range opportunity to prepare a core group of highly skilled academic geriatric social work researchers.

There are also federal resources to develop individual research capacity. But, few social workers, including those in aging, seek support from the broad array of National Institutes of Health research career development awards, which include pre-and post-doctoral fellowships, dissertation grants, career and research training awards, and minority enhancements and supplements. The NIA-funded program on "Social

Research Training on Applied Issues of Aging" at the University of Michigan School of Social Work stands as an example yet to be replicated at other schools of social work. Lack of institutional infrastructure, including appropriate mentors and oft-cited barriers to seeking and obtaining federal funding, such as stiff competition and lengthy lag times between submission and resubmission, may inhibit social work applications, particularly at junior levels (National Association of Deans and Directors, 1997). It is hoped that development of current and future scholars through the John A. Hartford Foundation initiative will better prepare gerontological social work researchers to secure federal funding in aging.

Promoting Gerontology Within National Social Work Research Organizations

In conjunction with enhancing individual research capacity, it is important for gerontological social work researchers to organize and promote their efforts through existing organizational structures. The Institute for the Advancement of Social Work Research (IASWR), the central component of a national research support infrastructure for social work, was created in 1993 by the Association of Baccalaureate Social Work Directors, National Association of Deans and Directors, Group for the Advancement of Doctoral Education, Council on Social Work Education, and National Association of Social Workers. The mission of IASWR is, "to advance the scientific knowledge base of social work practice by enhancing the research capacity of the profession; to promote use of research to improve practice, program development and policy; and to strengthen the voice of the profession in public education and public policy determinations by ensuring that social work is represented within the national scientific community" (IASWR, 2001).

IASWR exists to promote advancement of all social work research constituencies. Gerontologists are well represented in the organization's leadership, and in 2000, IASWR sponsored an invitational meeting with NIA staff to discuss strategies for forging links with social work researchers. The organization also regularly distributes information on aging-related conferences and funding opportunities to the membership's listserve.

Two other aforementioned social work organizations, the Society for Social Work and Research (SSWR) and the Association for Gerontological Education in Social Work (AGE-SW), are also highly relevant to gerontological social work research. SSWR was founded in 1994 to create a support and linkage network for social workers in research and to encourage social workers to engage in research. This organization also advocates for research funding and research training programs and endorses evidence-based social work practice. Gerontological social workers are prominent among SSWR membership, leadership, and conference participants. Plans to establish a special aging interest group within SSWR have been discussed sporadically but have not yet been realized.

Membership in AGE-SW has grown steadily in recent years and the organization has sponsored a number of research activities. For example, members revitalized the flagging Gerontology Symposium at the CSWE Annual Program Meeting in the mid 1990s, established a mentoring program to assist junior faculty and doctoral students with research and teaching in aging. Saltz-Corley and Kropf, past and current presidents of AGE-SW respectively, co-edited a special volume of *Research on Social Work Practice* on aging in 1998, and Damron-Rodriguez and Corley conducted a CSWE Millennium project on interdisciplinary collaboration in the field. AGE-SW also publishes a newsletter on its activities and maintains an active website (www.agesocialwork.org). There is a long-standing research committee in AGE-SW, but its organization and activities have been uneven over the years. Rejuvenation of this committee could provide an appropriate and useful forum for advancing a unified gerontological social work research agenda.

Developing and Advancing a Research Agenda

Austin (1998) has argued for a systematic approach to social work research based on specific domains of expertise. He recommends that each social work domain assess the state of its knowledge, identify critical knowledge gaps, and establish research needs and opportunities to fill those gaps (p. 39). To advance gerontological social work research, a core research agenda of prioritized topics is needed. The selection of topics for such an agenda should be based on their centrality to the profession's mission and expertise within the context of societal need and available resources.

In conjunction with the John A. Hartford Foundation Faculty Scholars program, the authors of this paper (national research mentor and Faculty Scholar respectively) are currently conducting a project to frame a set of national research priorities for gerontological social work. Using a Delphi methodology, which provides a systematic means to elicit and correlate expert opinions on an issue, we have enlisted two expert panels to develop these priorities. The first comprises 46 academic geriatric social workers identified through the extensive Hartford network, and the second consists of about 60 nominated expert practitioners. Ultimately, we will conduct three rounds of data collection with each panel in order to identify, prioritize, and gain consensus on a limited number of high priority research topics for social work in aging.

The top priority identified by the academic panel was "developing and testing psychosocial interventions across specific populations and conditions of older adults and their families" (Morrow-Howell, Burnette, & Chen, 2001). This finding is consistent with recommendations for research in other social work domains and is core to practice. Using 1990-1996 proceedings of the Gerontological Society of America annual scientific meetings, Grenier and Gorey (1998) conducted a meta-analysis on the effectiveness of social work with older persons. They found that 69% of older clients or their caregivers participating in a social work intervention fared better than the average comparison group participant. Yet, as our review of published social work research above shows, rigorous effectiveness studies of gerontological social work interventions are sparse, and the field needs more refined and rigorous intervention research. Once the practitioner panel of the Delphi study is completed, a comparison of the two panels will help illuminate concordant and discrepant aspects of practitioner and researcher agendas and will inform the development of specific practice-relevant research priorities.

In advancing our research agenda, social workers must attend to interfacing and overlapping areas with other social, behavioral, and biomedical sciences. Two recent national research agendas are illustrative. The National Research Council (NRC) report on the National Institutes of Health Committee on Future Directions for Behavioral and Social Science Research (Singer & Ryff, 2001) identifies ten research priorities that span NIH boundaries, underscoring the significance of behavioral and social science research for multiple disease outcomes and health promotion. The priorities are pre-disease pathways; positive health; environmentally induced gene expression; personal ties; healthy communities; inequality and health outcomes; population health; interventions; methodological priorities; and research infrastructure/training.

Similarly, the National Institute on Aging Strategic Plan (2001-2005) lists four overarching research emphases (each with several sub-goals): improving the health and quality of life of older people; understanding healthy aging processes; reducing health disparities among older persons and populations; and enhancing resources to support high quality research. Clearly, several priority areas in these two reports are highly compatible with the concerns and expertise of gerontological social work researchers.

To summarize current initiatives, the John A. Hartford Foundation is funding a major national program to improve the number of well-trained gerontological social work researchers through its Faculty Scholars and Doctoral Fellows Programs. Efforts of the participants of these programs to advance knowledge can be greatly facilitated through a coherent, prioritized research agenda that involves collaboration on topics that span interdisciplinary lines. Optimal implementation of such an agenda will depend in large part on the ability of gerontological social workers to work effectively within existing aging and social work organizations.

CONCLUSIONS AND SUGGESTIONS
FOR FURTHER DEVELOPMENT

The various data sources we have examined suggest that gerontological social work researchers have established a small national presence in social work schools. The extent to which they are undertaking aging research, however, is unclear. Social work researchers are contributing to the multidisciplinary knowledge base in aging, as indicated by their manuscripts in *The Gerontologist,* although their contributions to this literature are incommensurate with their involvement in interdisciplinary practice. And, although gerontological social workers are investigating topics that are important to their field, attention to these topics is variable and a number of critical areas remain under-examined. Finally, social workers scarcely have a "toehold" in federally funded research in aging, but they may be faring better with some, but not all, private foundations. Taken together, these findings suggest that we still have far to go.

On the other hand, our consideration of current initiatives to enhance the field suggests that the scope and level of commitment to gerontological social work has increased and continues to do so. It is important to maximize and extend the timely opportunities of these initiatives, which provide motivation and resources to enhance the research capacity of gerontological social work faculty, promote aging within national research organizations, and develop and implement a coherent research agenda for the field. We offer several suggestions for consolidating and building on current gains to ensure the ongoing development of a vibrant, focused program of research.

Maximizing infrastructure opportunities for gerontological social work research. The Hartford Faculty Scholars and Doctoral Fellows programs represent an unprecedented opportunity to increase the number of geriatric social work researchers. For these individuals and those they mentor to realize their potential, parallel investments are needed in institutional infrastructure for social work research in aging. These programs could focus exclusively on aging, as in centers or institutes on aging, or they could build aging research into existing institutional structures. The latter approach is taken less often, but it could maximize resources, increase others' awareness of aging issues, and promote knowledge development on aging across substantive domains.

Federally supported projects for developing social work research infrastructure offer one way to build on existing resources. The National Institute of Mental Health (NIMH) has funded eight Social Work Research Development Centers. The National Institute on Drug Abuse (NIDA) also recently initiated a program to enhance research infrastructure for social work inquiry on drug abuse and related issues and has funded two Social Work Research Development Centers. None of the existing NIMH or NIDA Social Work Research Development Centers focuses on aging *per se,* yet there is ample opportunity to enhance aging research through these Centers. The NIMH Social Work Development Centers at Portland State and Washington University, for examples, include projects on mental health services and older adults, and the NIDA Center at Columbia University School of Social Work includes several projects on substance abuse and HIV/AIDS among older adults and their families.

Building on existing research infrastructures in other NIH Institutes does not, of course, preclude gerontological social workers exploring the feasibility of NIA-sponsored social work research development centers. But, more immediate and certain gains in gerontological social work research may be realized by working through existing NIMH and NIDA Centers. Gerontology faculty would need to cultivate opportunities to partner with mental health and substance abuse researchers on issues of older adults and their families. Collaborating with non-aging specialists would increase the number of social work faculty involved in aging research and expand the scope of research topics. Engaging researchers in children and youth, mental health, health, and substance abuse, whose numbers far outnumber gerontology faculty, could introduce fresh perspectives and additional resources to their own work through the current initiatives described above and other federal, public, and private funding sources in aging.

Enhancing Links to Funding Sources. Opportunities to build on existing resources in schools of social work described above notwithstanding, there is still a shortage of resources targeted to gerontological social work research. The long-range impact of current initiatives to strengthen and focus the field depends on the successful development of new and existing linkages to viable funding sources, including federal, state, and local agencies, philanthropic foundations, and internal resources of academic institutions. As noted, social work has had tenuous ties with the NIA. Improving this linkage could have a major impact on research funding, interdisciplinary collaboration, and training and career development for social work researchers. Additionally, it is an opportune time to strengthen ties with the NIMH, given that the Surgeon General's report on mental health included aging (U.S. Department of Health and Human Services, 1999) and that the Institute has a new initiative to assess and expand its research portfolio relating to aging (see <www.nimh.nih.gov/research/roundtable 2001>).

An invested and organized group such as AGE-SW could effectively target the development of NIA-sponsored social work research by working closely with national organizations that have a strong stake in enhancing social work research, notably IASWR and SSWR. We might also cooperatively explore opportunities for collaborative research with the Office of the Assistant Secretary for Aging, Administration on Aging, Health Care Financing Administration, Social Security Administration, Agency for Healthcare Research and Quality, Department of Veterans Affairs, and Substance Abuse and Mental Health Services Administration (Austin, 1998, p. 36; CSWE, 2001, p. 5).

As part of the Action Network for Social Work Education and Research (ANSWER), IASWR and SSWR are advocating for the National Center for Social Work Research Act. This Act (S 70/HR 663) would establish a Center to collect data on significant public health and social concerns and promote the investigation of prevention and treatment of related problems. The Center would provide research grants; establish traineeships; convene workshops and conferences for researchers and practitioners; and disseminate information to policymakers, service delivery professionals, and the general public. In joining the IASWR and SSWR lobby for a National Research Center, gerontological social workers could define their own areas of priority and expertise. Again, AGE-SW could be instrumental in this activity, perhaps through a subcommittee to collect, organize, monitor, and disseminate information on lobbying efforts.

Enhancing key areas of gerontological social work research. Establishing a research agenda may encourage gerontological social work researchers to increase attention to under-examined key areas of the profession. For instance, our review of social work-authored publications showed scant attention to policy analysis. Given their first-hand knowledge about the impact of social policy on older clients and their families, social workers should be major players in the formulation, implementation, and evaluation of policy (Fahey, 1996). Yet their lack of demonstrated interest and expertise largely excludes them from public policy dialogue.

Attention to development of psychosocial outcomes measures and the testing of psychosocial interventions at the individual, family, group, and community level is also clearly deficient. This is particularly troubling given the widening appeal for increased research that directly informs practice. Austin (1998) notes, "The most important issue for the immediate future is to bring the practice effectiveness concerns of social work practitioners together with the resources represented by social work researchers" (p. 27). Similarly, the SAGE-SW blueprint for improving the quality of life for older adults and their families in the new millennium recommends two foci for gerontological social work research–increased opportunities and support for research and increased emphasis on practice-based, measurable research (CSWE, 2001, pp. 4-5). This report further calls for researchers to develop strategic outreach and incentives to faculty and field supervisors to conduct practice-based research and to assist in developing practice protocols.

To summarize, to address the psychosocial needs of our aging society, gerontological social workers must increase production of practice-and policy-relevant research. To accomplish this goal requires more skilled gerontological social work researchers who have adequate support to investigate a range of topics and to contribute to the knowledge base of gerontology. We need to assume leadership on interdisciplinary research teams in our areas of expertise and in developing research agendas for the 21st century. Knowledge development activities should be conducted in collaboration with practicing gerontological social workers.

NOTES

1. This project is a core component of the Hartford Foundation's *Strengthening Geriatric Social Work* initiative, which is described more fully below (Anita Rosen, personal communication, May, 2001). A form was distributed to faculty at social work and gerontology conferences and mailed to key contacts in social work schools nation-

ally. All faculty members with an interest in aging were invited to submit the form indicating interest in aging.

2. We first eliminated any project that was biomedical, according to the title and abstract, given the high likelihood that the PI was not a social worker. We then reviewed the titles and affiliations of the PIs of the remaining projects. We supplemented information in the CRISP system with the internet to identify discipline. This process may not pick up social work PIs jointly funded by NIA and another institute when NIA is not first listed; and we know at least one social worker funded by the National Institute of Nursing Research and the NIA.

REFERENCES

Austin, D.M. (1998). *A report on progress in the development of research resources in social work*. Washington, D.C.: Institute for the Advancement of Social Work Research.

Berkman, B., Silverstone, B., Simmons, J., Volland, P., & Howe, J. (2000). Social work gerontological practice: The need for faculty development in the new millennium. *Journal of Gerontological Social Work, 34*, 1-23.

Council on Social Work Education. (2001). *Strengthening the impact of social work to improve the quality of life for older adults and the families: Blueprint for the new millennium*. Washington, D.C.: Author.

Curl, A. *(acurl@cswe.org)*. (2001, May 7). RE: Request for statistics. E-mail to N. Morrow-Howell *(nancymh@gwbmail.wustl.edu)*.

Fahey, C. (1996). Social work education and the field of aging. *The Gerontologist, 36*, 36-41.

Grenier, A.M., & Gorey, K.M. (1998). Effectiveness of social work with older people and their families: A meta-analysis of conference proceedings. *Social Work Research, 22* (1), 60-64.

Institute for the Advancement of Social Work Research. (2001). *Strategic Plan 2001-2003*. Washington D.C.: Author.

Lennon, T. (2001). *Statistics on Social Work Education in the United States:1999*. Washington, D.C.: Council on Social Work Education.

Lubben, J. (2001). The Hartford Doctoral Fellows Program in Geriatric Social Work. *Journal of Gerontological Social Work* (in preparation for a special issue).

Morrow-Howell, N., Burnette, D., & Chen, L. (2001). *Research priorities for gerontological social work: Setting a national agenda*. Presentation at the Society for Social Work Research Annual Meeting, Atlanta, Jan. 21, 2001.

National Association of Dean and Directors of Schools of Social Work Task Force on Administrative Research Infrastructures within Social Work Education Programs. *Challenges and opportunities for promoting federally funded research in social work programs*. April, 1997.

National Institute of Mental Health Task Force on Social Work Research. (1991). *Building social work knowledge for effective services and policies: A plan for research development*. Austin: School of Social Work, University of Texas at Austin.

Rosen, A. *(aroswn@cswe.org)*. (2001, June 19). Email to N. Morrow-Howell *(nancymh@gwbmail.wustl.edu)*.

Saltz, C.L. & Kropf, N.P. (1998). Special issue "Empirical Research on Gerontological Social Work" *Research on Social Work Practice, 8* (1).

Scharlach, A., Damron-Rodriguez, J., Robinson, B., & Feldman, R. (2000). Educating social workers in an aging society: A vision for the 21st century. *Journal of Social Work Education, 36* (3), 521-538.

Singer, B.H. & Ryff, C.D. (2001.) *New horizons in health: An integrative approach.* National Research Council Commission on Behavioral and Social Sciences and Education. Washington, D.C.: National Academy Press.

U.S. Department of Health and Human Services. *Mental health: A report of the Surgeon General.* Rockville: Maryland: U.S. Department of Health and Human Services, Substance Abuse and Mental Health Services Administration, Center for Mental Health Services, National Institutes of Health, National Institute of Mental Health, 1999.

Demographics and Reality:
The "Disconnect" in Social Work Education

Anita L. Rosen, PhD, MSW
Joan Levy Zlotnik, PhD, MSW

SUMMARY. Social work education has neglected gerontology at the same time that the demand for aging-competent practitioners has increased. Surveys, focus groups, and other sources of data from the John A. Hartford Foundation SAGE-SW project at the Council on Social Work Education indicate a lack of current curriculum content, little encouragement for students, limited gerontological expertise among faculty, and more interest by students in gaining gerontological knowledge than expected. Suggested actions for practitioners and field agency supervisors are provided. *[Article copies available for a fee from The Haworth Document Delivery Service: 1-800-HAWORTH. E-mail address: <getinfo@haworthpressinc.com> Website: <http://www.HaworthPress.com> © 2001 by The Haworth Press, Inc. All rights reserved.]*

Anita L. Rosen is Director of Special Projects at the Council on Social Work Education and Project Manager of the John A. Hartford Foundation's grant project SAGE-SW, c/o Council on Social Work Education, 1725 Duke Street, Suite 500, Alexandria, VA 22314 (E-mail: arosen@cswe.org).

Joan Levy Zlotnik is the Executive Director of the Institute for the Advancement of Social Work Research and former principle investigator for Phase I of the CSWE/SAGE-SW project, c/o IASWR, 750 First Street NE, Suite 700, Washington, DC 20002 (E-mail: jlziaswr@naswdc.org).

The authors wish to express grateful appreciation to the John A. Hartford Foundation of New York City and its Hartford Geriatric Social Work Initiative.

[Haworth co-indexing entry note]: "Demographics and Reality: The "Disconnect" in Social Work Education." Rosen, Anita L., and Joan Levy Zlotnik. Co-published simultaneously in *Journal of Gerontological Social Work* (The Haworth Social Work Practice Press, an imprint of The Haworth Press, Inc.) Vol. 36, No. (3/4), 2001, pp. 81-97; and: *Gerontological Social Work Practice: Issues, Challenges, and Potential* (ed: Enid Opal Cox, Elizabeth S. Kelchner, and Rosemary Chapin) The Haworth Social Work Practice Press, an imprint of The Haworth Press, Inc., 2001, pp. 81-97. Single or multiple copies of this article are available for a fee from The Haworth Document Delivery Service [1-800-HAWORTH, 9:00 a.m. - 5:00 p.m. (EST). E-mail address: getinfo@haworthpressinc.com].

KEYWORDS. Social work education, gerontological social work, gerontological competencies, social work curriculum, student interest, practitioners and education

The preparation of social work students for practice has been an important goal of social work education. Yet, until recently, social work education has neglected gerontological education at the same time that the demand for aging-competent practitioners has increased (Peterson, 1990; Rosen & Zlotnik, 2001). Social work is not unique in this gerontological education dilemma (Fulmer, Flaherty & Medley, 2001; Blanchette & Flynn, 2001), but social work must find its unique way to address the disconnect between demographic reality and a contemporary educational environment that does not prepare most social workers for a growing aging population.

Though social work is well-suited to meet the needs of a growing aging population, the disconnect between inattention to gerontology in the social work curriculum and the actual practice needs of social workers could jeopardize the health of the profession and the role of social workers in the future. Practitioners, students, and educators are challenged to recognize the demographic imperative and practice demands of a growing aging population and change the culture and content of social work education.

In 1999, the Council on Social Work Education (CSWE) was provided with a grant from the John A. Hartford Foundation of New York City's Geriatric Social Work Initiative that, in part, sought a comprehensive assessment of the current state of gerontological social work education. Through the CSWE project, *Strengthening Aging and Gerontology Education for Social Work* (SAGE-SW), a variety of data and information were gathered, made available in CSWE/SAGE-SW newsletters (see <*www.cswe.org/sage-sw/*>) and culminated in an action agenda, entitled "A Blueprint for the New Millennium" (CSWE/SAGE-SW, 2001a).

Data were gathered for this assessment from a thorough review of the literature (CSWE/SAGE-SW 2001b), a national competencies survey, a student survey, focus groups, and expert technical advisors. Although there have been occasional efforts to focus gerontological attention on social work (Schneider, 1984; Kosberg, 1979), in general, until the advent of the John A. Hartford Geriatric Social Work Initiative in 1999, social work education was found to be inattentive to the demographic changes that should inform the preparation of social workers for practice (CSWE/SAGE-SW, 2001a).

What follows in this paper is an attempt to make use of the data gathered by the CSWE/SAGE-SW project in assessing the contemporary need for social work competence in aging and the response of social work education. The discussion also illustrates that the social work profession is well suited to work with older adults and their families, and that there are a variety of opportunities to strengthen aging and gerontology education for social work.

THE DEMOGRAPHIC DEMAND

The dramatic growth of the aging population affects all aspects of society and creates new and growing demand for a variety of health, mental health and social services. This growth in the aging population is well documented (Administration on Aging [AoA], 2000), including the rapid growth of those people 85 and older, which has doubled people 100 and older having tripled.

Of significance is that this increase in the number of people in the oldest-old (85+) category substantially increases the demand for health, mental health, and social services because this population group has higher incidence of dependency and disability than those aged 65-84 (Administration on Aging [AoA], 2000). The unique characteristics of the old-old present non-traditional medical problems in the health care system that are often misdiagnosed, and are exacerbated by "social isolation, emotional vulnerability, and poverty" (Blanchette & Flynn, 2001).

In addition to rapid growth of the oldest-old, there is a significant increase in the diversity of the aging population (Administration on Aging [AoA], 2000). Social workers in health and mental health care, child welfare and social services are increasingly involved with a diverse population of older clients, their families and caregivers (Peterson & Wendt, 1990; Damron-Rodriguez & Lubben, 1997; Wallace, 2001).

The growth of the aging population and accompanying changes in health care are a prime opportunity for social work to demonstrate its place on the interdisciplinary health or social service team. Social work is unique among health and mental health professions because its practitioners consider an integrated view of clients–the physical, mental, and social aspects of a person. Social work education and practice value such constructs as client self-determination, mobilizing the family system, and a comprehensive approach to human development that is essential in the provision of services to older adults and their families

(Greene, 2000). Social work, unlike other health and mental health professions, has focused on underserved populations, diversity and community-based care (Berkman, Damron-Rodriguez, Dobrof & Harry, 1996), all critical skills for work with older adults and their families. One such example is in the area of supportive housing, where the addition of social workers can bring such expertise as comprehensive case management expertise, coordination of health, mental health and social services, clinical services and counseling to help older people age in place (Ivry, 1995).

The aging of the population provides new challenges to the health, mental health, and social services system. Work with older adults and their families requires the comprehensive, psychosocial skills that are the focus of social work practice (CSWE/SAGE-SW, 1999). With an increasing number of intergenerational families composed of three, four, and five generations and with a growing number of grandparents raising their grandchildren, social workers can provide critical assistance to families juggling the demands of multigenerational caregiving. Social workers can also address issues of loss, grief and bereavement that are often associated with aging persons and families. These social work skills with older persons and their families have been shown to be effective (Gremier & Gorey, 1998) through a meta-analysis of published studies evaluating social work interventions. The eighty-eight studies examined by Gremier and Gorey (1998) demonstrated the efficacy of a broad range of social work interventions that work in a variety of settings with diverse populations.

The demographics of aging clearly indicate a need and a demand for social workers that specifically work in services to the aged (Barusch, Greene and Connelly, 1990; NIA, 1987; Peterson & Wendt, 1990), and also suggest that all social workers need basic aging-practice competence. In order for the social work profession to effectively respond to the changing needs of a growing aging population, social work education must assume the responsibility of adequate educational preparation that acknowledges these demographics. Social workers must be prepared to provide services across the lifespan.

GERONTOLOGY EDUCATION IN SOCIAL WORK TODAY

The most recent Council on Social Work Education (CSWE) statistics (Lennon, 1999) indicate that approximately 23 or 16% of Masters of Social Work (MSW) programs have a gerontology specialization,

7 (5%) have sub-concentrations, 17 (12%) offer aging as a specified "Field of Practice" and 6 (4%) offer a certificate in gerontology. However, despite the fact that the population is aging, today there are fewer specialty programs than 7 years ago (Damron-Rodriquez, Villa, Tseng & Lubben, 1997).

In education, too few programs provide gerontology curriculum at the bachelor's (BSW) level or specialization at the master's (MSW) level (Damron-Rodriquez & Lubben, 1997). Only 10% of students take a gerontology course when available (Damron-Rodriquez, Villa, Tseng & Lubben, 1997). Focus groups conducted by CSWE/SAGE-SW staff to assess the current state of gerontological social work education, indicated that, in most programs, unless a student entered the program with knowledge or interest in aging issues, they had little opportunity to acquire it at the MSW level. In addition, there are few opportunities for working professionals to participate in continuing education on aging through academic-sponsored courses. CSWE recognizes that competing interests are a normal part of professional education in any field, but the current situation does little to expand gerontology education in order to place it on equal footing with the other age groups across the lifespan. This is necessary since most social workers will have practice opportunity with older people or with their families (Reed, Beall & Baumhover, 1992).

AGING CURRICULUM CONTENT AND STUDENT INTEREST

The need for teaching gerontology is clear. The reality is that there is limited interest and activity to expand gerontological education through specialization. An alternative to specialization is that of integration or infusion of aging content into the basic social work curriculum. This would suggest that all social work students should be provided some basic competency and exposure to gerontology content. The CSWE/SAGE-SW project has not found substantial evidence to indicate that aging content is broadly integrated or infused in the social work curriculum, though students have interest in acquiring gerontology knowledge.

CSWE/SAGE-SW conducted a survey in October 1999 of approximately 400 social work students from 17 social work education programs in the Mid-Atlantic Region who were participating in a daylong conference in Washington, DC. Of the 221 respondents completing the survey, 135, or 61% percent were BSW students and 80, or 36% were

MSW students. In addition, CSWE/SAGE-SW conducted six focus groups with BSW, MSW and doctoral students.

The data provided from these efforts indicated that:

- There was interest in gaining knowledge about aging, though most students did not want to specialize in the area;
- There was some infusion or integration of aging content, primarily in Human Behavior and the Social Environment (HBSE) and Policy courses, but quantity and quality of content varied considerably (from no content to a high of about 15%); and
- Students have contact with older people in field practica.

This last point was a welcome finding in that previous studies indicate that exposure to specific client groups may increase interest in working with that population (Kane, 1999). However, if students are being exposed to older clients in field practica, social work education programs do not appear to be preparing them for services to older people as reflected in foundation course content or assignments.

Other information gathered from the student survey included the fact that 65 or 49% of BSWs and 28 or 36% of MSWs had taken or plan to take a course in aging. This interest is not borne out in the statistics quoted earlier of numbers of BSW and MSW students who take an aging course while in school. There is clearly a disconnect between interest, especially of BSWs and the opportunity to gain competence and exposure to aging while in social work school.

The survey also showed that 68% (87) of BSW students and 49% (36) of MSW students would accept employment in gerontological social work. When asked if aging was one of their top fieldwork placement choices, 40 or 30% of BSWs and 23 or 28% of MSWs answered affirmatively. Of the 147 (66%) students surveyed with no interest in aging, 52 or 35% would take a field placement in aging if they were offered a stipend.

The survey results suggest that there are many more students with an interest in working with an older population than previously thought, and many more with interest in gaining knowledge and skills related to aging. However, available data (Damron-Rodriguez & Lubben, 1997) indicate that this interest is often ignored in social work education.

The lack of attention to aging within social work education may account for the fact that only about 16% of baccalaureate social workers (BSWs) and 4% of masters of social work (MSW) graduates work specifically in services to the aged (Gibelman & Schervish, 1997; Teare &

Sheafor, 1995). Only about 5,000 National Association of Social Workers' 150,000 members indicate aging as their primary area of practice. Most practicing social workers have received little or no prior knowledge or skills in gerontology (Klein, 1996), as explicated in the White Papers and conference held by the Bureau of Health Professions Geriatrics Branch in 1995. Yet this same conference also suggests that data on social work practice with older people significantly underestimates the numbers of social workers that practice with older people (Berkman, Damron-Rodriguez, Dobrof & Harry, 1996), since the majority of social workers in health care settings serve predominately older persons (Damron-Rodriguez & Lubben, 1997). In fact, in a National Association of Social Workers (NASW) survey 62% of all respondents reported the need for gerontological knowledge (Peterson & Wendt, 1990). Fewer than 1200 MSW students, approximately 3%, are in an aging concentration (Lennon, 1999) although Scharlach, Damron-Rodriguez, Robinson and Feldman (2000) suggests that there is a demand for 5000 per year or 24% of all MSW students.

It is notable that if 16% of all BSW graduates do work in aging (Gibelman & Schervish, 1997; Teare & Sheafor, 1995), it would appear to be educationally prudent to integrate aging content in the foundation curriculum, particularly for BSW students. Yet, the CSWE/SAGE-SW student survey and focus groups do not indicate efforts to provide gerontology content.

THE CSWE/SAGE-SW COMPETENCIES SURVEY

Another illustration of the seeming disconnect between the need for basic aging competence and what is taught in social work education is found in the results of the CSWE/SAGE-SW competencies survey (CSWE/SAGE-SW, 2000). The overall purpose of this survey was to enable the CSWE/SAGE-SW program to adequately assess gerontological curricular needs for social work students, by analyzing sixty-five social work gerontological competencies that had been derived from a thorough review of the literature and input from technical experts. This national survey was conducted during winter 2000 and asked a sample of 2,400 social work practitioners and academics, both with and without aging interest, to give their opinion on which of the 65 gerontological social work competencies all social workers need and which only advanced practitioners and specialists need. The competencies list contained only those items related to gerontological social work knowledge and practice, and excluded competencies items that pertain to generic social work skills, knowledge or professional practice issues. The survey was seen as a way to generate interest in competent gerontology practice. The broad, national sample of academics and practitioners was drawn from:

- Social workers who have taken one of four licensing examinations (Basic, Intermediate, Advanced and Clinical) from the American Association of State Social Work Boards (AASSWB);
- National Association of Social Workers (NASW) members who indicated their primary field of practice was aging;
- CSWE individual membership; and,
- All 200 members of the Association of Gerontology Education in Social Work (AGE-SW), an organization for social work gerontology educators.

These four groups were chosen to provide input from a broad array of stakeholders, and validity beyond a small group of experts. The survey also was conducted to provide opportunity to promote education for practice and to enhance visibility of the SAGE-SW project.

The CSWE/SAGE-SW staff completed a thorough review of the literature and consultation with a group of seven expert researchers and practitioners, who were identified as national leaders in gerontological social work. From this work, sixty-five items were included in the survey (CSWE/SAGE-SW, 2000). These items are specific to gerontological social work in three major professional domains: (1) knowledge about elderly people and their families; (2) professional skill; and (3) professional practice. The overall adjusted response rate for the survey was 51%. The survey and accompanying demographic data provide a substantial amount of information. The most significant, as they pertain to this discussion are highlighted below.

Competencies are needed by all social workers. Over half the competency items were ones that the majority of respondents thought were needed by ALL social workers, BSWs and MSWs. These findings would suggest that basic social work foundation curricula should infuse or integrate content on aging in order for all social workers to gain the knowledge and skills needed to be competent professionals in a country with a rapidly growing aging population.

Social work faculty lack training. The respondent group of social work faculty was least likely to have special training or education in relation to aging. This suggests that a major barrier to infusing or integrating content into the basic curriculum is lack of faculty knowledge about gerontology. Information gathered from focus groups with faculty conducted by CSWE/SAGE-SW staff further suggests that such issues as resistance, limited interest, or few professional incentives are significant reasons that faculty do not pursue further training in gerontology. In addition, those focus groups revealed that faculty with little or no interest in aging also demonstrated limited knowledge of the range of career opportunities in aging or the variety of practice issues related to work with older people and their families.

Sources of specialty training. For all groups sampled, the primary source of specialty training in aging is continuing education-not social work courses. While the survey does not provide an explanation for this result, the CSWE/SAGE-SW researchers involved in the data collection and analysis, proposed at least three explanations for why social work education programs are not a primary source of specialty training:

- social workers often are not aware of the need for aging knowledge and skills until they begin working in the field;
- there is a lack of available aging electives, minors or certificates; and
- there is a lack of curricular flexibility that allow for electives, especially at the MSW level, so that unless students specialize in aging there is no opportunity to take an aging course, if it were offered.

For those who did report taking a specific course in aging while in school, the highest percentage were respondents from the AASSWB Basic examination pool. Responses from this group, comprised almost exclusively of recent BSW graduates, imply that it is more likely BSWs will elect to take an aging course than MSWs.

CORE COMPETENCIES AND CURRICULUM CONTENT FOR PRACTICE

The national competencies study, a literature review, and technical experts who consulted with the CSWE/SAGE-SW program provided some guidance in relation to those competencies that all social work students may need and those that may only be needed by MSW students in an aging concentration. Following are the ten competencies for all social workers–BSW and MSW–that gained the highest agreement from the national competencies survey (CSWE/SAGE-SW, 2000):

1. Assess one's own values and biases regarding aging, death and dying.
2. Educate self to dispel the major myths about aging.
3. Accept, respect, and recognize the right and need of older adults to make their own choices and decisions about their lives within the context of the law and safety concerns.
4. Understand normal physical, psychological, and social changes in later life.
5. Respect and address cultural, spiritual, and ethnic needs and beliefs of older adults and family members.
6. Examine the diversity of attitudes toward aging, mental illness, and family roles.
7. Understand the influence of aging on family dynamics.
8. Use social work case management skills (such as brokering, advocacy, monitoring, and discharge planning) to link elders and their families to resources and services.
9. Gather information regarding social history such as: social functioning, primary and secondary social supports, social activity level, social skills, financial status, cultural background, and social involvement.
10. Identify ethical and professional boundary issues that commonly arise in work with older adults and their caregivers, such as client self-determination, end-of-life decisions, family conflicts, and guardianship.

The ten items most agreed upon for students specializing in aging were (CSWE/SAGE-SW, 2000):

1. Conduct clinical interventions for mental health and cognitive impairment issues in older adults.
2. Assess for dementia, delirium, and depression in older adults.
3. Understand basic pharmacology and the interaction of medications affecting the elderly.
4. Adapt psychoeducational approaches to work with older adults.
5. Assess short-term memory, coping history, changes in socialization patterns, behavior, and appropriateness of mood and affect in relation to life events of those who are aging.
6. Demonstrate knowledge and ability to use relevant diagnostic classifications such as the DSM-IV for use with older persons.

7. Identify legal issues for older adults, including: advanced directive, living wills, powers-of-attorney, wills, guardianship, and Do Not Resuscitate (DNR) orders.
8. Develop strategies to address service fragmentation and barriers within the aging services delivery system.
9. Identify mental disorders and mental health needs in older adults.
10. Demonstrate knowledge about policies, regulations, and programs for older adults in health, mental health, and long-term care.

Another area of curriculum content that has emerged as critical for social work with a growing aging population is interdisciplinary practice. The complex needs of old clients often require multiple interventions from multiple professions or paraprofessionals. Participants in the CSWE/SAGE-SW focus groups strongly indicated that those social workers that work primarily in aging are often the only social worker in their agency, organization, or specialty service. Some examples of these settings are senior centers, adult day care, and nursing homes. These social workers have little or no opportunity to relate to other social work professionals on a daily basis. They may instead relate primarily to staff from other professions, or persons with no professional training at all. Others who work in settings with social workers often find themselves relating primarily to those in other professions such as medicine, nursing, long-term care administration, or law, as in the case of hospital social workers or those in adult protective services.

Many workplaces and payors do not recognize the need for interdisciplinary practitioner training, and college and university organizational cultures often do not foster interdisciplinary educational efforts such as interdisciplinary or team taught courses in professional schools (Klein, 1996; Netting & Williams, 1998). In addition, field practica or internships in health care settings, for physicians, nurses, occupational therapists, pharmacists, and social workers, often have students on differing rotations that make interdisciplinary field training quite difficult. Some health care students are on two or four week rotations, and others six weeks. Social workers usually are in the same placement for an entire semester or year.

Other professionals and social workers alike often misunderstand the social work role on the interdisciplinary geriatric team (Netting & Williams, 1998). Social workers generally are not prepared to work in the growing interdependent, interdisciplinary environment of aging services, and will be hard-pressed to provide leadership in interdisciplinary settings (Scharlach et al., 2000).

CURRENT EFFORTS TO ADDRESS THE "DISCONNECT"

Data gathered by the CSWE/SAGE-SW project would appear to make a convincing case for preparing social work students to address the needs of a growing aging population. The data also indicate that, until recently, social work education programs, at both the BSW and MSW levels generally have been inattentive to preparing their students for practice in an aging society. A variety of reasons have been forward for this lack of attention, including negative attitudes about work with older adults, lack of resources, and limited availability of stipends or research support for social work (Scharlach, Damron-Rodriguez, Robinson, & Feldman, R., 2000). Whatever the reasons, the centers for learning the social work profession have an obligation to, through their missions and culture, to address important social and demographic needs.

Social work education now has the opportunity to effect change through the John A. Hartford Foundation's Geriatric Social Work Initiative (www.jhartfound.org). The Foundation seeks to improve the health care of older persons by strengthening the health care professions, including social work. Among major initiatives are to develop a cadre of faculty scholars who can provide mentoring and leadership to other social work faculty; a field initiative that seeks to examine best-practice models of aging enrichment in MSW field practica; and a doctoral dissertation program that provides support and encouragement to future DSWs to attract interest in aging and practice research. At the CSWE, the John A. Hartford Foundation has provided two initiatives that are focused on strengthening or changing the social work education environment so that all students are prepared to meet the needs of a growing aging population.

The CSWE projects center on several key components:

1. Development and dissemination of resources and educational materials that allow for the infusion of aging content throughout the BSW and first year MSW program or in related courses, such as health care;

2. Development of competencies, materials, and networking opportunities that will strengthen the gerontology content in both aging and non-aging courses;
3. Provision of numerous faculty development institutes to enable faculty with little or no aging knowledge to infuse or integrate aging content into basic social work courses; and
4. Provision of money and technical support to social work programs, both BSW and MSW, that wish to transform their programs so that gerontology becomes a visible, equal content partner throughout the curriculum.

The John A. Hartford Geriatric Social Work Initiative is a critical step in helping to address the disconnect between demographic demand and the current reality of social work education. However, the Hartford project is only a beginning, and the social work profession cannot rely solely on the foundation to take leadership in preparing social workers for practice with an aging population.

Major issues to address are highlighted below and suggestions are set forth for significant change in the culture of social work education in order to bridge the gap between demographic realities and preparation of students (Scharlach et al., 2000; Rosen and Zlotnik, 2001; CSWE/SAGE-SW 2001a). Broad issues to address would have impact on social work education. Among them is the need for:

- Sustainable leadership to change the culture of social work in relation to aging;
- A committed national organization that provides a central point of information, linkage, educational resources, and communication;
- Increased visibility for the roles, settings, practice opportunities, and value of social work and aging; and
- Enhanced support for social work research in aging, particularly outcome-oriented, practice-based research.

Important issues related specifically to education include:

- Expand the number of BSW and MSW programs with the faculty and monetary resources to impact their educational curriculum;
- Expand opportunities for and models of interdisciplinary education and continuing education;
- Expand continuing education and certificate programs in aging and gerontology from social work education programs;

- Create incentives for faculty and students to increase attention to aging.

Unless practitioners and educators with interest in aging take leadership in changing the educational environment, the Hartford Initiative will have limited impact. Fortunately, some of this leadership is occurring in social work education. The National Association of Deans and Directors (NADD) and the Association for Baccalaureate Social Work Program Directors (BPD) have both developed aging committees and have indicated a willingness to support and promote aging within social work education. The Association for Gerontology Education in Social Work (AGE-SW), a 20-year-old organization comprised largely of social work educators with interest in aging, has worked closely with CSWE/SAGE-SW to support increased attention to social work and aging.

Many leadership ideas do not necessitate foundation or government support. In fact, there can be very low-cost strategies for increasing attention to aging in both BSW and MSW programs. In July 2000, the CSWE/SAGE-SW project held a meeting of 25 invited practitioners and educators from around the country to provide the project with technical advice and discussion in relation to preliminary results from the national competencies survey. The brainstorming and workgroups during the two-day meeting provided a wealth of information and ideas, many of which can be used immediately by those interested in advancing gerontological competency. A number of them are listed below and can be used by, and for, social work faculty, field supervisors and practitioners:

INCREASING STUDENT INTEREST

- Provide mentoring and support of students interested in gerontology by collaborating with practitioners and graduates who have skills in gerontology;
- Get students involved in the local aging network through class projects and assignments;
- Promote a clear role in gerontological social work for group workers, community workers and those interested in indirect practice;
- Advocate for loan forgiveness for students who specialize in gerontological social work; and;
- Invite guest speakers with gerontological background in all social work foundation courses.

ATTRACT FACULTY INTEREST

- Connect aging content and competencies on an interdisciplinary level (e.g., family violence, family health, women's issues);
- Suggest places where aging content easily can be added without revising the whole curriculum;
- Suggest opportunities for research, collaboration, and student projects; and,
- Reach out to faculty who teach core curriculum classes, including "Introduction to Social Work";
- Attract the interest of aging-related agencies and the aging practice community to social work education programs;
- Attract the interest of social work faculty in the research and teaching opportunities related to agencies and programs that serve older clients;
- Encourage faculty members to participate in the local aging network;
- Recommend guest speakers to other faculty members to inspire students with current "real" examples and learn about field placement opportunities;
- Use faculty as field supervisors so that non-traditional settings can serve as field placements (e.g., businesses are sensitive to caregiving needs of their employees but often do not have MSWs on their staff to supervise students);
- Seek out "Best Practices" agencies for collaboration to bridge the knowledge gap of academia;
- Encourage collaboration and incentives for field agencies (e.g., free courses for field instructors); and,
- Encourage more formal mechanisms for institutionalizing the interactions between field and practice in a sustainable way for meaningful collaboration.

These "doable" suggestions require that practitioners and field agency supervisors must take leadership in changing social work education. They also suggest that faculty with interest in aging also must take leadership within their social work programs to help effect a change in how social work students are prepared for practice.

The social work profession is challenged to ensure that all social work students have basic competency to address the realities of a growing population and that all students with interest in aging are provided curricula and field practica that strengthen their abilities to work with older people and their families. It is long past the time to be discussing the "disconnect" between demographics and the current social work education environment, and time to make gerontology competency a part of social work education.

REFERENCES

Administration on Aging [AoA] (2000). *A Profile of Older Americans* [Online]. Available: <*www.aoa.gov/aoa/stats/profile/default.htm*>.

Barusch, A., Greene, R., & Connelly, J. (1990). *Strategies for Increasing Gerontology Content in Social Work Education*. Washington, DC: Association for Gerontology in Higher Education.

Berkman, B. Damron-Rodriguez, J., Dobrof, R. & Harry, L. (1996) Social work, in S. Klein (Ed.). *A national agenda for geriatric education: White papers*. Rockville, MD: Health Resources and Services Administration.

Blanchette, P. & Flynn, B. (2001). Geriatric Medicine: An approaching Crisis. *Generations 25* (1), 80-85.

CSWE/SAGE-SW (1999). *Social Work with Older People [brochure]*. Council on Social Work Education, publications department. [Online] Available at: <*www.cswe.org/sage-sw/careerbrochure.htm*>.

CSWE/SAGE-SW (2000). *CSWE/SAGE-SW Aging Competencies Survey Report.* [Online] Available at: <*www.cswe.org/sage-sw/competenciesreport.htm*>.

CSWE/SAGE-SW (2001a). *Strengthening the Impact of Social Work to Improve the Quality of Life for Older Adults & their Families: A Blueprint for the New Millennium*. Alexandria, VA: Council on Social Work Education. [Online] Available: <*www.cswe.org/sage/sw/*>.

CSWE/SAGE-SW (2001b). *Annotated Working Bibliography in Social Work and Aging*. [Online] Available: <*www.cswe.org/sage/sw/*>–listed under Blueprint.

Damron-Rodriguez, J., Dorfman, R. & Lubben, J. (1992). A Geriatric Education Center Faculty Development Program Dedicated to Social Work. *Journal of Gerontological Social Work, 18* (3/4), 187-201.

Damron-Rodriguez, J., & Lubben, J. (1997). The 1995 White House Conference on Aging: An agenda for social work education and training. In C. Saltz (Ed.), *Social work response to the 1995 White House Conference on Aging: From issues to actions* (pp. 65-77). New York: The Haworth Press, Inc.

Damron-Rodriguez, J., Villa, V., Tseng, H., & Lubben, J. (1997). Demographic and organizational infludes on the development of gerontological social work curriculum. *Gerontology and Geriatrics Education, 17* (3), 3-18.

Fulmer, T, Flaherty, E., & Medley, L. (2001). Geriatric Nurse Practitioners: Vital to the Future of Healthcare for Elders. *Generations 25* (1), 72-75.

Gibelman, M., & Schervish, P. (1997). *Who We Are: A Second Look*. Washington, DC: NASW Press.

Greene, R. (2000). *Social Work with the Aged and Their Families* (2nd ed.). New York: Aldine de Gruyter.

Grimier, A. & Gorey, K. (1998). The effectiveness of social work with older people: a meta-analysis of conference proceedings. *Social Work Research, 22* (1), 60-64).

Ivry, J (1985). Aging in place: the role of geriatric social work. *Families in Society: The Journal of Contemporary Human Services, 76* (2), 76-85.

Kane, M. (1999). The Factors Affecting Social Work Student's Willingness to Work with Elders with Alzheimer's Disease. *Journal of Social Work Education, 35* (1), 71-85).

Klein, S. (Ed.). (1996). *A national agenda for geriatric education: White papers.* Rockville, MD: Health Resources and Services Administration.

Kosberg, J. (Ed.) (1979). *Working with and for the Aged: Readings in Social Work Series.* NASW Press.

Lennon, T. (1999). *Statistics on Social Work Education in the United States: 1998.* Alexandria, VA: Council on Social Work Education.

National Institute on Aging [NIA](1987). *Personnel for Health Needs of the Elderly Through the Year 2020.* Bethesda, MD: Department of Health and Human Services, Public Health Service.

Netting, F. E., & Williams, F. (1998). Can We Prepare Geriatric Social Workers to Collaborate in Primary Care Practices? *Journal of Social Work Education, 34* (2), 195-210.

Peterson, D. A. (1990). Personnel to Serve the Aging in the Field of Social Work: Implications for Educating Professionals. *Social Work, 35* (5), 412-415.

Peterson, D. A. & Wendt, P.F. (1990). Employment in the Field of Aging: A Survey of Professionals in Four Fields. *The Gerontologist, 30,* 679-684.

Reed, C. C., Beall, S. C., & Baumhover, L. A. (1992). Gerontological education for students in nursing and social work: Knowledge, attitudes, and perceived barriers. *Educational Gerontology, 18* (6), 625-636.

Rosen, A., & Zlotnik (2001). Social Work's Response to a Growing Older Population. *Generations 25* (1), 69-71.

Scharlach, A., Damron-Rodriguez, J., Robinson, B., & Feldman, R. (2000). Educating Social Workers for an Aging Society: A Vision for the 21st Century. *Journal of Social Work Education, 36* (3), 521-538.

Schneider, R.(Ed.) (1984). *Gerontology in Social Work Education: Faculty Development and Continuing Education.* Council on Social Work Education.

Teare, R., & Sheafor, B. (1995). *Practice-sensitive Social Work Education.* Alexandria, VA: Council on Social Work Education.

Wallace, G. (2001). Grandparent Caregivers: Emerging Issues in Elder Law and Social Work Practice. *Journal of Gerontological Social Work, 34* (3), 127-136.

US Bureau of Census (May, 1999) Sixty-five Plus in the United States: A Statistical Brief. [Online} Available at: <*http://www.census.gov/socdemo/www/agebrief.html*>.

Mental Health Services Policy
and the Aging

Brian Kaskie, PhD
Carroll L. Estes, PhD

SUMMARY. With the continued expansion of managed behavioral healthcare and the imminent increase in the number of older adults with mental illness, the intersection between managed behavioral healthcare and the aging population presents several challenges. Yet this intersection has not been explored in great detail. Managed behavioral healthcare has contained the costs of providing specialty mental health

---

Brian Kaskie is Assistant Faculty Member, Department of Health Management and Policy, University of Iowa. His primary interest concerns the pathways to health and social services for older persons with dementia and other forms of mental illness. Prior to arriving in Iowa, Dr. Kaskie competed a PhD in Gerontology and Public Policy at the University of Southern California in 1998, and a postdoctoral fellowship in health services research at the University of California, San Francisco.

Carroll L. Estes is Professor of Sociology, Department of Social and Behavioral Sciences, School of Nursing, University of California, San Francisco, 3333 California Street, San Francisco, CA 94118 (E-mail: cestes@itsa.ucsf.edu), and Director of the Institute for Health and Aging. Dr. Estes, whose PhD is from the University of California, San Diego, conducts research on aging policy, health and long-term care policy, older women, fiscal crisis, and devolution.

Address correspondence to: Brian Kaskie, PhD, Department of Health Management and Policy, University of Iowa, 2700 Steindler Building, Iowa City, IA 52242-1008 (E-mail: brian-kaskie@uiowa.edu).

[Haworth co-indexing entry note]: "Mental Health Services Policy and the Aging." Kaskie, Brian, and Carroll L. Estes. Co-published simultaneously in *Journal of Gerontological Social Work* (The Haworth Social Work Practice Press, an imprint of The Haworth Press, Inc.) Vol. 36. No. (3/4), 2001, pp. 99-114; and: *Gerontological Social Work Practice: Issues, Challenges, and Potential* (ed: Enid Opal Cox, Elizabeth S. Kelchner, and Rosemary Chapin) The Haworth Social Work Practice Press, an imprint of The Haworth Press, Inc., 2001, pp. 99-114. Single or multiple copies of this article are available for a fee from The Haworth Document Delivery Service [1-800-HAWORTH, 9:00 a.m. - 5:00 p.m. (EST). E-mail address: getinfo@haworthpressinc.com].

services to older adults but a number of other objectives remain unexamined. How, for example, does managed behavioral healthcare affect access and clinical outcomes for older adults with mental illness? We suggest that a more comprehensive policy agenda be pursued–access to specialty mental healthcare must be increased and clinical outcomes monitored more closely. *[Article copies available for a fee from The Haworth Document Delivery Service: 1-800-HAWORTH. E-mail address: <getinfo@haworthpressinc.com> Website: <http://www.HaworthPress.com> © 2001 by The Haworth Press, Inc. All rights reserved.]*

KEYWORDS. Aging, managed behavioral healthcare, mental health services, mental illness, older adults

INTRODUCTION

The United States Surgeon General (1999) proclaimed that mental health is fundamental to health and well being, and the detrimental effects of mental illness can be just as disabling as arthritis, cancer, and other serious health problems. Mental illness impairs functional ability, limits occupational and leisure opportunities, lowers health status, and may be a source of stress and burden to significant others and caregivers. Mental illness also represents a significant cost to the individual and to society. The Surgeon General suggested that one in five adult Americans (44 million) experienced a diagnosable mental disorder in the past year, and when substance abuse disorders were included, the proportion of diagnosable illnesses rose to 28% of the US adult population.

Within this context, managed behavioral healthcare organizations (MBHOs) have emerged and assumed primary responsibility for the delivery of specialty mental health services. In 1995, MBHOs administered specialty mental health services for 102 million Americans; by 1998, more than 160 million Americans obtained specialty mental health services from a managed behavioral healthcare organization (Sturm, 1999). Arguably, some aspect or characteristic of managed behavioral healthcare has been incorporated into every type of specialty mental health service delivered in the United States (Ma & McGuire, 1998).

Concurrent with the emergence of managed behavioral healthcare, the challenges of population aging have arrived. One of the most compelling is the growing number of older adults with moderate to severe forms of mental illness. The Epidemiological Catchment Area surveys conducted by the National Institute of Mental Health (Regier et al., 1988) indicated that the rate of mental illness among persons 65 years and older was 5.5% for anxiety disorders, 2.5% for clinical depression, 1.7% for substance abuse, and .02% for schizophrenia. Moderate to severe cognitive impairment among older adults reached 4.9%. Mental illness constitutes the fourth or fifth most debilitating health problem among older adults (Kaskie & Ettner, 2001).

The Surgeon General confirmed that mental illness among the elderly represents a major public health problem. As the proportion of the US population aged 65 and older rises from 13% to 20% by 2030, the older population will become more diverse in terms of racial and ethnic composition, education and income, living arrangements, and physical health (Administration On Aging, 2001). Indeed, the imminent increase in the number, proportion, and diversity of older adults with mental illness is disquieting, and the intersection between managed behavioral healthcare and population aging merits further attention.

From here, we focus upon the emergence and growth of managed behavioral healthcare, identify key characteristics of behavioral healthcare, and consider how the aging population intersects with managed behavioral healthcare. We conclude by advancing a policy agenda concerning the provision of specialty mental health services to older adults within managed behavioral healthcare organizations.

The Origins of Managed Behavioral Healthcare

Mirin and Sederer (1996) reported that the average annual cost of providing specialty services to a person with mental illness rose from $163 in 1987 to more than $400 in 1992. Goldman, McCulloch, and Sturm (1998) added that aggregate costs of mental health services rose 30% between 1988 and 1990. This growth outpaced aggregate healthcare expenditures over the same period, and the proportion of spending for specialty mental health services reached 10% of all healthcare expenditures in 1990. In 1996, total US direct service costs exceeded $99 billion for mental illness, addictive disorders, and dementia (U.S. Department of Health & Human Services, 1999).

Rising costs were linked with two circumstances. On one hand, costs increased because public policies were enacted that expanded access to mental health services. During the 1980s, 28 states passed legislation that required the inclusion of mental health services in all health insurance programs (Mirin & Sederer, 1996). Access to services increased further (and costs rose) as the list of professionals authorized to provide mental health services was expanded. In 1989, the Medicare program established that mental health services could be provided by licensed clinical psychologists and licensed clinical social workers as well as medical doctors. Rosenbach (1997) reported that the number of older Medicare beneficiaries who used a specialty mental health service increased more than 50% between 1987 and 1992.

On the other hand, the 1980s brought forth the era of managed healthcare. As administrative, organizational, and procedural applications were introduced into the delivery of healthcare, direct costs were reduced. However, since managed care techniques generally were not applied to the delivery of specialty mental health services, the costs of mental health services continued to rise unhindered.

In the early 1990s, the purchasers of mental health services (e.g., employers, government agencies) concluded that the rising costs of mental health services could be contained by limiting excessive use and access to the most expensive forms of inpatient mental health treatment (Goldman, McCulloch, & Sturm, 1998). The purchasers also determined that managed behavioral healthcare organizations were most qualified to reach the cost containment goal.

Although the Medicare program has never contracted a managed behavioral healthcare organization to provide mental health services, the program implements policies and techniques that are characteristic of behavioral healthcare management. For example, the Health Care Financing Administration requires 50% co-payments and still imposes service use limitations on inpatient and outpatient care.

Estes (1995) argued that focusing on containing the cost of specialty mental health care drastically changed the access to and outcomes of mental health service delivery. Yet, managed behavioral healthcare organizations have not fully documented how clinical processes and outcomes have changed. How Medicare policies affect service use and outcomes remains unexplored as well.

What Is Managed Behavioral Healthcare?

Managed behavioral healthcare organizations can be defined as carve-in or carve-out models (Cuffel, Snowden, Masland, & Piccagli, 1994). A carve-in refers to an agreement where the purchaser (i.e., the employer, state Medicaid program) contracts with a healthcare organization to administer specialty mental health services to a group of beneficiaries. Since the healthcare organization provides all other beneficiary health services within the same administrative structure, this is referred to as a mental health carve-in.

In a carve-out model, a purchaser decides that specialty mental health services should be administered separately from healthcare services, and then contracts with an independent managed behavioral healthcare organization. Beneficiaries in a carve-out plan access mental health services through a managed behavioral healthcare organization that is organized and administered separately from all other healthcare services.

Another critical feature of managed behavioral healthcare concerns how services are paid for (Lourie, Howe & Roebeck, 1996). In one financing arrangement, the purchaser reimburses the service provider on a fee-for-service schedule. This follows the tradition in which clinical practice (and the related fees) were defined by the practice provider. There is no management of service delivery or the costs thereof.

Another method can be defined as capitated financing. In this approach, the purchaser offers the provider organization (e.g., the MBHO) a fixed-fee for the delivery specialty mental health services to a defined beneficiary population. Oftentimes, the payments are calculated as a per person per month (PPPM) rate. Under this contract, the administrative organization and professional providers profit if service costs are less than the PPPM allocations. However, if service costs exceed PPPM allocations, the administrative organizations and providers are liable.

A third form of financing mental health services constitutes a hybrid of these two arrangements. In this approach, the purchaser and provider agree to a capitated financing contract that curtails the amount of profits or losses that can be incurred. This approach removes the incentive to curtail service delivery as well as manage inefficiencies in service use.

Finally, managed behavioral healthcare is characterized by policies and techniques that are theoretically designed to increase the efficiency and effectiveness of specialty mental health services. Telephone screening and intake interviews, treatment authorizations, clinical guideline implementation, case management, service coordination, concurrent review, and outcome evaluation constitute some examples of policies and techniques widely applied by MBHOs (Goldman, McCulloch, & Sturm, 1998; Wells, Astrachan, Tischler, & Unutzer, 1995). Figure 1 and Table 1 feature the organizations and providers that are involved in managed behavioral

TABLE 1. Three Critical Dimensions of Managed Behavioral Healthcare

Dimension	Characteristics
Organizational Structure	-Carve-In -Carve-Out
Service Financing	-Retrospective Payment (fee-for-service) -Prospective Payment (PPPM capitation) -Mixed (profit/loss limits)
Clinical Care Management	-Telephone Screening -Intake Assessment -Treatment Review -Outcome Evaluation

FIGURE 1. Organization of Managed Behavioral Healthcare

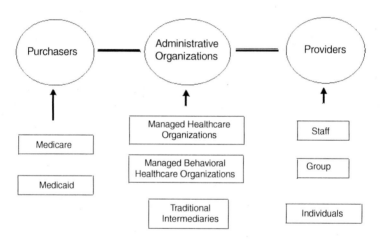

healthcare and list the different types of techniques that are used to manage behavioral healthcare.

What Does Managed Behavioral Healthcare Do?

The rising costs of providing mental health services were associated with a deliberate public policy effort to increase service access and a comparative lack of service management. Managed behavioral healthcare emerged as a response to unchecked access and an apparent lack of service management. Accordingly, researchers have focused on how managed behavioral healthcare met these challenges.

Mechanic (1998) confirmed that managed behavioral healthcare organizations initially focused on reducing access to inpatient services. Inpatient services were not always the most appropriate, least restrictive form of care. Inpatient services also constituted the most costly form of care and accounted for more than 50% of all mental health service outlays. Conwell, Nealson, Kim, and Mazure (1989) reported that the average length of stay (LOS) for older adults who required inpatient mental health services was 53 days. Managed behavioral healthcare set out to curb access to inpatient services and reduce the length of stay among those who were admitted. In so doing, total costs for providing mental health services would be contained.

Goldman, McCulloch, and Sturm (1998) evaluated the provision of mental health services in the three years before and after a managed behavioral healthcare organization assumed authority to administer specialty services. They found that in the three years prior to the implementation of managed behavioral healthcare, service costs increased 30%. Afterwards, total costs dropped 43%. These substantial cost reductions were attributed to two factors. First, the managed mental health organization reduced the probability that any person would be admitted to an inpatient facility. Inpatient admission rates dropped from 6.5 to 3.0% of the beneficiary population. Second, among the persons who were admitted to an inpatient facility, the MBHO reduced the average length of stay from 26 to 8 days.

Other researchers also have found that the management of inpatient care corresponded with reduced costs of mental health service delivery. Ettner (1998) compared inpatient service use among older Medicare beneficiaries with a diagnosed mental illness. She found that the average costs and length of stay were less within administrative organizations that received a prospective reimbursement fee. The average length of stay in traditional fee-for-service setting was 15 days longer, and the costs were 25% higher. In comparing inpatient service use before and after prospective payment was applied to diagnose cases of depression among older Medicare beneficiaries, Wells and his colleagues (1993) found that average length of stay decreased. Moreover, Christianson, Lurie, Finch, Moscovice, and Hartley (1992) as well as McGuire, Hodgkin, and Shumway (1995) reported how behavioral managed care contained the costs of delivering mental health services to Medicaid beneficiaries in Utah and New Hampshire.

Beyond shaping the type of services being provided, managed behavioral healthcare changed the staffing pattern for mental health service delivery. Mechanic (1996) argued that the number of psychiatrists who provided specialty services remained constant, but the number of master and bachelor level professionals providing services increase significantly. The increase among non-doctoral level providers changed the way specialty mental health services were delivered (Dial, Bergsten, Karton, Buck & Chalk, 1996; Scheffler & Ivey, 1998). Within managed behavioral healthcare organizations, medical doctors, psychiatrists, and clinical psychologists more often supervise clinical care and oversee prescription therapy rather than conduct intensive psychotherapy. The master and bachelor level professionals were involved with phone intake, initial assessment, and providing group rather than individual therapy.

Researchers have suggested that managed behavioral healthcare succeeded in curbing inappropriate inpatient service use and reducing total costs, but no one has resolved if and how the quality of specialty mental health services changed under managed behavioral healthcare (Manderscheid & Henderson, 1996). The researchers who have addressed this issue have not yet provided any definitive conclusions.

Johnson and MacFarland (1994) suggested that managed behavioral healthcare controls the costs of direct services by imposing inappropriate service restrictions on the most seriously and persistently mentally ill. Mechanic (1998) reported that functional outcome ratings were lower among individuals who received managed behavioral healthcare services especially those with serious and persistent mental illness. Colenda, Banzak and Mickus (1998) suggested that the prevalence of mental health was lower among Medicare managed care beneficiary populations, and suggested that the administrative organizations were recruiting older adults selectively and not providing access to specialty mental health services.

However, Goldman, McCulloch, and Sturm (1998) found that self-reports completed by individuals who obtained mental health services administered by a managed behavioral healthcare organization reflected a high amount of satisfaction. Wells et al. (1993) reported that the application of managed care processes improved the quality of care provided to depressed older adults–they found that readmission rates and secondary complications were lowered when services were managed more closely.

Managed Behavioral Healthcare and the Aging Population

Wells et al. (1993) and Ettner (1998) reported that, as the Medicare program monitored access to inpatient care and applied other managed behavioral healthcare techniques, Medicare service costs for mental health services were contained without compromising the quality of patient care.

The Medicare program continues to manage specialty mental health services, and contract with managed healthcare organizations that carve-in specialty mental health. The intersection between managed behavioral healthcare and the aging population expands further as state Medicaid programs continue to contract with managed behavioral healthcare organizations. With a primary goal of cost containment, how exactly Medicare and Medicaid affect access to and outcomes of specialty care remains relatively unexplored. It is not enough to know that costs are contained without knowing anything about access and the quality of clinical outcomes.

We find it puzzling that Medicare and Medicaid continue to pursue cost containment almost exclusively, especially since other serious problems in providing specialty mental health services to older adults have been identified (Estes, 1995). Kaskie and Ettner (2001), for example, reported that fewer than 25% of older adults who need mental healthcare ever received treatment, and this lack of treatment provision to older adults has been found across all service settings–community based services, inpatient hospitals, residential care and nursing facilities.

Managed behavioral healthcare must move beyond containing costs, and respond to the other challenges presented by the growing population of older adults with mental illness. Access to services, cost containment, patient education, professional training, and clinical outcomes should all be pursued vigorously–especially since Gatz and her colleagues (1998) identified several well-established and probably efficacious psychological treatments for older adults confirmed that the use of community based mental health services by older adults was substantially lower than other populations. Lebowitz, Light, and Bailey (1986) added that 28% of Community Mental Health Organizations (CMHOs) did not retain a geriatric staff specialist or target any programs to older individuals suffering with any mental illness including dementia. Estes, Binney, and Linkins (1994) found that only 15% of CMHOs even listed the older population as a service priority.

Among older persons who did obtain psychiatric treatment, less than half were treated in the mental health specialty sector. Ettner and Hermann (1998) documented that the majority of inpatient psychiatric care provided to older adults occurred within general hospitals, and this care often was provided in hospital scatter-beds instead of designated psychiatric units. Burns et al. (1993) reported that nearly two-thirds of older nursing home residents have a diagnosable mental illness but less than 5% received specialty mental healthcare.

So why would managed behavioral healthcare limit access to any form of specialty mental healthcare? This question is especially relevant to the aging population since Knight (1990) and Scheffler (1985) suggested that intensive inpatient care actually was appropriate for many older individuals who experienced several morbidities. The clinical treatment of older adults with mental illness often requires a certain combination of health, mental health, and social services. While some older adults should be deterred from inappropriate inpatient service use, we are certain that many other older adults with mental illness receive no form of specialty care whatsoever. Access to mental health services of any kind should be increased rather than curtailed.

We also would be puzzled if managed behavioral healthcare continued to focus on cost containment as a primary objective. Expenditures for specialty mental health services provided to older adults were never excessive. Medicare outlays for mental health services have never amounted to more than 5% of total costs (Reference). In short, expenditures for older adults with mental illness are half as much as the national average. Why should managed behavioral healthcare focus solely upon containing costs?

As the intersection between managed behavioral healthcare and the aging population expands, efforts should be directed towards reaching several goals. For example, efforts should be directed towards implementing empirically supported clinical treatment guidelines. Gatz and her colleagues (1998) identified several well-established and probably efficacious psychological treatments for older adults. These included therapy for older persons with depression, treatment for sleep disorders, and memory training for persons with dementia. Schneider (1995) listed a number of pharmaceutical interventions that were effective with older adults diagnosed with anxiety, depression, mania, and other mental illnesses. Small et al. (1997) identified pharmaceutical therapies (e.g., tacrine, donepezil) for the treatment of dementia of the Alzheimer's type. Borson and Raskind (1997) reported that anti-psychotic drug therapies were effective in reducing secondary behavioral problems such as aggressiveness and hostility among persons with dementia. At this time, it is entirely unknown whether or not managed behavioral healthcare apply any of these in clinical settings (Gottlieb, 2000).

Barriers should be removed that prevent older adults with mental illness from obtaining specialty treatment. Blixen (1988) suggested that older adults might be reluctant to seek out care because of the stigma that has been attached to mental illness. Knight, Woods, and Kaskie (1998) added that older adults may be discouraged from obtaining specialty services because they are embedded within a perplexing array of medical and long-term care service organizations that may not provide access to mental healthcare. Moreover, older adults with no prior history of mental illness may not recognize symptoms that correspond with a late-onset disorder such as dementia. They interpret psychological symptoms as physical problems, and seek out a healthcare provider. Narrow et al. (1993) reported that the majority of older adults with mental illness initially sought treatment from a general medical provider. Certainly, the aging population would benefit from any effort to promote mental health, prevent mental illness, and provide effective treatment.

Still, even if older adults actively sought specialty treatment or primary care providers recognized mental illness and referred individuals to mental health professionals appropriately, Gatz and Finkel (1995) argued that the needs of older adults with mental illness would not be met because of the pervasive lack of professionals with clinical expertise in aging populations. There simply are not enough geriatric psychiatrists, gero-psychologists, and clinical social workers that are expert in the diagnosis and treatment of aging populations. How effective is managed behavioral healthcare in hiring experts or training master and bachelor level professionals to become experts in aging populations remains unexplored.

In short, managed behavioral healthcare must respond to several challenges presented by the aging population. Access to services, cost containment, patient education, professional training, and clinical outcomes should all be pursued vigorously.

The Substance Abuse and Mental Health Services Administration (2000) has taken a critical step forward by supporting a multi-site demonstration program focusing on the delivery of services to older adults with mental illness.

THE COURSE AHEAD

Whether or not managed behavioral healthcare can reach these multiple objectives depends on how well certain obstacles are met. Estes

(1995) and her colleagues (Estes et al., 1994) have identified seven key factors that may impede the pursuit of policy objectives for managed behavioral health care and the aging population. These include rationalization, privatization, competition, deinstitutionalization, trans-institutionalization, medicalization, and informalization.

The rationalization of mental health care, intended to achieve productivity and efficiency gains, is marked by the growth of managed care and the contracting for mental health services. Privatization and increased competition among for-profit behavioral health and managed care entities have intensified efficiency and profitability goals in the provision of mental health care (Estes & Alford, 1990: Dorwart & Epstein, 1993: Schlesinger & Dorwart, 1984). Services are more market-oriented, and the behavior of insures, employers, and practitioners is more driven by their own economic well-being, while diminished attention is given to access to care and their broader societal function (Brown& Cooksey, 1989: Dorwart& Epstein, 1993). A dilemma is that there is no standardization in how mental health services are provided under these service trends (Gottlieb, 1993). Efforts to improve the role of managed behavioral healthcare for the aging must consider how such efforts support the "bottom line" profitability.

Frank (1989) suggested that these obstacles can be avoided if policy objectives concerning the delivery of mental health services to older adults are defined by organized advocacy efforts consisting of consumers, their caregivers, professional providers, service administrators, and purchasing authorities. The Administration On Aging (2001), the National Coalition on Mental Health and Aging (2001) and the United States Surgeon General (2000) all have advanced a comprehensive policy agenda concerning mental health services policy and the aging. These efforts should be applauded and encouraged.

In advancing the policy agenda concerning managed behavioral healthcare services and the aging population, we suggest that careful consideration be directed towards developing the means to monitor the purchasers, administrative organizations, and providers of mental health services. What exactly are the limitations imposed on mental health services by purchasers? How are these distinct from those imposed by administrative organizations? Are any concessions made for the unique needs of older adults? Do any purchasers finance the transportation of frail older adults to and from specialty mental health services?

At this time, such critical questions cannot be addressed because public information about the costs, use, and outcomes of mental health service delivery to older adults has been difficult to capture. Rosenbaum, Silveri, and Wehr (1998) reported that fewer than 20% of the managed behavioral healthcare organizations collect individual data on costs and service use. Estes, Kaskie, and Linkins (2000) determined that public oversight of how Medicaid and other state agencies provide mental health services to older adults is altogether absent. They reported that fewer than ten states counted the number of older adults who received publicly financed mental health services, and absolutely no states collected quantitative information from the managed behavioral healthcare organizations about services delivered to older adults. Without this information, purchasers, administrative organizations, and providers cannot be monitored in a way that encourages the delivery of the most appropriate mental health services.

In conclusion, we suggest that any new efforts to expand the public policy agenda concerning the delivery of services to older adults with mental illness should embrace six points:

1. Policy makers should recognize that mental illnesses will become the second or third most common problem experienced by the older adult population over the next 20 years, and the lack of service use must be recognized as a serious problem (Surgeon General, 1999).
2. Efforts to promote mental health and prevent mental illness among the elderly should be expanded. Education efforts should be targeted so the stigma associated with mental illness is dispelled. Americans also should become familiar with the symptoms of mental illness, and know how to seek effective professional help.
3. The rights of older individuals with mental illness must be protected (Administration On Aging, 2001). Older persons with mental illness should be given the right to plan their treatment and dictate the application of advance directives. Persons with mental illness will be able to obtain insurance coverage that is comparable to other forms of health insurance (i.e., mental health parity).
4. Since effective treatments for mental illnesses have been identified, a more concerted effort must be taken to increase service delivery to older persons. Policy makers must recognize that two deterrents to the provision of effective treatment for the elderly are a lack of funding and a lack of service coordination.
5. Policy aimed at increasing funding for services must resolve three issues. One is Medicare reimbursement policy only pays for 50%

of the cost of mental health treatment costs, while 80% of other medical services are reimbursed under Medicare. The high out-of-pocket patient cost for mental health is a serious impediment to need care. A second is the lack of economic incentives to provide specialty mental health services. Medicare reimbursement rates for mental health services fall below market-level. Thirdly, is to address the bias in providing mental healthcare in general healthcare settings. Medicare reimbursement policies, for example, encourage the delivery of inpatient psychiatric services in general hospitals rather than in specialty care settings.

6. The provision of effective mental health services must follow the objectives outlined in the Olmstead decision: persons who require mental healthcare must be provided services in the most appropriate, least restrictive setting. Older persons with mental illness must access services in a variety of community settings.

A promising legislative proposal is the recent Medical Mental Health Modernization Act of 2001 which would (1) Provide equal coverage for mental and physical illness by eliminating the 190-day lifetime cap for inpatient services and reducing the 50 percent co-pay for outpatient mental health services to the 20 percent level that is standard for numerous medical services. (2) Create Medicare mental health coverage for evidence-based community support-services, such as crisis residential programs, psychiatric rehabilitation, substance abuse intervention and other non-institutional mental health care (Polyak, 2001). Although the Act does not in and of itself address managed care, it goes along way to address mental illness, which is defined by the Surgeon General as "a major public health problem."

AUTHOR NOTE

The authors gratefully acknowledge invaluable research assistance provided by Aileen McLeod and Winston Tseng in the preparation of this article. The authors are grateful for research support from three projects at the Institute for Health & Aging, UCSF that contributed to this paper. They are also indebted to the Institute of Gerontology at the University of Denver for Karen Linkins and valuable information, and to the Lewin Group Inc., for their work on this topic.

REFERENCES

Administration on Aging (2001). *Older Adults and Mental Health: Issues and Opportunities.* Wahington DC: Department of Health and Human Services.

Cuffel, B., Snowden, L., Masland, M. & Piccagli, G. (1994). Managed mental health care in the public sector. Unpublished manuscript.

Dorwart, R. A., & Epstein, L. (1993). *The Privatization of Mental Health Care.* Westport, CN: Auburn House.

Estes, C.L. (1995). Mental Health Services for the Elderly: Key Policy Elements. In Margaret Gatz (Ed.) *Emerging Issues in Mental Health & Aging.* American Psychological Association, Washington, D.C., pp. 303-327.

Estes, C.L., & Alford, R. (1990). Systemic Crisis and the Nonprofit Sector: Toward a Political Economy of the Nonprofit Health and Social Services Sector. *Theory and Society, 19*, 173-198.

Gatz, M., Fiske, A., Fox, L.S., Kaskie, B., Kasl-Godley, J., McCallum, T.J., and Wetherell, J. (1998). Empirically validated psychological treatments for older adults. *Journal of Mental Health and Aging.*

Goldman, W., McCulloch, J. & Sturm, R. (1998). Cost and use of mental health services before and after managed care. *Health Affairs, 17, 2*, 40-52.

Kaskie, B. & Ettner, S. (2001). *The promotion of mental health, prevention of mental illness and provision of effective treatment to older Californians: A report submitted to the Older Californians Strategic Planning Initiative.* Sacramento, CA: California Health and Human Services Agency.

Lourie, I., Howe, S., & Roebeck, L. (1996). Lessons learned from two behavioral managed care approaches with special implications for children, adolescents, and their families. U.S. Department of Health and Human Services.

Ma, C.A., & McGuire, T.G. (1998). Costs and incentives in a behavioral health carve-out [see comments]. *Health Affairs, 17, 2*, 53-69.

Mehrent, T. & Krauss, H. (1989). Cost benefits of a medically supervised day treatment program for patients with Alzheimer's disease and other forms of dementia. *The American Journal of Alzheimer's Care and Related Disorders and Research, 2*, 4-6.

Mirin, S., & Sederer, L (1996). "Mental health care: Current realities and future directions." *Psychiatric Quarterly, 65, 3*, 161-175.

Polyak, K. (2001). AAGP Joins with Stark and Wellsone to present comprehensive Medicare mental health party bill. *Press Release. April 2, 2001.* American Association for Geriatric Psychiatry.

Regier, D., Boyd, J., Burke, J., Rae, D., Myers, J., Kramer, M., Robins, L., George, L., Karno, M., & Locke, B. (1988). One month prevalence of mental disorders in the United States: Based on the five epidemiological catchment area sites. *Archives of General Psychiatry, 45*, 977-986.

Rosenbach, M. (1997). Trends in Medicare Part B Mental Health Utilization and Expenditures: 1987-1992. *Health Care Financing Review, 18, 3*, 19-42.

Sturm, R. (1999). Tracking changes in behavioral health services: How have carve-outs changed care? *Journal of Behavioral Health Services & Research, 26. 4*, 360-371.

U.S. Department of Health and Human Services (2000). *Mental health: A report of the Surgeon General*. Rockville, MD: Author.

Wells, K., Astrachan, B., Tischler, G., & Unutzer, J. (1995). Issues and approaches in evaluating managed mental health care. *The Milbank Quarterly, 73, 1*, 57-75.

Wells, K., Rogers, W., Davis, L., Kahn, K., Norquist, G., Keeler, E., Koscoff, J., & Brook, R. (1993). Care of hospitalized depressed elderly patients before and after implementation of the Medicare prospective payment system. *American Journal of Psychiatry, 150*, 12, 1799-1805.

Social Work with Older Adults
in Health Care and Residential Settings
in the New Millennium:
A Return to the Past

Elizabeth S. Kelchner, MSW, ACSW

SUMMARY. Social Work has a long history of working with older adults in health care and residential settings. The responsibilities of social workers in these settings have varied over time, and are often determined by the economic needs of the organizations rather than the psychosocial needs of the recipients of services. Demographics indicate that the population of older adults will increase dramatically over the next several decades. This article provides a brief look at past practices and argues for a stronger advocacy role for social workers to help to insure a better quality of care for the clients of these programs and services. *[Article copies available for a fee from The Haworth Document Delivery Service: 1-800-HAWORTH. E-mail address: <getinfo@haworthpressinc.com> Website: <http://www.HaworthPress.com> © 2001 by The Haworth Press, Inc. All rights reserved.]*

Elizabeth S. Kelchner is a doctoral candidate at the Graduate School of Social Work, University of Denver, and adjunct faculty member. She was previously the Director of Social Work and Assistant Administrator for a long-term care facility in upstate New York.

Address correspondence to: Elizabeth S. Kelchner, MSW, ACSW, School of Education and Human Development, State University of New York, P.O. Box 6000, Binghamton, NY 13902-6000.

The author wishes to thank Audrey Weiner for her review of the manuscript.

[Haworth co-indexing entry note]: "Social Work with Older Adults in Health Care and Residential Settings in the New Millennium: A Return to the Past." Kelchner, Elizabeth S. Co-published simultaneously in *Journal of Gerontological Social Work* (The Haworth Social Work Practice Press, an imprint of The Haworth Press, Inc.) Vol. 36, No. (3/4), 2001, pp. 115-125; and: *Gerontological Social Work Practice: Issues, Challenges, and Potential* (ed: Enid Opal Cox, Elizabeth S. Kelchner, and Rosemary Chapin) The Haworth Social Work Practice Press, an imprint of The Haworth Press, Inc., 2001, pp. 115-125. Single or multiple copies of this article are available for a fee from The Haworth Document Delivery Service [1-800-HAWORTH, 9:00 a.m. - 5:00 p.m. (EST). E-mail address: getinfo@haworthpressinc.com].

KEYWORDS. Health care and residential settings, aging, advocacy and older adults and families, social work and health care, social work and long-term care

INTRODUCTION

As we enter the new millennium, Americans are living longer, healthier lives. However, old age continues to be associated with an increased risk for certain diseases and disorders, and health care continues to be an important issue for older adults. Sensory losses, such as hearing and vision, can cause older adults to require assistance with activities previously accomplished independently. Chronic diseases, such as diabetes, heart disease, and high blood pressure, can lead to acute episodes that further impact functional independence. Although this cohort (age 65+) represents approximately 13% of the U.S. population, they account for 36% of all hospital stays, with longer average lengths of stays than those under age sixty-five (Duncker & Greenberg, 2001). While a majority of adults over the age of sixty-five live in the community, including family settings, alone, and with non-relatives (Duncker & Greenberg), the need for residential options, specifically nursing homes and assisted living facilities, represent another significant issue for older adults and their families.

Over 90% of nursing home residents are age 65 and older, however, only a small number of individuals in this cohort, just over 4%, lived in nursing homes in 1997 (Gabrel, 2000). Due to the aging of the baby boomers, some projections indicate that this number will increase by at least 57 percent by the year 2030 (Siegel, 1996). Although the number of older adults living in nursing homes is relatively small, it is estimated that as many as 45% of older adults will reside in a nursing home at some point in their lives (Garner, 1995).

Assisted living facilities provide another option for housing when living alone or other community options are no longer possible or desirable. A recent study indicated that at the beginning of 1998 there were over 11,000 assisted living facilities in the United States, providing care for approximately 520,000 individuals (Hawes, Rose, & Phillips, 1999). This article will summarize issues related to social work practice in these two key health and residential care facilities and suggest the need for a more pro-active role for social work as we move through the 21st century.

HISTORICAL ROLE OF SOCIAL WORK IN HEALTH CARE

Social work has a long history of practice within health care, but our history of working with the elderly is less committed. For example, outdoor relief workers were employed to clear wards and free hospital beds in 1900 in Cleveland (Poole, 1995), and in 1905 Massachusetts General Hospital opened the first hospital-based social work department (Oktay, 1995). At the turn of the last century, social workers were also involved in the prevention of conditions that led to poor health (Poole). Early in the 20th century socioeconomic conditions caused the elderly to be viewed as a social problem (Dunkle, 1984). Social workers were involved in the "expansion of a system of insurance for meeting welfare needs," (Dunkle, p. 9), including those of older adults. The Social Security Act of 1935, and the Health Insurance for the Aged Act (which created Medicare and Medicaid) and the Older Americans Act, both signed into law in 1965, afforded opportunities for social work to become actively involved in the provision of services to this cohort. Additionally, the Nursing Home Reform Act of 1987 mandates the provision of medically-related social services in nursing facilities. However, social workers have not shown much interest in working with older adults, and our role in working with this cohort has not been strong. In 1997, only 3.4% of master's degree social work students enrolled in gerontological social work as a field of practice (Lennon, 1998). A similar percentage, (3.5%), of the membership of the National Association of Social Workers claim aging as "their primary area of practice" (Rosen & Zlotnik, 2001).

TRADITIONAL ROLE OF SOCIAL WORK

Today, social workers provide services to older adults and their families through a number of health related settings, including hospitals, nursing homes, assisted living facilities, mental health agencies, and home health care services. Hospital social work includes information and referral, discharge planning and psychosocial intervention (Poole, 1995), while the services provided in nursing homes have been described as "assistance to residents and their families in handling social, environmental, and emotional problems" (Gabrel, 2000, p. 4). Social workers have also traditionally been involved in the nursing home admissions process. However, as the nursing home industry has become more competitive, the role of social work in this critical area has been challenged. Numerous facilities have turned to nursing and marketing staff to attract potential residents and more importantly, their families. Some assisted living facilities offer the services of a social worker, although the nature and intensity of involvement varies (Kane & Wilson, 1993). Described as "host settings," the nature of social work services (Kruzich & Powell, 1995) and staff perception of functions that are "distinctive of social work" (Cowles & Lefcowitz, 1995, p. 279) differs in these programs. The sometimes tenuous relationship between social work and those who define the organizational mission along with the reality of a prospective payment system can lead both social workers and managers to view the role of social work in these settings as less than it could and should be for the benefit of the clients of these programs and services.

Within the nursing home setting, social workers perform a variety of functions. In addition to conducting psychosocial assessments (Nathanson & Tirrito, 1998), social workers address resident and family psychosocial needs (Peak, 2000; Vourlekis, Greene, Gelfand, & Zlotnik, 1992), work to resolve family conflicts with staff (Iecovich, 2000; Vinton, Mazza, & Kim, 1998), and address problem behaviors of nursing home residents (Tirrito, 1996). Nursing home staff social workers indicate that the direct provision of services to residents and their families to help meet psychosocial needs is a priority function, especially during the transition period (Vourlekis et al.).

WORK WITH FAMILIES

Peak (2000) found that families responded positively to a group approach to addressing the placement process and family adaptation to the environment of a nursing home. Group members provided needed social support to each other and were able to use the group process to address difficulties they were experiencing in psychosocial functioning.

Conflicts between family members and nursing home staff can be a significant concern and occur for a number of reasons, including "miscommunications, misconceptions, [and] reasons inherent in the facility's policies and procedures" (Iecovich, 2000, p. 74). Additionally, some family members have difficulty relinquishing "authority and control" of their relative to facility staff (Vinton et al., 1998). Social workers in health care settings are uniquely qualified to use multiple interventions in helping to resolve these conflicts. Residents with difficult to manage behaviors can provide a challenge to staff. Facility staff often call upon social workers to offer interventions to deal with disruptive behaviors of nursing home residents, even though some social workers lack the knowledge needed to deal with these difficult situations (Tirrito, 1996).

BEYOND THE REGULATIONS

Often modeled after hospitals (Reinardy & Kane, 1999), nursing homes typically follow a medical model approach, considered the "state of the art" method of practice for social work and other professions. Regulations, however, offer the minimum standards of compliance for nursing homes, and social workers can take a different approach in these settings. According to William Thomas, founder of the Eden Alternative, nursing home residents often face "the three plagues of loneliness, helplessness and boredom" (Oriol, 2001, p. 9). Research has identified that as we age, life satisfaction includes feeling needed, believing that we are respected, and realizing the expectations we had about our old age (Ghusn, Hyde, Stevens, Hyde, & Teasdale, 1996). Working within the framework of an interdisciplinary team, we can consider the needs of this cohort from a strengths rather than deficit perspective.

TRUE EMPOWERMENT

Lacking technical knowledge, it may be difficult for older adults to self-advocate, but with assistance, they can learn how to survive in the systems that affect their lives and how to exercise their rights. An empowerment-oriented approach includes a sense of control and quality of life, opportunities for choice, personal decision making, and the presence of support systems.

Several approaches have been utilized in an empowerment approach with older adults, including storysharing (Thorsheim & Roberts, 1990), community work (Kam, 1996), one on one (Meredith & Wells, 1994), and group-oriented empowerment strategies (Cox & Parsons, 1996). Group work, a preferred method by some practitioners, and community work share some important characteristics. Group work utilizes group work methods to empower older adults in their community (Cox & Parsons), while community work attempts to empower older adults through participation in one's community (Kam). Using a broad definition of community that includes nursing homes and assisted living facilities, group and community work can be appropriate models in these settings.

Having power over one's life is more complex than simply having choices in particular situations (Kapp, 1989). It is knowledge that creates power. If individuals are empowered to be able to make decisions regarding their life and what is important to them, it is imperative that we ensure that they have the means to obtain adequate information with which to make decisions.

Although empowerment of older adults has been proven to be effective, there are some limitations and problems associated with this process. In some cases, practitioners themselves may represent a limitation (Kam, 1996). Attitudes and beliefs about and towards older adults may prove to be a barrier to empowerment practice with this cohort. Professionals who work with older adults are not immune from the negative images commonly held about them. Whether or not the elderly are valued as individuals can determine whether efforts of empowerment will be successful. Obstacles to this process may also include the process of aging itself. Difficulties in hearing and vision, ability to communicate, mobility, and mental ability can all contribute to a considerable challenge to the empowerment-oriented social worker and interdisciplinary team. In addition, environmental concerns, such as lighting, temperature, and acoustics, can present considerable barriers.

Institutional settings can also present challenges to older clients and workers. Individuals living in residential programs may fear reprisals if they "complain" about conditions or treatment. The social worker's values may not reflect those of the administration, and communication between all involved parties may be difficult. Defining the "real problem" may be complicated, with different opinions and agendas (Coppola & Rivas, 1985; Meredith & Wells, 1994; Thorsheim & Roberts, 1990).

Empowerment-oriented practitioners need to be clear that the individuals with whom they are working agree with their assessment that to be empowered will enhance their lives. This can pose a difficulty in some situations, and it behooves the practitioner to not rush in too quickly or be too aggressive in their desire to be of help. Some groups and individuals may need to first understand the situation under which they are existing and the possible alternatives. Consciousness-raising is an important aspect of empowerment oriented practice. Older adults have the right to decent and appropriate health care services. This right is being threatened by misinformation and myths of aging held by old and young alike, and fears harbored by younger cohorts about the future of our health care systems. Empowering older adults so that they are able to fully participate in the discussions and decisions about their care is an important activity for social work in long-term care settings.

FAMILIES AS PARTNERS IN CARE

Contrary to the myth that families abandon the elderly to institutional settings, they continue to play an important role in the lives of nursing home residents (Naleppa, 1996). Family involvement enhances the well being of institutionalized elders and their families when specific issues are addressed. It is important for families to be able to visit without apprehension or anxiety. Nursing home staff can help to demonstrate that they are a caring community by encouraging families to share in the care of their relative and by establishing cooperative and interdependent relationships between family members and nursing assistants. Additionally, the involvement of family members can assist residents in enhancing their sense of self (Tobin, 1995).

CULTURE CHANGE

In addition to the strategies mentioned earlier, social workers need to be aware of the movement towards consumer directed care. As baby boomers and their parents' age, the recipients of services will be more involved then ever in what care looks like and how it is provided. Nursing homes today offer little in the way of privacy, with the majority of residents living in double rooms that offer little in the way of personalization. Contrary to the popular moniker, "nursing homes" are more institution-like than home-like, and are less likely to provide an environment where one can exercise "control, autonomy, and self-care" (Eustis, 2000, p. 13). If we look to alternatives to the medical model, such as the Eden Alternative and other social models of care, social work will be an equal partner rather than an enabler of medicine.

Social workers in these settings also have a role to play as educators, of the residents, families, staff, social work students, and the community at large. Many of us experience anxiety when involved in health care encounters that have unclear outcomes. Uncertainty about our health can cause us to feel vulnerable, frightened, and alone. Older adults, many of whom face chronic as well as acute illness and disease, may also experience discrimination when seeking care and assistance.

Health care providers' attitudes towards and interests in working with older adults can effect the quality of care provided. Older adults have many strengths that are often ignored and/or unnoticed by younger individuals and by the older adults themselves. All too often, decision making is left to others, including family members and health care professionals, because elders are perceived as being helpless, vulnerable, and labeled as being frail. Caring family members and professionals, including social workers, often have paternalistic or even pejorative attitudes towards the elderly. As with other oppressed groups, older adults begin to believe that they are incapable of self-direction, that their advancing age prevents them from functioning independently, and that they are worthless and a burden to society. As part of our advocacy work and as educators we can help older adults, health care providers, family members and the community to have a more appropriate view of the contributions and abilities of this cohort.

CONCLUSION

The skills we possess as social workers and the values of our profession place us in the position of playing a lead role in determining how care is provided in hospitals, nursing homes and assisted living facilities. We need to take a pro-active approach in enhancing our role in these residential programs. As practitioners, we need to document our interventions and conduct practice-based research studies to determine the efficacy of our approaches. To ensure quality of life for the elderly we need to strongly advocate for a balance between medical and psychosocial methods of care, using both a micro, "case advocacy," and macro, "social advocacy," perspective (Carlton-LaNey, 1997). To enhance family involvement, we need to work to strengthen and empower them so that they can advocate for their family members. Community involvement does not end with institutional placement, and social workers have the skills and abilities to make sure that community connections are not lost upon residential placement. Through our advocacy, we need to ensure that residents are allowed more autonomy and decision-making, that their rights are not violated, and that access to families is encouraged and facilitated.

In order to accomplish our goals we need to be involved in policy making that includes increased funding geared to improved quality of life for residents, support of demonstration models of care such as the

Eden Alternative as well as the development of other resources, and increased and improved geriatric training for staff of these facilities.

Social work skills include the development and accessing of resources, working with interdisciplinary teams, as team members and as leaders, providing staff development programs and educational information for families, and advocating for our clients. By using the skills of our profession we can help to ensure that as we move through the 21st century, older adults and their families will have appropriate residential options that offer quality services in a warm, caring, and personal environment.

As social workers, we must help to ensure that need for residential placement in advanced age does not mean that life has ended, but rather that another stage of life has been entered, one that can be both rich and rewarding.

REFERENCES

Carlton-LaNey, I. (1997). Social workers as advocates for elders. In M. Reisch & E. Gambrill (Eds.), *Social work in the 21st century* (pp. 285-295). Thousand Oaks, CA: Pine Forge Press.

Coppola, M., & Rivas, R. (1985). The task-action group technique: A case study of empowering the elderly. In M. Parnes (Ed.)., *Innovations in social group work: Feedback from practice to theory* (pp. 133-147). NY: The Haworth Press, Inc.

Cowles, L. A., & Lefcowitz, M. J. (1995). Interdisciplinary expectations of the medical social worker in the hospital setting: Part 2. *Health and Social Work, 20,* 279-286.

Cox, E. O., & Parsons, R. J. (1996). *Empowerment-oriented social work practice with the elderly.* Pacific Grove, CA: Brooks/Cole Publishing Company.

Duncker, A., & Greenberg, S. (2001). *A profile of older Americans: 2000.* Washington, DC: Administration on Aging, U.S. Department of Health and Human Services.

Dunkle, R. E. (1984). An historical perspective on social service delivery to the elderly. *Journal of Gerontological Social Work, 7* (3), 5-17.

Eustis, N. N. (2000). Consumer-directed long-term-care services: Evolving perspectives and alliances. *Generations, 24* (3), 10-15.

Gabrel, C. S. (2000). *An overview of nursing home facilities: Data from the 1997 national nursing home survey. Advance data from vital and health statistics; no. 311.* Hyattsville, MD: National Center for Health Statistics.

Garner, J. D. (1995). Long-term care. In *The encyclopedia of social work* (Vol. 2, pp. 1625-1634). Washington, DC: NASW Press.

Ghusn, H. G., Hyde, D., Stevens, E. S., Hyde, M., & Teasdale, T. A. (1996). Enhancing satisfaction in later life: What makes a difference for nursing home residents? *Journal of Gerontological Social Work, 26* (1/2), 27-47.

Hawes, C., Rose, M., & Phillips, C. D. (1999). *A national study of assisted living for the frail elderly. Executive summary: Results of a national survey of facilities.* Washington, DC: U.S. Department of Health and Human Services.

Iecovich, E. (2000). Sources of stress and conflicts between elderly patients, their family members and personnel in care settings. *Journal of Gerontological Social Work, 34* (2), 73-88.

Kam, P.-K. (1996). Empowering elderly people: A community work approach. *Community Development Journal, 31,* 230-240.

Kane, R. A., & Wilson, K. B. (1993). *Assisted living in the United States: A new paradigm for residential care for frail older persons?* Washington, DC: American Association of Retired Persons.

Kapp, M. B. (1989). Medical empowerment of the elderly. *Hastings Center Report, 19,* 5-7.

Kruzich, J. M., & Powell, W. E. (1995). Decision-making influence: An empirical study of social workers in nursing homes. *Health and Social Work, 20,* 215-222.

Lennon, T. M. (1998). *Statistics on social work education in the United States: 1997.* Alexandria, VA: Council on Social Work Education.

Meredith, S. D., & Wells, L. (1994). An empowerment perspective: A key factor in meeting the challenge of gerontological social work. In L. Gutiérrez & P. Nurius (Eds.), *Education and research for empowerment practice* (pp. 137-147). Seattle, WA: Center for Policy and Practice Research, University of Washington.

Naleppa, M., J. (1996). Families and the institutionalized elderly: A review. *Journal of Gerontological Social Work, 27* (1/2), 87-111.

Nathanson, I. L., & Tirrito, T. T. (1998). *Gerontological social work: Theory and practice.* New York: Springer Publishing Company, Inc.

Nursing Home Reform Act of 1987, Pub. L. No. 100-203, 101 Stat. 1330 (1989).

Oktay, J. S. (1995). Primary health care. In *The encyclopedia of social work* (Vol. 3, pp. 1887-1894). Washington, DC: NASW Press.

Oriol, W. E. (2001). Eden Alternative founder Thomas: Nursing home industry 'crumbling.' *Aging Today* [On-line]. Available: <www.asaging.org/at/at-213/thomas.html>.

Peak, T. (2000). Families and the nursing home environment: Adaptation in a group context. *Journal of Gerontological Social Work, 33* (1), 51-66.

Poole, D. L. (1995). Health care: Direct practice. In *The encyclopedia of social work* (Vol. 2, pp. 1156-1167). Washington, DC: NASW Press.

Reinardy, J., & Kane, R. A. (1999). Choosing an adult foster home or a nursing home: Residents' perception about decision making and control. *Social Work, 44,* 571-585.

Siegel, J. (1996). *Aging into the 21st century.* Washington, DC: Administration on Aging, U.S. Department of Health and Human Services.

Thorsheim, H., & Roberts, B. (1990). Empowerment through storysharing: Communication and reciprocal social support among older persons. In H. Giles, N. Coupland, & J. M. Wiemann (Eds.), *Fulbright Papers: Vol. 8, communication, health and the elderly* (pp. 114-125). Manchester, England: Manchester University Press.

Tirrito, T. (1996). Mental health problems and behavioral disruptions in nursing homes: Are social workers prepared to provide needed services? *Journal of Gerontological Social Work, 27* (1/2), 73-86.

Tobin, S. S. (1995). Fostering family involvement in institutional care. In G. C. Smith, S. S. Tobin, E. A. Robertson-Tchabo, & P. Power (Eds.), *Strengthening aging families: Diversity in practice and policy* (pp. 25-44). Thousand Oaks, CA: SAGE Publications.

Vinton, L., Mazza, N., & Kim, Y-S. (1998). Intervening in family-staff conflicts in nursing homes. *Clinical Gerontologist, 19,* 45-68.

Vourlekis, B. S., Greene, R. R., Gelfand, D. E., & Zlotnik, J. L. (1992). Searching for the doable in nursing home social work practice. *Social Work in Health Care, 17,* 45-70.

Challenges in Elder Mistreatment Programs and Policy

Paulette St. James, PhD, LCSW

SUMMARY. Programs serving victims of elder mistreatment face numerous policy challenges including unclear definitions of key terms, an insubstantial and methodologically weak research base, underdeveloped causal theories and practice models, porous statutes and policies, and the absence of federal or other unified funding and directing mechanisms. Elder mistreatment issues provide numerous opportunities for gerontological social work participation and calls for the unique contributions that the profession of social work brings to an increasingly multidisciplinary effort. *[Article copies available for a fee from The Haworth Document Delivery Service: 1-800-HAWORTH. E-mail address: <getinfo@haworthpressinc.com> Website: <http://www.HaworthPress.com> © 2001 by The Haworth Press, Inc. All rights reserved.]*

Paulette St. James is Administrator of Adult Protection for the State of Colorado. Dr. St. James has worked extensively in the specialty areas of health and human services policy development and evaluation and complex organizational analysis for over 20 years.

Address correspondence to: Paulette St. James, c/o Colorado Adult Protective Services, 1575 Sherman Street, Ground Floor, Denver, CO 80203 (E-mail: Paulette.stjames.state.co.us).

The author wishes to thank Wendy Lustbader and Joanne Otto for their reviews of the manuscript.

This article does not necessarily represent the perspectives of other Colorado State personnel or administrators of other State adult protective services programs.

[Haworth co-indexing entry note]: "Challenges in Elder Mistreatment Programs and Policy." St. James, Paulette. Co-published simultaneously in *Journal of Gerontological Social Work* (The Haworth Social Work Practice Press, an imprint of The Haworth Press, Inc.) Vol. 36, No. (3/4), 2001, pp. 127-140; and: *Gerontological Social Work Practice: Issues, Challenges, and Potential* (ed: Enid Opal Cox, Elizabeth S. Kelchner, and Rosemary Chapin) The Haworth Social Work Practice Press, an imprint of The Haworth Press, Inc., 2001, pp. 127-140. Single or multiple copies of this article are available for a fee from The Haworth Document Delivery Service [1-800-HAWORTH, 9:00 a.m. - 5:00 p.m. (EST). E-mail address: getinfo@haworthpressinc.com].

KEYWORDS. Elder abuse, elder mistreatment, abuse and neglect, adult protective services, gerontological social workers

This policy-oriented discussion broadly examines what elder mistreatment is, its causes, its prevalence, how the programs that address it are structured and regulated, and the interventions or actions being taken to respond to it. The purpose of this wide sweep inventory and status update is to illuminate the array of challenges in the elder mistreatment program area to help organize and direct future policy actions. Recommendations are offered for social work involvement in program development policy and determination.

ELDER MISTREATMENT DEFINITIONS

A repeated theme of authors and a prefacing caveat in many studies is the recognition that definitions of elder mistreatment are both conceptually and functionally confusing. However, the major categorical distinctions of elder mistreatment are fairly consistent in the literature and among elder protection programs. They include abuse, caregiver neglect (including abandonment), self neglect, sexual abuse, emotional or psychological abuse, and financial or material exploitation. Typically, both abuse and neglect are included as part of the same overall framework. This entanglement of acts of commission with acts of omission perpetuates a definitional dilemma (Galbraith, 1989). Including self-neglect in the elder mistreatment catchall definition further increases confusion (Wolf, 1996). The aforementioned major categories of mistreatment are diverse, do not precisely identify the criteria of behaviors included in each category, and are not mutually exclusive.

Definitions of elder abuse are generally those of white, middle-class professionals (Hudson & Carlson, 1998), but sometimes vary by race, ethnic background, geographic location (Valentine & Cash, 1986) and occupation (Payne et. al, 1999). It might also be assumed that a chasm exists between lay public and professional definitions. One study (Hudson & Carlson, 1998) highlights the agreement between professionals and public representatives on the most essential components of the theoretical definition of elder abuse (only) when definitions of the term are made clear. This lends optimism to the possibility of reaching shared understandings. Because it is awkward to refer to the broad array of behaviors by repeatedly naming each aspect of the problem such as abuse, neglect and exploitation each time the subject matter of this article is mentioned, elder mistreatment is used as the collective descriptor for these behaviors.

It is very difficult to devise prevention strategies, formulate causal theories or administer successful interventions without knowing the internal structural characteristics or the external parameters of the problem. Further, interoccupational and intraoccupational differences in meaning and definition impede professionals from collaboratively identifying or reaching goals, or even gauging their distance from goal attainment. Research and knowledge building are also compromised by a lack of definitional uniformity.

NEED FOR SERVICES

Inherent in solving any social problem is the identification of need, in this case, the need for investigation, protective measures, and services to achieve safety or reduce risk. Social problems are a complex construct selected from multiple realities as a matter of societal concern (Stone, 1984). This social constructivist lens enables us to recognize that the scope and character of problems and policy responses are strongly shaped by those who have the political power and authority to define the problems and to claim responsibility for solving them.

Social services programs, specifically adult protection, hold the largest claim in addressing needs arising from elder mistreatment. Failure to address elder mistreatment within the context of definitional trends and larger policy and cultural contexts limits the understanding and ability to provide resolution, and may limit the legitimate right of social services agencies to claim responsibility for solving the elder mistreatment problem.

Professionals that address elder mistreatment concerns must be actively involved, along with the clients they serve, in shaping problem definition. One avenue to pursue in defining need includes examination of the opposition from persons who consider protective measures as a privacy invasion, such as for example, some groups of younger persons with disabilities that are included in the state adult protection statutes in over three quarters of the states.

The limited involvement of elderly persons in front line lobbying and intervention activities for elder protection programs is another trail for exploration. While elders act as consultants and participate on governmental and agency boards and committees, it is striking that the professionals are the primary driving force in defining, directing and intervening in elder mistreatment issues (Harbison, 1999). Further, elder persons tend to defer to professionals even when their own ideas and resolutions are likely to be more successful, so the self-definitions of elder persons concerning their life situations are important to definitions of abuse (ibid).

Acting on someone else's behalf under any condition in which that person is able to act on his own behalf runs counter to the value of self-determination, a widely respected practice standard value held by adult protection workers and advocates of elder persons, and a tenet of most state adult protection legislation. Professionals must define conditions under which their involvement is warranted.

Social workers should also be attuned to recognizing situations that reflect problem redefinition, such as those due to budget constraints that force a second level determination of eligibility or informal categorical exclusions. This may take the form of managing by resources or reducing the scope or penetration of services. Applying scales or screens, such as those related to risk or dependency, to further delineate and prioritize levels of need is an example of a common practice used to alter the boundaries of who may receive protective services.

EXTENT OF ELDER MISTREATMENT

The scope of elder mistreatment is unknown. Some literature suggests that the incidence and prevalence of elder mistreatment is overestimated and over reported. Methodological flaws, duplicate counts by social services departments that define each report as a new case and varied interpretations about what constitutes a case are reasons cited for an inflated estimation (Galbraith, 1989, Administration on Aging, 1998). More commonly, others purport the "iceberg" theory of elder mistreatment whereby only a small portion of the magnitude of mistreatment is exposed. The most comprehensive national estimate is that the incidence of non-institutional elder abuse and neglect may occur as much as four to five times more than what is reported (Administration on Aging,1998).

Attempts to determine the extent of elder mistreatment, as well as many other facts and features about elder abuse, are frequently based on information that is collected from State adult protection programs. Many states do not have adequate information management systems, are not automated, and do not have standardized definitions for counties that report the statistics to states for compilation. In a paper presented to the National Academy of Science (Otto, 2001), it was reported that most States could not reliably respond to many survey questions about such things as the number of investigations conducted, gender, race and age of victims and perpetrators, percent of cases in court action, and funding sources.

The research on elder mistreatment is sparse and methodologically weak. Many studies are based on small, purposive samples. Generalizability and comparability of findings are impaired. Wolf (1996) has noted that little more was known about elder abuse in the mid 1990's than was revealed 10 years prior. There are no federal public policy directives that require states to develop uniform data management systems or provide financial support to do so. There are few demonstration projects and a diminutive presence of gerontological programs in higher education that might contribute to basic and evaluative research. Thus, the elder mistreatment knowledge base continues to be grossly underdeveloped.

CAUSES OF ELDER MISTREATMENT

Literature regarding the causes of mistreatment has routinely fallen into the following major areas: caregiver stress, victim dependency, intergenerational abusive family patterns, isolation of the victim, and psychopathology of the abuser (Wolf & Pillemer, 1989; Quinn & Tomita, 1997). These most popularized factors fade under scrutiny to sufficiently demonstrate causal links to elder mistreatment. Further, single-cause explanations cannot speak to the varied types of abuse and neglect and are over simplistic in their application to a complex problem.

The caregiver stress view emphasizes caregiver or family stress as a major underlying cause of elder mistreatment. Caregiver stress, brought on by a heavy workload, many sacrifices, and a multitude of forces is undeniable, but does not hold as a dominant risk factor in reviews of studies of elder mistreatment (Quinn & Tomita, 1997; Anetzberger, 2000). The particular external stresses that may be related to abusive conditions, and the internal stresses that both the caregiver and care recipient experience in the relationship require further study with methods that are sensitive to reach beyond surface explanations.

Proponents of the domestic violence model that interpret elder abuse as a point on the domestic violence continuum are likely to reject the caregiver stress rationale and to see elder abuse as a power and control issue that blames the victim for being too needy. Brandl (2000) cautions against unwittingly colluding with the abuser by directing resources toward the abuser in the form of social supports rather than toward the victim's safety and empowerment.

Victim dependency as a common subset of the caregiver stress perspective has also been consistently replaced with assertions that the perpetrator, rather than the victim, is more likely to lack self-sufficiency or be dependent (Wolf & Pillemer, 1989). This dilution of the victim dependency factor thins the explanatory value of the social exchange model. Previously, it was thought that when caregivers did not receive their due rewards in the relationship, they retaliated with abusive behavior.

Intergenerational transmission of violence has often been accepted as an element in the elder mistreatment equation but it has not been substantiated in elder abuse cases (Wolf, 1996). With its basis in social learning theory, it is a widely accepted maxim that children who are victims of abuse are prone to become abusive parents. In the case of adult children abusing their parents, the cycle of violence must take a different form since the abuser was not first an abused elder (Pillemer, 1986). In kind "paybacks" by abused sons or daughters may also be a factor to consider in cyclic family violence when parents are abused. Elder abuse by non-family members represents an additional deviation from the intergenerational transmission theory.

Because elder mistreatment is perceived as illegitimate behavior, social support may have a deterring effect (Pillemer, 1986). Abused elders tend to have fewer social contacts and feel less satisfied with their social relationships than non-abused elders, but isolation in itself cannot be reliably considered as a cause of mistreatment (ibid). A close examination of the reasons for isolation is required to predict a profile of isolated elders who are vulnerable to be abused. Loss of family and friends due to death or relocation, alienation from family, being separated from supports such as one's community of faith or being homebound are areas to explore.

The psychopathology of the abuser continues to be explored as an elder mistreatment cause. With the exception of alcohol use and some studies that report a considerable degree of mental illness, the role of intra-individual dynamics is unclear (Pillemer,1986). Little is known about what the characteristics of the elder abuser are, and rarely, does research include a focus on the perpetrators or the intra-individual characteristics of the abused. One recent study found that typical abuse cases are characterized by both a caregiver with a history of difficult interpersonal relationships and a care recipient with a history of being abused (Reis, 2000).

STATUTORY CONSIDERATIONS

There are numerous features of elder mistreatment statutes that can be delineated into discernable categories. These include definitions of elder abuse/neglect/exploitation, age ranges of the victims, requirements for law enforcement or legal coordination, assessment and intervention response times, scope of services, and mandatory versus an urged or unspecified duty to report (Tatara, 1995). Only duty to report is considered here because it particularly lends itself to further examination for social work practice and policy determination.

Mandatory versus voluntary reporting of adult or elder mistreatment has raised much controversy among adult protection workers and administrators, legislative representatives, and interest groups. At present, all but six states (Colorado, New Jersey, North Dakota, New York, South Dakota, and Wisconsin) have mandatory reporting requirements for specified occupational groups. The categories of persons most often designated by State laws as mandatory reporters are social workers, physicians, nurses, and law enforcement or police officers, mental health professionals, nursing home personnel, dentists, and more rarely, personnel of financial institutions. States with mandatory reporting laws generally grant immunity to reporters and define failure to report as a misdemeanor with specified fines.

A rationale to support mandatory reporting is that it is considered to be an effective way, second to public education, to identify cases of elder abuse (U.S. Congress, 1991). Issues associated with mandatory reporting are whether it takes decision-making rights away from older persons, violates privacy, autonomy and confidentiality, or promotes negative stereotypes of elderly persons (Galbraith, 1989, Sellers et al., 1992). Mandatory reporting is patterned after the child protection model (Rinkle, 1989). Some critics of mandatory reporting suggest that a parental relationship between the victim of elder abuse and social services programs is especially ageist (Harbison, 1999).

In a survey of adult protective service administrators, only 60% of the 47 states that participated favored a mandatory reporting requirement (NAAPSA, 1994). One concern expressed about mandatory reporting was that it is ineffective without adequate funding for staff and services. Those that did not favor mandatory reporting thought that it misdirected limited resources, were concerned if it undermined client self-determination, or questioned if such a mandate is helpful in identifying or preventing abuse or neglect.

Despite the presence of elder mistreatment laws, there is evidence that underreporting or failure to report is an extensive practice among mandated reporters and further, criminal enforcement is virtually non-existent (Moskowitz, 1998). Reasons that some have given for not reporting include concerns about alienating the abused, concerns about confidentiality, professional loyalty, fear of recrimination, the absence of protocols for training (Davies, 1997), and the desire to avoid timely court appearances (Moskowitz,1998 in reference to physicians).

Whether reporting is mandatory or voluntary, once an allegation is reported, the investigation is always mandatory. Thus, in some cases, the violation of privacy aspect of the self-determination principle kicks in when the investigation of alleged elder mistreatment is already underway since the initial victim contact is often made uninvited by the alleged victim or unannounced by the protective services worker.

PROGRAM STRUCTURE

In 1974, adult protection was included in the Title XX allocation structure, legitimizing the use of federal funds for the purposes of adult protection. However, no other comprehensive supportive actions toward a federally directed program were ever enacted. State and local programs operate primarily on the basis of their adult protective services legislation.

All states have programs to provide adult protective services, although there is much variance and fragmentation among programs. Programs are administratively arranged in a variety of organizational configurations. More than half of the programs are located in State Departments of Social Services. Within this structure, adult protection is a state administered program with state employees housed in regional or county offices. Elsewhere, local governments have responsibility for providing adult protection services under State supervision. In this more autonomous arrangement, programs further vary by county or region, as states generally do not have any sanctioning or directing authority over the local entities. Many adult protection programs are also located in state units on aging that provide or coordinate an array of other programs under the Older Americans Act, such as ombudsman and elder rights programs.

Funding sources of adult protection programs vary among states. Title XX funds represent the largest portion of Adult Protection Service budgets, and local funds combined with a fraction of funds from other sources such as the Older Americans Act make up the remainder (NAAPSA, 1997). Of the Title XX block grant funds that are allocated to states, only about 3% ($83 million) of the expenditures are for adult protective services (Department of Health and Human Services, 1998). Much progress has been made in improving the identification of elder mistreatment and in calling attention to the horrors of elder abuse. However, due to diminishing funds and a focus on the problem of abuse rather than on the institutional solutions, adult protective services are becoming more invisible (Otto, 2000).

INTERVENTIONS

The primary functions of adult protective services are to receive and investigate reports of adult or elder mistreatment, to assess client need, to coordinate or deliver services to victims, and to pursue legal action when indicated (Anetzberger, 2000). While statutes include the provision of such services as a stated expectation, the content and process of intervention are largely discretionary.

Interventions fall into a few large categories of activity such as providing or arranging services toward a long term care plan to reduce risk and increase safety, counseling the individual and family about resource choices and ways to alleviate specifically identified issues leading to mistreatment, or removing the victim of mistreatment from the harmful situation.

One interesting aspect of adult protection services is that program eligibility and the precise mix of services are not strictly determined by categorical inclusion or exclusion. For example, some programs provide a law based or interpretative qualifier directing that interventions be made only when persons are deemed incapacitated. Yet, in some cases, latitude is exercised by providing a host of services to persons who do not precisely meet the criteria for program admission. This elastic feature of eligibility differs from most social services programs that carry tight gatekeeping restrictions.

Statutes typically mandate narrow timeframes for investigating instances of elder mistreatment but lack protocols for service delivery. A typical case handling method of social services programs is a processing of cases through an evaluation procedure that assumes a comprehensive assessment with minimal contact, sometimes by phone or in a few face-to-face contacts. Many programs accentuate admission but due to gross staff and financial resource limitations, either provide limited intervention or deflect the problem to other social service programs. Many states enormously exceed nationally accepted caseload size standards (NAAPSA, 1997) and therefore do not have the capability to provide in-depth and ongoing intervention. Further, program evaluation measures may imply that the less time a case is open, the more favorable the program outcome, thereby encouraging workers whose performance is measured by such criteria to provide only the most essential services.

The effectiveness of interventions is unknown. However, adult protection programs are not uncommonly accused by professionals themselves, clients, and the community at large with "having done nothing." In one study, workers rated their interventions to restore safety and stability to elder abuse victims as very helpful in only 18.9% of the cases (Dolan & Blakely, 1989). Hudson (1986) reviewed several studies that document that resolutions have high rates of dissatisfaction. Contributing factors to such assessments are many. Interventions and services are considered by some recipients to be a violation of rights, are frequently refused, are a misaligned or limited package of services to address the breadth and depth of problems, are financially unaffordable, are of too short a duration for continued monitoring to sustain the value of intervention, and are devised on a shaky causal foundation.

DISCUSSION

Numerous factors strangulate efforts to protect elders from mistreatment. Specifically, the primary issues that affect adequate policy development and implementation include: Ambiguous, non-consensual definitions of key terms that infiltrate all action to address elder mistreatment problems; differences in the quantitative and qualitative methods used to determine need that result in conflicts and limits on who is served, by whom, and with what strategies; ethical dilemmas inherent in actions that seek to both protect victims and honor self-determination; theoretically insubstantial and methodologically weak extant research, fragmented program policies and services that result from State and local autonomy; the lack of federal commitment to adequately fund and coordinate States in developing, implementing, and evaluating protective services programs; and vague, unenforced, and under-funded directives that are inadequate to provide helpful interventions to elder mistreatment victims and further, may increase worker and State liability for improper decision-making.

Several priority actions where gerontological social workers can play an active role are indicated. Because of the prescriptive nature of definitions, the challenge to clear definitional fog is the most fundamental. Focused attempts should be made to disintegrate the overarching descriptor of elder mistreatment, identify the nuances of the major categorical distinctions, and improve conceptual focus by attending to the behaviors that belong to each category.

Research in all areas of elder mistreatment is desperately needed and deserves both State level commitment and federal financial support. If there is indeed a correlation between the growth of the elderly population and the incidence of abuse, neglect, and exploitation, and further, if the incidence of these problems is rising at a rate far exceeding these parallels, then we are particularly ill prepared to deal with the avalanche of problems immediately at our heels. Research on causes, intervention strategies, and models for worker training must be accelerated. Social work faculty and those interested in the area of gerontology are urged to prioritize elder mistreatment issues as a research focus. Universities and State departments must be encouraged to co-sponsor joint research and training programs to test theories and guide social workers in administrative and direct service delivery responsibilities.

The development and evaluation of program policies must always consider the ethical aspects of professional intervention. The balance of self-determination and duty to protect is a practice dilemma that presents a difficult challenge for social workers and other professionals who must accurately determine on a case-by-case basis where the line of the responsibility to protect intersects with an individual's civil liberties. Policy efforts must be constructed in a way that allows the value of self-determination to be operationalized while achieving the goal of protection. Further, the advocacy representatives of persons served must come from the membership of groups served, with serious attention to their definitions of rights and needs.

The onus for policy direction, formulation, and refinement should remain with existing adult protective services programs. The claim that social workers, or more generally, the departments of social services, hold on the elder mistreatment problem may be tenuous. Groups that hold partial claims to the elder mistreatment problem, such as law enforcement, the courts, and advocacy organizations have the potential to expand their territories into a primary directing role. While collaboration with other service agencies is an absolute prerequisite, the extensive experience of social services programs in the social problem-solving arena creates the strongest foundation for organizational placement of the elder mistreatment problem. Privatization of adult protection programs is also a potential threat to the structure of service delivery.

Social workers and others must actively be involved in political and legislative activity to preserve our privilege to serve victims of mistreatment. We must be savvy in legislative processes to secure program support and we must participate in activities to amend porous statutes to adequately address program needs.

Involvement with professional and advocacy organizations is an effective strategy for informing the public, governmental policy makers, and other professionals about the issues of elder mistreatment and the programs that address them. Despite variances in administrative structure, mandates, and service provision approaches, efforts have been made toward unified program development. For example, NAAPSA (National Association of Adult Protective Services Administrators), which currently includes representatives from most states, has joined with five other partners to comprise the National Center on Elder Abuse to coordinate and facilitate social and political action toward elder mistreatment solutions.

Finally, for the purposes of strong and unified policy, stable funding, equity in the protection of victims, development of training standards and training funds, and closer accountability of the efforts taken by programs to address elder mistreatment, a federal role must be seriously considered as a primary pillar of support for future viability of adult protection programs.

CONCLUSION

As we have seen, a matrix of problems and issues confront those dedicated to addressing elder mistreatment policy and program development. The complexity of problems necessitates the involvement of a network of various occupational groups such as law enforcement and mental health workers, and further, includes professionals other than social workers who routinely occupy positions in adult protection programs. Thus, the determination of program policy and service delivery has become a multidisciplinary effort.

It is essential that the profession of social work assert its considerable strengths and vitality in confronting elder mistreatment challenges. In particular, gerontological social workers, with their grounding in the knowledge base of aging, bring critically significant values of a client-centered problem-solving orientation, empowerment of those most affected by our policy actions, cultural sensitivity, and a strengths-based philosophy toward intervention.

Finally, issues related to elder mistreatment present rich opportunities for both ground breaking and expanded social work participation in elder rights advocacy, research, training and higher education, direct service delivery, clinical and program development, policy determination, and political action.

REFERENCES

Administration on Aging. (1998). *National elder abuse incidence study.* Washington, D.C.

Anetzberger, G. J. (2000). Caregiving: Primary cause of elder abuse? *Generations*, 24(2), 46-51.

Brandl, B. (2000). Power and control: Understanding domestic violence in later life. *Generations*, 24(2), 39-45.

Davies, M. (1997). Key issues for nursing: The need to challenge practice. In P. Decalmer & F. Glendenning (Eds.), *The Mistreatment of Elderly People* (pp. 175-185). London: Sage Publications.

Department of Health and Human Services. (1998). *SSBG Program Annual Report on Expenditures and Recipients.* Washington, D.C.

Dolan, R. and Blakely, B. (1989). Elder abuse and neglect: A study of adult protective services workers in the U.S. *Journal of Elder Abuse & Neglect*, 1(3), 31-49.

Galbraith, M.W. (1989). A critical examination of the definitional, methodological, and theoretical problems of elder abuse. In R. Filinson and S. Ingman (Eds.), *Elder Abuse Practice and Policy* (pp. 35-42). New York: Human Services Press.

Harbison, J. (1999). Models of intervention for "elder abuse and neglect": A Canadian perspective on ageism, participation, and empowerment. *Journal of Elder Abuse & Neglect*, 10(3/4), 1-17.

Hudson, M.F. (1986). Elder neglect and abuse: Current research. In K.A. Pillemer and R.S. Wolf (Eds.), *Elder Abuse: Conflict in the Family* (pp. 125-166). Dover, MA: Auburn House.

Hudson, M.F. and Carlson, J.R. (1998). Elder abuse: Expert and public perspectives on its meaning. *Journal of Elder Abuse & Neglect*, 9(4), 77-97.

Moskowitz, S. (1998). Private Enforcement of Criminal Mandatory Reporting Laws. *Journal of Elder Abuse & Neglect*, 9(3), 1-22.

NAAPSA. (1997). *APS Compilation of Workload Studies and Caseload Data.* San Antonio, TX.

Otto, J. M. (2000). The role of adult protective services in addressing abuse. *Generations*, 24(2) 33-38.

Otto, J. M. (2001). *Presentation to the elder abuse research panel*, National Academy of Science, May 24. Washington, D.C.

Payne, B.K., Berg, B.L. Byars, K. (1999). A qualitative examination of the similarities and differences of elder abuse definitions among four groups: Nursing home directors, nursing home employees, police chiefs, and students. *Journal of Elder Abuse & Neglect*, 10(3/4), 63-85.

Pillemer, K.A. (1986). Risk factors in elder abuse: Results from a case-control study. In K.A. Pillemer and R.S. Wolf (Eds.), *Elder Abuse: Conflict in the Family* (pp. 239-263). Dover, MA: Auburn House.

Quinn, M.J. and Tomita, S.K. (1997). *Elder Abuse and Neglect* (2nd ed.). New York: Springer Publishing.

Reis, M. (2000). An abuse-alert measure that dispels myths. *Generations*, 24(2), 13-16.

Rinkle, V. (1989). Federal Initiatives. In R. Filinson and S. R. Ingman (Eds.), *Elder Abuse Policy and Practice* (pp.129-137). New York: Human Services Press.

Sellers, C. S., Folts, W.E., & Logan, K.M. (1992). Elder mistreatment: A multidimensional problem. *Journal of Elder Abuse* & Neglect, 4(4), 5-23.

Stone, D. A. (1984). *The Disabled State*. Philadelphia: Temple University Press.

Tatara, T. (1995). *An Analysis of State Laws Addressing Elder Abuse, Neglect, and Exploitation*. National Center on Elder Abuse. Washington, D.C.

U.S. Congress. (1991). *Elder Abuse: Effectiveness of reporting laws and other factors*. Report to the Chairman, Subcommittee on Human Services, Select Committee on Aging. GAO Report HRD-91-74. Washington, D.C.

Valentine, D. and Cash, T. (1986). A Definitional Discussion of Elder Mistreatment. *Journal of Gerontological Social Work*, 9(3), 17-27.

Wolf. R.S. (1988). Elder abuse: Ten years later. *Journal of the American Geriatrics Society*, 36, 758-762.

Wolf, R.S. (1996). Elder abuse and family violence: Testimony presented before the U.S. Senate Special Committee on Aging. *Journal of Elder Abuse & Neglect*, 8(1), 81-96.

Wolf, R.S. and Pillemer, K.A. (1989). *Helping Elder Victims: The Reality of Elder Abuse*. New York: Columbia University Press.

Gerontological Social Work
with Older African American Adults

Marvella E. Ford, PhD
Bonnie Hatchett, PhD, ACSW

SUMMARY. The proportion of older adults in the U.S. population is growing. By the year 2050, 21% of all Americans aged 65+ years will be members of minority groups, with African Americans comprising the largest subgroup. Disparities in health status and mortality exist between older African American and Caucasian adults. The charge to gerontological social work in the new millennium is to develop effective means of reducing racial disparities in health status. This paper presents some of the key health issues facing older African American adults and describes approaches that could be used by gerontological social work practitioners and researchers in helping to close the widening racial gap in health status. *[Article copies available for a fee from The Haworth Document Delivery Service: 1-800-HAWORTH. E-mail address: <getinfo@haworthpressinc.com> Website: <http://www.HaworthPress.com> © 2001 by The Haworth Press, Inc. All rights reserved.]*

KEYWORDS. Aging, social work, African American adults, physical health, mental health

---

Marvella E. Ford is Associate Research Scientist, Henry Ford Health System, Center for Medical Treatment Effectiveness Programs, in Diverse Populations, One Ford Place, 3E, Detroit, MI 48202 (E-mail: mford1@hfhs.org).

Bonnie Hatchett is Associate Professor, Director of Social Work Program, University of Texas/El Paso (E-mail: hatchett@utep.edu).

[Haworth co-indexing entry note]: "Gerontological Social Work with Older African American Adults." Ford, Marvella E. and Bonnie Hatchett. Co-published simultaneously in *Journal of Gerontological Social Work* (The Haworth Social Work Practice Press, an imprint of The Haworth Press, Inc.) Vol. 36, No. (3/4), 2001, pp. 141-155; and: *Gerontological Social Work Practice: Issues, Challenges, and Potential* (ed: Enid Opal Cox, Elizabeth S. Kelchner, and Rosemary Chapin) The Haworth Social Work Practice Press, an imprint of The Haworth Press, Inc., 2001, pp. 141-155. Single or multiple copies of this article are available for a fee from The Haworth Document Delivery Service [1-800-HAWORTH, 9:00 a.m. - 5:00 p.m. (EST). E-mail address: getinfo@haworthpressinc.com].

INTRODUCTION

The beginning of the new millennium represents a unique opportunity to reflect upon some of the challenges facing the field of gerontological social work in working with older African American adults. The purpose of this paper is to discuss some of the key health issues facing older African American adults and the manner in which these issues can be addressed in gerontological social work practice. The need for this discussion is suggested by Jackson, Lockery and Juster (1996), who note that the overall increase in the standard of living among older Americans in the general population is not experienced similarly among older African American adults. This issue is of increasing importance, given the fact that the number of African American elders aged 65+ years increased from 2.1 million to 2.7 million (a 29% increase) between 1980 and 1995 and is expected to increase to 6.9 million by 2030 and to 8.6 million by 2050 (Miles et al., 1999).

Much of the current growth in the proportion of older adults in the U.S. population is due to a higher rate of increase among older African American adults, which is expected to be higher than the rate of increase among older Caucasian adults into the year 2025 (Sinclair, Hayes-Reams, Myers, Allen, Hawes-Dawson and Kington, 2000). Thus, as Jackson and George (1996) and Netzer, Coward, Peek, Henretta, Duncan and Dougherty (1997) suggest, older adults are becoming more ethnically diverse.

In this paper, the term "African American" refers to Blacks in the United States who are of African origin or descent. Caveats of this paper include the fact that although physical health and mental health issues are presented separately, it is important to note than these two areas are, in fact overlapping. Older African Americans are likely to have a number of physical health problems that may be associated with their mental health status (Cohen, 1993). In addition, a distinction is not made in this paper between primary depressive disorder, found among individuals who either have been well previously or whose only mental health issue is depression, and secondary depressive disorder, found primarily among patients with a physical illness or those who experience an adverse drug effect (Cohen, 1993).

The paper is organized in the following manner. First, physical health issues faced by older African American adults will be described, followed by a discussion of some of the mental health issues faced by members of this population. Next, implications of the information presented for gerontological social work practice and research are discussed. The paper concludes with a brief summary.

OLDER AFRICAN AMERICAN ADULTS
AND PHYSICAL HEALTH ISSUES

The physical health challenges facing older African American adults are numerous (Ory, Lipman, Barr, Harden, & Stahl, 2000; Jackson & George, 1998; Mitchell, Matthews, & Griffin, 1997). Indeed, older African Americans, compared to older Caucasians, have a higher incidence of hypertension, heart disease, stroke and end-stage renal disease (Jackson & George, 1998; Mouton, 1997; Kotchen, Shakoor-Abdullah, Walker, Chelius, Hoffman, & Kotchen, 1998; Kim, Bramlett, Wright, & Poon, 1998; Wallace, Levy-Stroms, Anderson, & Kington, 1997). In fact, the prevalence of hypertension is 50% higher in African American adults compared to their Caucasian counterparts (Kotchen, Shakoor-Abdullah, Walker, Chelius, Hoffman, & Kotchen, 1998).

Cancer, like the other diseases mentioned, affects African Americans in disproportionate numbers relative to their Caucasian counterparts. For example, African American men have the highest incidence and mortality rates of prostate cancer of any other racial or ethnic group, and this disparity continues to increase (Platz et al., 1999; Guo, Sigman, Borkowski, & Kyprianou, 2000; Powell et al., 2000; Collins, 1997; Smith, DeHaven, Grundig & Wilson, 1997; Powell et al., 1997). Prostate cancer rates are 30 percent higher among African American men aged 65 and older, compared with Caucasian men in the same age group (Mouton, 1997).

African American men tend to be diagnosed at a more advanced stage of lung cancer than Caucasian men, and have a 33% higher mortality rate due to lung cancer compared to Caucasian men (Greenwald, Polissar, Borgatta, McCorkle & Goodman, 1998; Bach, Cramer, Warren & Begg, 1999). In addition, African Americans have higher death rates due to colorectal cancer than Caucasians, and survival rates after surgical resection for colorectal cancer are lower for African Americans than for Caucasians (Demers, Severson, Schottenfeld & Lazar, 1997; Baquet & Commiskey, 1999; Tilley et al., 1997; Cooper, Yuan, Landefeld & Rimm, 1996). Among African Americans aged 45 years and older, relative survival has been found to decrease with increasing age (Wingo, Ries, Parker & Heath, 1998).

Racial disparities in mortality rates between older African American and Caucasian adults may be due to comorbidity, access to health services, knowledge, attitudes and beliefs about disease, and/or disease biology. As a result of racial disparities in the impact of disease, African Americans aged 65-74 years of age, compared to Caucasians in this age group, have an 80% greater risk of being disabled, a 20% greater chance at ages 74-84 years and a 60% greater chance at ages 85+ years (Cohen, 1993). Adequate access to medical care, which could help to alleviate the burden of disease on older African American adults, entails more than financial access. In a Milwaukee study, a high rate of uncontrolled hypertension was found even among African American adults with financial access to medical care (Kotchen, Shakoor-Abdullah, Walker, Chelius, Hoffman, & Kotchen, 1998). In order for health care to be most effective, it needs to be perceived as being available and accessible, and individuals need to feel that the benefits of seeking health care outweigh the risks associated with this care, whatever they may be. Clearly, this is an issue that demands further exploration.

While the effects of race vs. socioeconomic status (SES, indicated by education, occupation and income) on health outcomes may be debated, Mouton (1997) conducted a study that shows that while SES factors have a greater influence on mortality and functional status than race, older African American adults are in poorer health and have higher levels of financial strain and caregiver burden than Caucasian elders. Thus, socioeconomic status has been found to have an inverse relationship with health (Adler & Boyce, 1994). Differences in socioeconomic status (SES) between older African American and Caucasian adults may be reflective of their differential levels of educational attainment. For example, in 1999, 45% of all African Americans in the U.S. aged 65+ years had completed high school, compared with 73% of Caucasians aged 65+ years (Current Populations Reports, 1999). Differing levels of educational attainment by racial group are related to lower wages and pension benefits among African American adults (Conward & Hernandez, 1997). Thus, upon reaching retirement, many African Americans are forced to live on very low incomes.

In a study with a sample of 67 African American and 181 Caucasian adults aged 60-107 years conducted in Georgia as part of the Georgia Centenarian Study, Kim, Bramlett, Wright & Poon (1998) found that the African Americans study participants had significantly poorer self-perceived health ($p < 0.01$) compared to their Caucasian counterparts. However, when education and income were taken into account, these racial differences disappeared and a significant relationship was not found between race and health behavior (Kim, Bramlett, Wright, & Poon, 1998).

Similarly, data from a Milwaukee study that included a sample of 583 inner-city African American adults show that among women, prevalence of hypertension was inversely associated with SES (Kotchen, Shakoor-Abdullah, Walker, Chelius, Hoffman, & Kotchen, 1998). This inverse relationship was not found among African American men. Among the women in the sample, an inverse relationship was found between the likelihood of taking antihypertensive medication and SES. A similar but non-statistically significant trend was found for the men in the sample (Kotchen, Shakoor-Abdullah, Walker, Chelius, Hoffman, & Kotchen, 1998).

Low socioeconomic status is associated with a reduced level of access to medical care and with poor overall health status (Kim, Bramlett, Wright, & Poon, 1998; Kotchen, Shakoor-Abdullah, Walker, Chelius, Hoffman, & Kotchen, 1998; Williams & Collins, 1995). Unfortunately, African Americans are overrepresented in lower levels of SES relative to Caucasians (Oliver & Shapiro, 1997). According to reports from the U.S. Bureau of the Census (U.S. Bureau of the Census, 1999), in 1999, among households headed by persons aged 65+ years, African Americans reported a median income of $25,992, compared to a median income of $33,795 among Caucasians. In addition, in 1999, 22.7% of older (aged 65+ years) African Americans had incomes below the poverty line, compared to only 8.3% of older (aged 65+ years) Caucasians (U.S. Bureau of the Census, 1999).

OLDER AFRICAN AMERICAN ADULTS AND MENTAL HEALTH ISSUES

Before beginning a discussion of existing literature related to older African American adults and mental health issues, it is first necessary to state a caveat presented by Cohen (1993). That is, although higher rates of psychiatric disorder are reported among African Americans than among Caucasians when symptom measures are used, racial differences typically do not appear when diagnostic measures are used (Cohen, 1993). In addition, as Cohen (1993) notes, previous studies of mental health issues in older African American adults were typically based on low income, inner-city populations. Thus, paying attention in analyses to such factors as socioeconomic status (SES) and urbanicity is important in understanding mental health issues among older African American adults (Cohen, 1993).

Results from a study of depression among 2,840 older (aged 60+ years) African American and Caucasian individuals residing in Baltimore, MD (n = 1,157) and Durham-Piedmont, NC (n = 1,683) show that while the African Americans in the study were more likely than Caucasians in the study to report thoughts of death (but not suicidal ideation),

African Americans were also less likely to report sadness (Gallo, Cooper-Patrick, & Lesikar, 1998).

When depressive symptoms and depressive illness were examined among 96 older (aged 60+ years) African American community dwelling adults in urban and rural counties in the western portion of Tennessee, it was discovered that being female and having a low income were associated with CES-D scores that indicated depression (Baker, Okwumabua, Philipose, & Wong,1996). In addition, individuals who screened positive for depressive symptoms reported having fewer activities of daily living skills (such as requiring help with bathing) and were more likely to have hypertension, arteriosclerosis and circulatory disease, compared to individuals in the study who did not screen positive for depressive symptoms. Interestingly, social isolation was associated with likelihood of screening positive for depressive symptoms among urban study residents (Baker, Okwumabua, Philipose, and Wong, 1996).

As Cohen (1993) notes, an interesting research question that remains to be answered is whether older African Americans adults, given their higher prevalence of chronic diseases such as hypertension, diabetes and cardiovascular disease and associated disability than older Caucasian adults, have a correspondingly higher rate of secondary depressive disorder. Baker, Okwumabua, Philipose and Wong (1996) actually found that adults who exhibited depressive symptoms were more likely than others to have limited activities of daily living skills and to have hypertension, arteriosclerosis, and circulatory disease (Baker, Okwumabua, Philipose, & Wong, 1996).

The role of gender in depression among older African American adults was examined by Brown, Milburn and Gary (1992). These investigators used the Center for Epidemiologic Studies Depression Scale (CES-D) (Radloff, 1977) to examine depression in a sample of 1,018 study participants, 148 of whom were 65 years of age and older. Of this number, 69 (47%) were men and 79 (53%) were women. Brown and her colleagues (Brown, Milburn, & Gary, 1992) did not find a gender difference in depressive symptoms and attributed this result to the fact that the men and women in the study reported a similar number of stressful life events. Thus, it was speculated that having a similar number of stressful life events was related to the finding of similar levels of depression among the African American men and women in the study.

While incidence of depression was reported by Mouton (1997) to be lower among African American elders than among Caucasian elders, in another study examining multiple role participation and depressive symptoms among 547 older (aged 55+ years) African American women and 2,152 older (aged 55+ years) Caucasian women, it was found that the African American women reported higher levels of depressive symptoms than the Caucasian women in the sample (Cochran & Brown,1999).

A study examining the effects of race and gender on depression was conducted by Fernandez, Mutran, Reitzes and Sudha (1998). These investigators discovered that rates of depression were higher among retired African American men aged 58-64 years than among retired African American women, Caucasian women and Caucasian men in rather than this age range. This finding may be related to the lingering effects of work stressors experienced by African American men and by their lower rate of financial stability at retirement relative to their Caucasian counterparts (Fernandez, Mutran, Reitzes, & Sudha, 1998).

Turning from depression to dementia as a mental health outcome, Hendrie et al. (1995) conducted a study examining prevalence of Alzheimer's disease and dementia among Blacks in Ibadan, Nigeria and in the United States. The Nigerian sample consisted of 2,494 Yorubas, while the U.S. sample was composed of 2,212 community-dwelling individuals and 106 individuals residing in nursing homes. All study participants were aged 65+ years. The prevalence rates for both dementia and Alzheimer's disease were significantly lower in the Nigerian sample than in the U.S. sample, whether the data from the U.S. were combined (community-dwelling and nursing home residents) or examined separately (Hendrie et al., 1995). Despite the noted limitations of cross-cultural studies (i.e., language differences, differences in literacy levels), these data point to the influence of cultural factors rather than genetic factors on mental health (Hendrie et al., 1995).

Turning to the role of social support in the health status of older African American adults, it is important to note that social support can help to alleviate or mitigate the negative impact of disease and disability on overall well-being (Blazer, Hays, Fillenbaum, & Gold, 1997; Cohen, 1993). For example, social support has been found to serve a protective function in relation to suicide; suicide rates among African Americans are highest among those who live alone and who are not involved in family units (Gibbs, 1997).

Social support was examined in a study based on a stratified (by age and ethnicity) probability sample of 1,570 Caucasian, African American and Latino residents of New York City Medicare recipients aged 65 years and older (Cantor, Brennan, & Sainz, 1994). In this study, it was discovered that in contrast to the Caucasians and Latinos in the study, African Americans in the study had less inclusive social networks but tended to have many relatives living nearby. While Caucasians were the most likely of the three ethnic groups to report having a living spouse, which indicates a source of support and stability, Caucasians also reported significantly less face-to-face contact with their children than did members of the two other groups. Despite this fact, reports of degree of closeness to children was not found to vary by racial or ethnic group. Latino survey respondents reported the highest number of siblings residing nearby and tended to have narrower and more family-centered social networks than the African Americans or Caucasians in the study (Cantor, Brennan, & Sainz, 1994). Given the same levels of income and health status, it was discovered that African Americans and Latinos were more likely than Caucasians to receive higher levels of assistance from children, in terms of assistance with activities of daily living (Cantor, Brennan, & Sainz, 1994). In general, the study by Cantor, Brennan and Sainz (1994) highlighted the fact that need for assistance, rather than ethnicity, seemed to be the driving force between the types of social exchanges engaged in by the study respondents.

The role of grandparents in many African American families is a major issue related to social support among members of this group. These older adults, many of whom are coping with co-morbid health conditions, may have partial or full responsibility for raising their grandchildren (Ghuman, Weist, & Shafe, 1999; Minkler & Fuller-Thomson, 2000; Fuller-Thomson, 2000). Unfortunately, previous research demonstrates that the burden of parenting a second generation takes its toll; grandparents caring for grandchildren report higher levels of depression and physical health symptoms than their non-caregiving counterparts (Minkler & Fuller-Thomson, 2000; Fuller-Thomson, 2000).

IMPLICATIONS FOR GERONTOLOGICAL SOCIAL WORK PRACTICE AND RESEARCH WITH OLDER AFRICAN AMERICAN ADULTS

Physical health and mental health outcomes of older African Americans are impacted by socioeconomic status and social support systems. These factors must be taken into consideration if effective supportive services are to be provided to older adults to help them maintain a positive quality of life. Older African American adults can benefit from gerontological social work services. These services must form a continuum capable of meeting the needs of older African American adults in different phases of later years, accompanied with different demands and based on declining capabilities (Beaver & Miller, 1995). Social work practice with older adults typically includes three levels of intervention: primary, secondary and tertiary.

The goal of primary intervention is to assist older adults with maintaining a high level of functioning, to prevent problems from occurring, or to forestall decline as long as possible. As an example, relatively healthy older adults may require assistance in maintaining their level of physical functioning, such as making sure they eat well-balanced meals, exercise, and adhere to medical treatment regimens, including the use of prescription medications.

Various activities promote the health and well being of older adults. A health promotion program is an example of such an activity. For health promotion campaigns such as health fairs to be most effective with older African Americans, there are practical issues to be considered. Specifically, the location, transportation, time of day of the fair, means of advertising, as well as the font size and readability of printed material are important.

Health information presented at congregate meal sites may be effective in helping to promote positive health activities, especially if transportation is provided. Health campaigns that have the support of clergy may also be well received by older African American adults, due to the significance of religion in the lives of many members of this group. An example of another form of health promotion would be a campaign aimed at environmental issues, such as equipping homes with carbon monoxide and smoke detectors or incorporating the use of crime alerts and Neighborhood Watch programs that reduce the likelihood of victimization of older African American adults, especially those who live alone.

Secondary interventions focus on problems already identified or that have already begun, such as health impairments, that may become more evident as individuals age. Impaired older adults may require assistance in managing problematic chronic conditions, such as diabetes, for which dietary habits may need to be modified after diagnosis with this disease. An example of a secondary intervention might be disease management programs run by social workers that focus on diseases that affect African Americans in large numbers, such as diabetes or hypertension. Other types of secondary interventions include support groups for grandparents who have the responsibility for rearing grandchildren, due to the inability of their parents to care for them. This is especially crucial for many older African American adults, who may be faced with issues of changing health, social and economic status at a time when new responsibilities, such as raising grandchildren, are being incurred. Social workers could serve as political advocates by lobbying for bills that allow funds for these older adults who care for these children.

Tertiary interventions are two-fold, in that they include both disability limitations and rehabilitation activities, with the goal of minimizing effects of disability and providing rehabilitation to the greatest extent possible. Severely impaired individuals and their caregivers may benefit from social work services such as attending an Alzheimer's support group or receiving information regarding an array of services available for individuals with this disease.

In providing primary, secondary and tertiary interventions, social workers often function in many roles and on various levels of intervention. Case management refers to the coordination of a specified group of resources designed to produce multiple services to social clients with complex needs in a timely fashion (Encyclopedia of Social Work, 1987; Seltzer, Ivry, & Litchfield, 1987). Not all clients need case-management services, yet this approach is most useful when working with individuals who have complicated interacting problems, need assistance with bureaucratic issues and who are limited in their ability to access needed services (Sowers-Hoag, 1997). Case management clients who are older adults often have multiple chronic functional impairments associated with late life (Gwyther, 1988). This is typically the case with many older African American adults, who tend to concurrently experience a number of different chronic conditions.

Social workers, as case managers, play a critical role in the successful integration of formal services with services provided by families and other primary groups (Moore, 1990). Social workers serve to maximize the potential of individuals and primary groups to function independently as well as facilitate and negotiate the provision of services by linking individuals to social institutions, organizations and agencies (Lowry, 1985).

Typically, case managers are expected to develop an overall care plan for each client system. The care plan focuses on the progression of services to be provided over time and the linkages among them and between them and the informal support system (Encyclopedia of Social Work, 1987). Required services often include shopping, housekeeping, personal care, transportation, and bookkeeping.

Advocacy is an important, and often neglected, aspect of case management for older adults, particularly older African American adults. Recent research indicates that when social workers provide case management services, there is a greater emphasis on the advocacy function

(Douville, 1993). During the linking process, the client and case manager may encounter barriers to service. Advocacy involves an affirmative or assertive approach to assisting a client in receiving services or amenities that are being withheld unfairly (Rothman, 1991). Barriers can range from the more tangible problems of geographic inaccessibility to more subtle forms of practitioner resistance. To overcome these barriers, case managers must have sound advocacy skills and should be prepared to help clients move through bureaucratic rules and blocks and obtain benefits they are due (Rothman, 1991). Advocacy strategies include discussion, persuasion, prodding, educating, campaigning and confrontation. For example, social work advocates could press for recommends funding for programs that address the concerns of older African Americans regarding social insurance and health benefits (Gibbs, 1997). Such programs could help to reduce negative physical health and mental health outcomes among members of this population.

CONCLUSION

This paper has highlighted issues pertaining to the physical health and mental health issues facing older African American adults. A caveat is the fact that older (aged 65+ years) African Americans are a heterogeneous rather than a monolithic group. Individual differences may be related to state of origin, religious background, educational level attained and socioeconomic status, among other factors. Despite these individual differences, however, older African American adults share a similar experience of the racism and discrimination that pervaded U.S. society in previous years. This shared experience may have actually served to reduce the dispersion of socioeconomic status (SES) among older African Americans. That is, due to prevailing societal attitudes, ceiling effects on potential earnings may have been imposed, regardless of educational level attained. These ceiling effects appear to have a significant, enduring negative impact on the physical health status of African Americans at every stage of life, compared to their Caucasian counterparts. Thus, rather than facing their "golden years," many African Americans must spend their remaining time learning to cope with disease. However, it is encouraging to note that while older African Americans may report higher levels of physical symptoms and depression than older Caucasians, they also appear to have higher levels of life satisfaction and to be more heavily involved in their social support networks.

Gerontological social workers would do well to build upon the assets and strengths of African American communities while at the same time performing case management functions to help link individuals with needed formal health services. Also, in order to gain accurate data to reduce racial and ethnic disparities in health status, social work researchers could conduct additional research on physical health and mental health issues faced by older African American adults. Indeed, Sinclair, Hayes-Reams, Myers, Allen, Hawes-Dawson, & Kington (2000) point out the fact that older African Americans are underrepresented in health research. Thus, the actual needs of older African Americans may actually be far less than the currently known needs of members of this group.

To this end, Sinclair et al. (2000) have made recommendations regarding means of including older African American adults in health-related research. These recommendations include being aware of the concerns of members of this population, working with community "gatekeepers" to develop relationships, being aware of the impact of the demographic characteristics of research staff on the population being sought after for inclusion in research, providing transportation for research-related activities, addressing literacy needs, making research written materials culturally appropriate and addressing the concerns of potential participants regarding safety. Only by combining practice and research can gerontological social workers begin to address the often multi-faceted needs of older African American adults.

REFERENCES

Adler, N.E., & Boyce T. (1994). Socioeconomic status and health: The challenge of the gradient. *American Psychologist, 49,* 15-24.

Bach, P. B., Cramer, L. D., Warren, J. L., & Begg, C. B. (1999). Racial differences in the treatment of early-stage lung cancer. *New England Journal of Medicine, 341,* 1198-1205.

Baker, F. M., Okwumabua, J., Philipose, V., & Wong, S. (1996). Screening African American elderly for the presence of depressive symptoms: A preliminary investigation. *Journal of Geriatric Psychiatry and Neurology, 9,* 127-132.

Baquet, C. R., & Commiskey, P. (1999). Colorectal cancer epidemiology in minorities; review. *Journal of the Association of Academic Minority Physicians, 10,* 51-58. 1999.

Beaver, M. L., & Miller, D. (1995). *Clinical social work practice with the elderly: Primary, secondary and tertiary interventions.* Homewood, IL: Dorsey Press.

Blazer, D. G., Hays, J. C., Fillenbaum, G. G., & Gold, D. T. (1997). Memory complaint as a predictor of cognitive decline: A comparison of African American and white elders. *Journal of Aging and Health, 9,* 171-184.

Brown, D. R., Milburn, N. G., & Gary, L. E. (1992). Symptoms of depression among older African-Americans: An analysis of gender differences. *Journal of Gerontology, 32,* 789-735.

Cantor, M. H., Brennan, M., & Sainz, A. (1994). The importance of ethnicity in the social support systems of older New Yorkers: A longitudinal perspective (1970 to 1990). *Journal of Gerontological Social Work, 22,* 95-128. 1994.

Cochran, D. L., Brown, D. R., & McGregor, K. C. (1999). Racial differences in the multiple social roles of older women: Implications for depressive symptoms. *The Gerontologist, 39,* 465-472.

Cohen, G. D. (1993). African American issues in geriatric psychiatry: A perspective on research opportunities. *Journal of Geriatric Psychiatry and Neurology, 6,* 195-199.

Collins, M. (1997). Increasing prostate cancer awareness in African Americans. *Oncology Nursing Forum, 24*(1), 91-95.

Conward, H., & Hernandez, G. (1997). Ethnic issues in health care delivery to elderly people: Specific focus on black Americans and Hispanics. *Gerontology for Health Professionals 2nd Edition,* 111-129.

Cooper, G. S., Yuan, Z., Landefeld, S., & Rimm, A. A. (1996). Surgery for colorectal cancer: Race-related differences in rates and survival among Medicare beneficiaries. *American Journal of Public Health, 86,* 582-586.

Current Populations Reports. (1999). Educational Attainment in the United States. *Current Populations Report,* 20-528.

Davis, J. E., & Andes, N. (1995). Alaskan community characteristics and infant mortality. *Statistics in Medicine, 14,* 481-490.

Demers, R. Y, Severson, R. K, Schottenfeld, D., & Lazar, L. (1997). Incidence of colorectal adenocarcinoma by anatomic subsite. An epidemiologic study of time trends and racial differences in the Detroit, Michigan area. *Cancer, 79*(3), 441-447.

Douville, M. L. (1993). Case management-predicting activity patterns. *Journal of Gerontological Social Work, 20,* 43-55.

Encyclopedia of Social Work 18th Edition. (1987). *Case Management.* Washington, DC: National Association of Social Work Press, 212-222.

Fernandez, M. E., Mutran, E. J., Reitzes, D. C., & Sudha, S. (1998). Ethnicity, gender, and depressive symptoms in older workers. *The Gerontologist, 38,* 71-79.

Fuller-Thomson, E. (2000). African-American grandparents raising grandchildren: a national profile of demographic and health characteristics. *Health and Social Work, 25*(2), 109-118.

Gallo, J. J., Cooper-Patrick, L., & Lesikar, S. (1998). Depressive symptoms of whites and African Americans ages 60 years and older. *Journal of Gerontology, 53B,* 277-286.

Ghuman, H. S., Weist, M. D., & Shafe, M. E. (1999). Demographic and clinical characteristics of emotionally disturbed children being raised by grandparents. *Psychiatric Services, 50*(11), 1496-1498.

Gibbs, J. T. (1997). African American suicide: A cultural paradox. *Suicide and Life-Threatening Behavior, 27,* 68-79.

Greenwald, H. P., Polissar, N. L., Borgatta, E. F., McCorkle, R., & Goodman, G. (1998). Social factors, treatment, and survival in early-stage non small cell lung cancer. *American Journal of Public Health, 88*(11), 1681-1684.

Guo, Y., Sigman, D. B., Borkowski, A., & Kyprianou, N. (2000). Racial differences in prostate cancer growth: Apoptosis and cell proliferation in Caucasian and African-American patients. *Prostate, 42*(2), 130-136.

Gwyther, L. P. (1988). Assessment-content, purpose, outcomes. *Generations, 12*, 11-15.

Hendrie, H. C., Osuntokun, B. O., Hall, K. S., Ogunniyi, A. O., Hui, S. L., Unverzagt, F. W., Gureje, O., Rodenberg, C. A., Baiyewu, O., Musick, B. S., Adeyinka, A., Farloe, M. R.,Oluwole, S. O., Class, C. A., Komolafe, O., Brashear, A., & Burdine, V. (1995). Prevalence of Alzheimer's disease and dementia in two communities: Nigerian Africans and African Americans. *American Journal of Psychiatry, 152*, 1485-1492.

Jackson, J. S., & Lockery, S. A. (1996). Minority perspective from the health and retirement study. *The Gerontologist, 36*, 282-284.

Jackson, P. B., & George, L. K. (1998). Racial differences in satisfaction with physicians: A study of older adults. *Research on Aging, 20*, 298-316.

Kim, J. S., Bramlett, M. H., Wright, L. K., & Poon, L. W. (1998). Racial differences in health status and health behaviors of older adults. *Nursing Research, 47*, 243-250.

Kotchen, J. M, Shakoor-Abdullah, B., Walker, W. E., Chelius, T. H., Hoffman, R. G., & Kotchen, T. A. (1998). Hypertension control and access to medical care in the inner city. *American Journal of Public Health, 88*, 1696-1699.

Lowry, L. (1985). *Social Work with the Aging. The Challenge and Promise of the Later Years (2nd Edition)*. New York, NY, Lohgman Green.

Miles, T. P., Wang, E., Mouton, C. P., Henderson, J. N., Mui, A., Aranda, M. P., Kington, R. S., Levy-Storms, L., & Ting, M. (1999). *Full-Color Aging: Facts, Goals, and Recommendations for America's Diverse Elders*. Washington, DC: Gerontological Society of America, p. 6.

Minkler, N., & Fuller-Thomson E. (2000). Second time around parenting: factors predictive of grandparents becoming caregivers for their grandchildren. *International Journal of Aging and Human Development, 50*(3), 185-200.

Mitchell, J., Matthews, H. F., & Griffin, L. W. (1997). Health and community-based service use: Differences between elderly African-Americans and whites. *Research on Aging, 19*, 199-222.

Moore, S. T. (1990). A social work practice model of case management: The case management grid. *Social Work, 35*, 444-448.

Mouton, C. P. (1997). Special health considerations in African-American elders. *American Family Physician 55*, 1243-1253.

Mouton, C. P. (1997). Special health considerations in African-American elders. *American Family Physician, 55*(4), 1243-1253.

Netzer, J. K., Coward, R. T., Peek, C. W., Henretta, J. C., Duncan, R. P., & Dougherty, M. C. (1997). Race and residence differences in the use of formal services by older adults. *Research on Aging 19*, 300-332.

Oliver, M. I. and Shapiro, T. M. (1997). *Black Wealth/White Wealth: A New Perspective on Racial Inequality*. New York, NY: Routledge Press.

Ory, M. G., Lipman, P. D., Barr, R., Harden, J. T., & Stahl, S. M. (2000). A national program to enhance research on minority aging and health promotion. *Journal of Mental Health and Aging, 6,* 9-18.

Platz, E. A., Pollack, M. N., Rimm, E. B., Majeed, N., Tao, Y., Willett, W. C., and Giovannucci, E. (1999). Racial variation in insulin-like growth factor-1 and binding protein-3 concentrations in middle-aged men. *Cancer Epidemiology, Biomarkers, & Prevention, 8* (12), 1107-1110.

Powell, I. J. (1997). Prostate cancer and African-American men. *Oncology, 11*(5), 599-605.

Powell, I. J., Banerjee, M., Novallo, M., Sakr, W., Grignon, D., Wood, D. P., and Pontes, J. E. (2000). Prostate cancer biochemical recurrence stage for stage is more frequent among African-American than white men with locally advanced but not organ-confined disease. *Urology, 55*(2), 246-251.

Powell, I. J., Heilbrun, L. K., Sakr, W., Grignon, D., Montie, J., Novallo, M., Smith, D., & Pontes, J.E. (1997a). The predictive value of race as a clinical prognostic factor among patients with clinically localized prostate cancer: A multivariate analysis of positive surgical margins. *Urology, 49*(5), 726-731.

Radloff, L. (1977). The CES-D scale: a self-report depression scale for research in the general population. *Applied Psychological Measurement, 3,* 385-401.

Rothman, J. (1991). A model of case management: Toward empirically based practice. *Social Work, 36,* 520-528. 1991.

Sakr, W. A. (1999). Prostatic intraepithelial neoplasia: A marker for high-risk groups and a potential target for chemoprevention. *European Urology, 35*(5-6), 474-478.

Seltzer, M. M, Ivry, J., & Litchfield, L.C. (1987). Family members as case managers: Partnership between the formal an informal support networks. *Journal of Mental Health and Aging, 27,* 722-728.

Sinclair, S., Hayes-Reams, P., Myers, H. F., Allen, W., Hawes-Dawson, J., & Kington, R. Recruiting African-Americans for health studies: Lessons from the Drew-RAND Center on Health and Aging. *Journal of Mental Health and Aging,* 639-651.

Smith G. E., DeHaven, M.J., Grundig, J.P., & Wilson G.R. (1997). African-American males and prostate cancer: Assessing knowledge levels in the community. *Journal of the National Medical Association, 89,* 387-391.

Sowers-Hoag, N. (1997). Case management with the elderly. *Gerontology for Health Professionals (2nd Ed.),* 74-92.

Tilley, B. C., Vernon, S. W., Glanz, K., Myers, R., Sanders, K., Lu, M., Hirst, K., Smereka, C., & Kristal, A. R. (1997). Worksite cancer screening and nutrition intervention for high-risk auto workers: Design and baseline findings of the next step trial. *Preventive Medicine, 26,* 227-235.

U.S. Bureau of the Census. (1999). *Current Populations Reports: Poverty in the United States.* Washington, DC: U.S. Bureau of the Census, 60-210.

Wallace, S. P., Levy-Storms, L., Anderson, R. M., & Kington, R. S. (1997). The impact by race of changing long-term care policy. *Journal of Aging and Social Policy, 9,* 1-20.

Williams, D. R., & Collins, C. (1995). U.S. socioeconomic and racial differences in health: Patterns and explanations. *Annual Review of Sociology, 21,* 349-386.

Wingo, P. A., Ries, L. A., Parker, S. L., & Heath, C. W. (1998). Long-term cancer patient survival in the United States. *Cancer Epidemiology, Biomarkers & Prevention, 7*(4), 271-282.

Older Workers' Issues
and Social Work Practice

Alberta Dooley, PhD

SUMMARY. Gerontological social work practice has expanded greatly in the past two decades, however older workers' issues have not been a primary focus of gerontological social work practice, social work literature or social work associations. The issues and conditions of older workers are of critical importance to social workers concerned with the quality of life of the older population. This article will briefly outline key older worker issues and selected programs and will review current social work interventions and suggest a potential future role for social work in this arena of practice. *[Article copies available for a fee from The Haworth Document Delivery Service: 1-800-HAWORTH. E-mail address: <getinfo@haworthpressinc.com> Website: <http://www.HaworthPress.com> © 2001 by The Haworth Press, Inc. All rights reserved.]*

KEYWORDS. Social work and older workers, older workers issues, caregiving and older workers

---

Alberta Dooley is Associate Professor, School of Social Work, California State University, Chico. Prior to her appointment at Chico, she was an assistant professor at the University of Oklahoma School of Social Work. Dr. Dooley completed her MSW and PhD in social work and has several years of direct practice experience.

[Haworth co-indexing entry note]: "Older Workers' Issues and Social Work Practice." Dooley, Alberta. Co-published simultaneously in *Journal of Gerontological Social Work* (The Haworth Social Work Practice Press, an imprint of The Haworth Press, Inc.) Vol. 36, No. (3/4), 2001, pp. 157-164; and: *Gerontological Social Work Practice: Issues, Challenges, and Potential* (ed: Enid Opal Cox, Elizabeth S. Kelchner, and Rosemary Chapin) The Haworth Social Work Practice Press, an imprint of The Haworth Press, Inc., 2001, pp. 157-164. Single or multiple copies of this article are available for a fee from The Haworth Document Delivery Service [1-800-HAWORTH, 9:00 a.m. - 5:00 p.m. (EST). E-mail address: getinfo@haworthpressinc.com].

Gerontological social work practice has expanded greatly in the past two decades; however, older workers' issues have not been a primary focus of gerontological social practice effort, social work literature, or social work associations. The issues and conditions of older workers are of critical importance to social workers concerned with the quality of life of the older population. Not only do work and work-related issues affect the quality of life of employed older Americans, they also determine late life financial status for many. In addition, many older workers are caregivers to frail and/or disabled elders. Their ability to provide quality care for their elders is often strongly affected by work situations.

Many social workers have found that addressing older workers' issues is important to their clients needs. Some social workers are employed directly in programs serving older workers, such as employee assistance programs and older workers' programs. Others have become involved in these issues while working with families where income from older workers is key to family economic survival. This article will briefly outline key older worker issues, describe selected programs, review related current social work interventions, and suggest a potential future role for social work in this arena of practice.

WORKFORCE ISSUES

The 8.6 million older workers (60 and older) in the United States consists of characteristics very similar to the general population 60 and older, while retirees of this age group (2.6 million) include a racial breakdown of 82% white and 14% Black elders (National Academy on An Aging Society (NAAS), 2000). Almost 50% of white older workers report very good to excellent health, while among Black older workers less than one third report very good to excellent health. Men in both populations report better health that women. Income differences continue to be another key factor of diversity among older workers.

Older workers represent a dynamic heterogeneous and changing segment of the workforce, the challenges differ among subgroups of older workers, for example: (a) older workers who have been displaced from long-term positions (especially those with firm-specific knowledge and skills; (b) discouraged older workers who have experienced rejection in their employment-seeking efforts and are no longer looking for work but want to work; (c) older workers who are employed but feel that their training is inadequate for job retention and/or advancement; (d) older women without or with very little prior work experience who are seeking employment due to loss of special income through death or divorce; (e) older workers who regardless of health status or desire for employment require wages for survival; and (f) older workers who have adequate resources but are seeking supplemental income or the social/emotional benefits of continued productive work. While older workers are in diverse subgroups, many share common issues. Age discrimination, rapid technological advance that requires ongoing and rapid retraining (and consequent devaluation of long experience), increasing insecurity concerning the availability of retirement income (forced by high long-term-care costs, etc.), and changing concepts regarding appropriate retirement age are examples of such concerns.

Research on older workers' issues suggest that age discrimination remains strong in layoff strategies, hiring practices, promotion opportunities, and training opportunities. These practices are often supported by employer beliefs concerning older workers (LaVelle, 1998). Many employers continue to view older workers as resistant to change, uncreative, cautious and slow to make judgments, lower in physical capacity, uninterested in technological change, less productive, and untrainable. These beliefs are held despite contrary research findings that negate these factors and point to qualities of older workers as such positive attitudes toward change, loyalty, low rates of absenteeism, less on-the-job injuries, and ability to learn how to use new technology (Atchley, 2000). Vierk (1995) notes the fears of employers about the potential high costs of provision of health care for older workers and Couch (1998) notes that displaced elders often do not obtain health care coverage in their new places of employment. In sum, strong evidence exists to support the fact that many older workers face on-the-job discrimination, under-employment, and unemployment related to discrimination. The lack of adequate income and key benefits, specifically health care and retirement programs related to older workers' issues have an impact on their future quality of life, as well as current living status.

Older workers aged 55 and over who have experienced an involuntary job loss are much less likely than younger workers to be reemployed quickly (Chan & Huff, 2001). In the *Journal of Labor Economics* (2001), Chan and Huff note that job loss at age 50 or above has substantial and long-lasting employment effects. As these downsized workers encounter ageism and a labor market with increased demands for technical expertise, they become discouraged and the more time they spend unsuccessfully seeking employment, the more depleted their resources become. The loss of health insurance and pension benefits may increase the amount of time now necessary for these displaced workers to remain in the labor market (Chan & Huff, 2001). It is also important to acknowledge that work holds a central position in most older workers' lives that exceeds subsistence needs. The meaning of work for older workers was examined in a qualitative study of Senior Community Service Employment Service Program (SCSEP) older workers (Dooley, 1995). While all of the 30 participants in this study needed the income to supplement small social security benefits, they also reported that work provided social and health benefits and enhanced family functioning in their lives. Kaye, Alexander, and Kauffman (1999), in examining factors contributing to job quality and satisfaction among ethnically diverse, lower income, elderly part-time workers, found that interaction with others and staying active were more important to study participants than financial supplementation.

Selected Programs and Social Work Interventions

The concerns of older workers do not receive strong focus. Programs that assist older workers include special work and training programs, employee assistance programs, and the work of occupational social workers in a variety of settings.

Universal work and training programs are often not well equipped to meet the special needs of older workers. Special efforts to meet the needs of older workers have been developed by the department of labor. These efforts include special job training and finding programs administrated through the states and special programs to serve the low income elderly. Senior Community Service Employment Programs (SCSEP), a number of private initiatives to incorporate older workers into their businesses. SCSEP is a national employment and training program authorized under Title V of the Older Americans Act. The goals of SCSEP are to assist older workers, 55 years and older, in locating employment and to provide training and temporary part-time employment for older workers in community service jobs. This program has been very successful in assisting seniors, who must be at 125% of the poverty level to qualify, in locating employment in both the private and public sectors. This program meets needs for both the community and older workers and should be expanded in order to reach the many discouraged and displaced workers. Key strategies such as appropriate pace in training, the use of social support and attention to other psycho-social factors, related to late life important, have been stressed by these programs.

Employee Assistance Programs (EAPs) find the issues of older workers to be a primary part of their work. Issues of disability are often exaggerated by age. EAP counselors must help older workers make decisions related to retirement and income.

Older women, due to the gendered nature of caregiving, often have uneven work histories as a result of caring for children, spouses, and now aging parents. The balancing of elder care and work responsibilities can lead to emotional and physical strain. Lee, Walker, and Shoup (2001) note that employers may need to develop interventions that help employees cope with excessive caregiving duties. A number of employers have begun to develop caregiver training opportunities and instigate some employee supports, such as more flexible time constraints, will grow by 43% and the pool of female workers in the same age range will increase by 63%. EAP social workers are often in key positions to foster the development of these opportunities.

Rehner Iversen's (1998) article on "Occupational Social Work for the 21st Century" highlights the need for expanding the role of occupational social workers to address the welfare to work crisis, her emphasis on the need for advanced social work practice in work-enhancement programs is applicable to issues relating to older workers. Rehner Iversen's reformulation model includes: (1) work-specific social work roles similar in scope to advanced generalist practice in expanding the practice focus to group, organization, and policy levels, this formulation specifies work programs as the particular practice domain; (2) work-focused assessment, brief counseling, and referral; (3) work-focused advocacy. Occupational social workers in a work-focused advocacy role could team with corporate counterparts to facilitate improvements in organizational structure and resource management appropriate to poor and dislocated workers; (4) work-focused program development; (5) work-focused social activist initiate and support policy changes; (6) concurrent multilevel practice practitioners will engage in concurrent roles at the micro (individual), meso (small group and family), and macro (organization and community levels (pp. 6-8). In addition to EAP settings occupational social workers are also available to older workers in a few rehabilitation programs.

Mor-Barak and Tynan (1993) suggest areas for social work intervention that include advocacy for the promotion of continued employment and rehiring of older workers, linking older job seekers with interested employers, advising companies on work arrangements and training programs, and counseling older workers and their families (p. 45). Occupational social workers will need to be informed regarding where to find older workers, what companies are dedicated to hiring older workers, what resources are available to older workers in terms of training and employment pursuit assistance, and the factors associated with successful on-going employment.

Work environments have undergone major changes during the last quarter of the 20th century resulting in the need for adaptive behaviors by employees (Yeatts, Folts, & Knapp, 2000). These authors suggest specific actions that provide support for older workers such as: (1) accessible training and education, (2) management and coworker support as in publicizing the achievements and contributions of older workers, (3) recognizing that older employees have needs, values, and interests that must be met by their jobs for them to choose to remain employed, and (4) personnel policies affecting older workers and age discrimination. Other work design changes as suggested by Griffiths (1999) include establishing life span models of work design as opposed to "age-free" models and to emphasize contextual research that evaluates workplace interventions instead of cross-sectional studies.

CHALLENGES TO SOCIAL WORK AND SOCIAL WORK EDUCATION

Emphasis on the value of diversity is a primary focus in social work education. Age diversity, as we prepare for an aging workforce, "may well be the most conflict-ridden diversity issue of the 21st century" (Hanks & Icenogle, 2001). How can social work education address this anticipated issue? Research indicates that despite the aging population, students in the helping professions continue to give low priority to working with older adults (Hanks & Icenogle, 2001). Hanks and Icenogle suggest intergenerational conflicts will be rooted in differences in the work ethic and life experience of the Baby Boomers and Generation Xers rather than in ageist attitudes. These authors believe that both younger and older workers need to have anticipatory socialization experiences as preparation for positive interactions in an age-diverse workforce by participating in educational interventions that are designed to reflect the realities of age and cohort differences. Traditionally intergenerational service-learning programs involve working with the frail elderly with scant emphasis on active adults (Hanks & Icenogle, 2001). The Council on Social Work Education mandates the infusion of diversity issues in all social work curricula; expanding curricula to include the study of intergenerational diversity would fulfill a larger societal purpose by strengthening the community at large. Social work field education also offers an ideal opportunity for students to become advocates for older workers seeking to re-enter the workforce who have become discouraged by rejection, for older women with little or no past work histories or training, and for older workers preferring to remain in the workforce. Iversen Rehner (1998) suggests "Integrated occupational curricular offerings in more graduate programs, instead of individual elective courses, would buttress the professional domain" (p 11).

Social work practitioners must first examine their own internalized ageist attitudes. Reio, Jr., and Sander-Reio (1999) found that ageism continues to significantly impact decision making in the workplace. These authors demonstrate how both managers and adult educators inadvertently sustain ageism by grouping workers by age rather than other factors such as experience or behavior. The ageist myth is so prevalent that as with other marginalized groups the majority's biases may be internalized resulting in lower self-esteem and loss of power among older workers. While recent research indicates physiological issues associated with aging are offset by increases in judgment and well-honed evaluative skills in considering the value of information, studies continue to indicate managers and even trainers believe that older workers do not perform as well as younger workers (Reio, Jr. & Sander-Reio, 1999). These unsubstantiated biases result in lower job performance evaluations that older workers may not challenge due to their own internalization of beliefs about aging. Occupational social workers are in unique positions to combat ageist practices in the workplace by advocating for the older worker with management and by helping workers reclaim their sense of worth.

CONCLUSIONS

While the issues and concerns of older adults related to employment have not been a central focus of gerontological social work, these issues are of critical importance. Late life work opportunities have significant impact on quality of life and the social work profession has both the professional mandate and the knowledge and skills to address these issues from all levels of practice. As social workers encounter active older adults with problems, an assumption regarding work and "retirement" that is often made is that they no longer desire or need to work. These assumptions need to be thoroughly looked into to eliminate the possibility of ageism in the workplace resulting in a discouraged worker, caregiving responsibilities that hinder outside employment, and the absence of appropriate training that may be hindering employment. Social workers must be knowledgeable about available resources and actively involved in policy decisions that affect older workers currently in the labor market and those seeking to re-enter an ever-changing workplace. This is an area of practice that is rich in complexity and warrants further study and attention.

REFERENCES

Atchley, R. (2000). *Social Forces and Aging*. Belmont, CA: Wadsworth Thomson Learning.

Chan, S. & Huff. S.A. (2001). Job loss and employment patterns of older workers. *Journal of Labor Economics, 19* (2).

Couch, K. A. (1998). Late life job displacement. *The Gerontologist, 38*, (1), 7-17.

Dooley, A. (1995). Unpublished dissertation. University of Denver.

Griffiths, A. (1999). Work design and management–the older worker. *Experimental Aging Research, 25* (4).

Hanks, R. S., & Icenogle, M. (2001) Preparing for an age-diverse workforce: Intergenerational service-learning in social gerontology and business curricula. *Educational Gerontology, 27* (1).

Kaye, L.W., Alexander, L.B., & Kauffman, S. (1999) Factors Contributing to job quality and satisfaction among ethnically diverse, lower income elderly part-timers. *Journal of Gerontological Social Work, 31* (1/2).

Lavelle, M. (1998). On the edge of discrimination. In Cox, H. (Ed.), *Aging* (12th ed.). Guilford, CT: Dushkin/McGraw-Hill.

Lee, J. A., Walker, M., & Shoup, R. (2001). Balancing elder care responsibilities and work: The impact on emotional health. *Journal of Business & Psychology, 15*(2).

Mor-Barak, M. & Tynan, M. (1993). Older workers and the workplace: A new challenge for occupational social work. *Social Work, 38* (1).

National Academy on An Aging Society (NAAS), 2000. *Do Young Retirees and Older Workers Differ by Race?* (No. 4). Washington, DC: NAAS.

Rehner Iversen, R. (1998). Occupational social work for the 21st century. *Social Work, 43* (6).

Reio, Jr., T. G. & Sanders-Reio, J. (1999). Combating workplace ageism. *Adult Learning, 11* (1).

Vierk, B. (1995). Cost, Cost and Cost: The Top Barriers to Employment for Older Workers: Results of a Survey to Older Workers Employment Agencies. *Unpublished Report Prepared for the Department of Labor*.

Yeatts, D. E., Folts, W. E., & Knapp, J. (2000). Older workers' adaptation to a changing workplace: Employment issues for the 21st century. *Educational Gerontology, 26* (6).

Changing the Paradigm:
Strengths-Based and Empowerment-Oriented Social Work with Frail Elders

Rosemary Chapin, PhD, MSW
Enid Opal Cox, DSW

SUMMARY. Empowerment-oriented and strengths based practice with older adults who face physical, mental and resource related challenges in late life have gained recognition in recent decades. This article explores the basic tenets of these approaches to practice and suggests their similarities, differences and potential contributions from the perspective authors who each advocate one model. Both approaches stress work across various levels of practice (personal, interpersonal and political) and the potential of older adults to be active participants in decisions and actions that affect their quality of life. *[Article copies available for a fee from The Haworth Document Delivery Service: 1-800-HAWORTH. E-mail address: <getinfo@haworthpressinc.com> Website: <http://www.HaworthPress.com> © 2001 by The Haworth Press, Inc. All rights reserved.]*

Rosemary Chapin is Associate Professor, University of Kansas, School of Social Welfare, 304 Twenty Hall, Lawerence, KS 66045-2510 (E-mail: rchapin@ukans.edu). She directs the Office of Aging and Long Term Care Research and Training.

Enid Opal Cox is Professor of Social Work and Director Institute of Gerontology University of Denver Graduate School of Social Work, 2148 South High Street, Denver, CO 80208-2886 (E-mail: ecox@du.edu).

[Haworth co-indexing entry note]: "Changing the Paradigm: Strengths-Based and Empowerment-Oriented Social Work with Frail Elders." Chapin, Rosemary, and Enid Opal Cox. Co-published simultaneously in *Journal of Gerontological Social Work* (The Haworth Social Work Practice Press, an imprint of The Haworth Press, Inc.) Vol. 36, No. (3/4), 2001, pp. 165-179; and: *Gerontological Social Work Practice: Issues, Challenges, and Potential* (ed: Enid Opal Cox, Elizabeth S. Kelchner, and Rosemary Chapin) The Haworth Social Work Practice Press, an imprint of The Haworth Press, Inc., 2001, pp. 165-179. Single or multiple copies of this article are available for a fee from The Haworth Document Delivery Service [1-800-HAWORTH, 9:00 a.m. - 5:00 p.m. (EST). E-mail address: getinfo@haworthpressinc.com].

KEYWORDS. Empowerment-oriented practice, strengths-based practice, aging and empowerment, strengths and aging, empowerment and frail elders, self-help and aging

INTRODUCTION

Approaches to social work practice with frail elders that equate aging with disability and conceptualize the helping process based on a medical model of the frail elder as passive recipient of expert services, face increasing challenges from professionals seeking a shift to a very different practice paradigm. A growing literature reflecting the relevance and application of empowerment-oriented and strengths-based practice perspectives for gerontological social workers has been evident throughout the past decade (Cox, 1999; Fast & Chapin, 2000, 2001; McInnes-Dittrich, 1997; Perkins & Tice, 1995; Cox & Parsons, 1994). This article is written by two authors each representing one of these perspectives and explores the contributions these two practice approaches can make as we shape gerontological social work practice in the twenty-first century.

Empowerment-oriented and strengths-based practice approaches have many characteristics in common. Both include the basic assumption that elders, including those experiencing a severe physical disability, and all but extreme levels of dementia, possess the capacity to be active participants in the helping process. Elders, family members, and/or caregivers can benefit from these strengths-based and empowerment-oriented interventions. These interventions have been introduced in a variety of age-related settings and with older persons facing special issues (e.g., nursing homes, senior centers, senior clinics, case-management agencies, caregiving and care-receiving issues, older workers' issues, and various health related situations). Cox (1999) notes that social justice provides an overall guiding principle for empowerment-oriented practice. Most proponents of this approach stress a knowledge base that includes a historical view of oppression; an ecological view of individual and group functioning; ethnic, class, and feminist perspectives that illuminate the political aspects of issues; and a cultural perspective that enhances understanding of values, beliefs, behaviors, and an overall critical perspective (Lee, 2001; Breton, 1994; Estes, 1999). Empowerment practice is also reinforced by social science theory including macro theories such as conflict-based critical analysis that guide our understanding of classism, racism, ageism, sexism, and other forms of discrimination. Both empowerment and strengths-based practice are informed by postmodern critiques of social values and more mezzo level theories related to powerlessness, oppression, self-efficacy, and social support and related practice theories.

The strengths perspective posits that the strengths and resources of people and their environment rather than their problems and pathologies should be the central focus of the helping process in social work. It is a philosophical stance for social work practice that places emphasis on individuals' inner and environmental strengths. Social work academicians and practitioners have actively explored the utility of the strengths perspective since the 1980s (e.g., Rapp & Chamberlain, 1985; Weick, 1987; Weick, Rapp, Sullivan & Kisthardt, 1989; Saleebey, 1997). The strengths perspective has been applied to mental health, child welfare, work with older adults, women's issues, substance abuse, and policy.

The social problems foundation of social work practice can be recast in the basic human needs tradition of Towle (1945, 1987). Gerontological practice can then be viewed as a tool for helping people meet basic human needs. As with empowerment-oriented practice, social work practitioners, faculty, and students around the country have been exploring methods for actually integrating the strengths perspective into gerontological social work practice, policy, and research (Chapin, 2001; Fast & Chapin 2000, 2001; Perkins & Tice 1995). Potentially, integration of the strengths perspective and empowerment-oriented interventions into gerontological social work can provide practitioners with new tools for conceptualizing social needs or problems, a more inclusive approach to formulation of the helping process, and an expanded array of empowering practice options. Strengths-based practice proponents stress values that encompass human potential to grow, heal, learn, and identify wants. Individual uniqueness, self-determination, and strengths of person and environment are also strongly acknowledged (Fast & Chapin, 1997). Systems theory and ecological perspectives are frequently relied upon knowledge bases (Saleebey, 1997). The philosophical values base and knowledge bases of both practice models support a strengths approach to assessment and intervention.

When clients are viewed as people with strengths rather than as pathological or deficient, then the absolute necessity of their inclusion in problem definition at both the direct practice and policy practice level cannot be denied. Social workers can then clearly see that efforts to assure that client voices are heard and understood are fundamental to effective practice. The importance of ensuring inclusion of clients' voices becomes clear when the problem definition process is viewed in this way, and the focus is on the strengths rather than the deficits. Work to reframe the issue so that client needs are normalized rather than pathologized, is central to this process. For example, instead of a primary focus on risk factors in doing assessment, empowerment and strengths-based social work require a focus on determining strengths and helping older adults maintain agency over their lives. Assertive outreach and efforts to ensure resource acquisition sufficient to create an environment supportive of individual and community strengths are key to strengths-based practice.

ELDERS AND THEIR SOCIAL CONTEXT

In order to assess the need for a new practice paradigm, it is necessary to examine the current social context elders experience. Attaining the age of 65 is a testament to resilience, to capacity to survive hardship, particularly for women and people of color, who compose the majority of social work clients. However, social workers as well as other professionals who hold the keys to needed resources continue to view elders through a problem lens. Indeed, aging is conceptualized as a problem and the paradigm of midlife decline is well documented and reinforced daily through advertisements as well as in textbooks used to educate the next generation of professionals (Chapin, 2001). The paradigm of midlife decline must be replaced with one that creates expectation of continued growth and development through all stages of life.

Although healthy elders are increasingly portrayed as leading productive lives, when elders become disabled, images of dependency permeate our understanding of their life experience. The elders that social workers see are typically ones with needs that the elder cannot meet, often due to disability and or serious lack of economic resources, including health care access. Additionally, elder client populations are becoming more ethnically diverse as noted by Torres-Gil in his article in this special edition.

DISABILITY RELATED ISSUES

For frail elders who experience disability, the old stereotypes stressing dependency and the overriding need for protection once again become paramount. We continue to allow this view of disabled elders to dominate our vision of their potential to live life fully and joyfully until the end. Although younger people with disabilities have demanded individualized accommodations so that they can live in a least restrictive environment, elders with disabilities often no more severe than those routinely accommodated in the community for younger people, can be found in many of our nursing facilities. Social workers who could be their allies in seeking community options are often in roles that don't support a new vision of the strengths of disabled elders. Hospital social workers are expected to facilitate rapid discharge from the hospital, and the nursing facility may be part of the same complex. Social workers in nursing facilities are often charged with keeping beds filled. Discharge of residents can mean loss of needed revenues, and depending on the reimbursement system in place in the state, loss of higher functioning residents can mean discharging those people who are the most profitable to retain. Additionally, social workers' efforts to facilitate client choice are often not supported by their employers. Until the dominant view in the society is one of individualization of elders with disabilities, counter pressures that would insist on attention to least restrictive environment for elders will be insufficient to correct the bias toward institutionalization.

RESOURCE RELATED ISSUES

Economic security of elders and the additional supports they need are most clearly understood in the context of their life cycle. Policies and programs do little to equalize or improve life status for most older adults. Older women are often by-passed in a society that rewards only work that is directly market related. People age 45 and older are often faced with age discrimination and older women and members of minority ethnic groups especially, are affected due to the influence of diminished earlier employment opportunity. Social Security, pensions, and other sources of late-life income are consequently restricted for many older women whose life work was related primarily to family caregiving functions. Older men who have been relegated to low-income jobs that provided limited retirement related benefits also find themselves with inadequate resources in late life.

Over 3 million people 65 and over, have incomes below the poverty line. While many data sources report that only 10-12% of elders are living below the poverty line, more in-depth analysis suggest that over 50% of these older adults find themselves economically challenged related to increased housing costs, health related costs (especially the costs of medicines and long-term-care needs), and other increasing costs of living. In sum, lack of survival resources and poor mental and physical health in old age are often predicated on a life of lower economic resources, higher stress, and limited health care (Tran & Dhooper, 1997; Estes, 1999;). Age is not the great equalizer.

How then do social workers begin to re-image old age? It is in the day to day experience of direct practice with elders that social workers, alert to the possibility of re-imaging old age, can begin to develop more positive visions for themselves and the elders they serve. The stories of older adults who have lived life fully until their deaths, despite physiological and resource decline, need to be heard again and again.

STRENGTHS-BASED
AND EMPOWERMENT-ORIENTED RESPONSE

Strengths-based and empowerment-oriented interventions simultaneously focus on client strengths and environmental strengths and strategies that include education (transfer of knowledge and skills, often among individuals in similar circumstances), self-help, enhancing social networks, advocacy, and social action. Empowerment-oriented practice maintains special focus on consciousness-raising (regarding the personal and political dimensions of issues), multi-level intervention strategies and change, and collectivity in problem solving and action. Both perspectives strongly support client participation in all aspects of the decision-making processes affecting their lives and seek egalitarian working relationships between social worker and client.

The value base and philosophical perspective of empowerment-oriented and strengths-based practice models, reinforced by selected social science theories, suggested above, guide empowerment and strengths-based practice with older adults. The very nature of these approaches requires focus on personal, interpersonal (family, friendship, community networks), organizational, and political levels of issues.

In summary, commonalities between the strengths perspective and empowerment-oriented intervention approaches include: a knowledge base rooted in post–modernism, critical political/economy and moral perspectives; emphasis on participatory knowing (critical consciousness) and action; commitment to acknowledging worth of traditionally oppressed populations and cultural diversity; action strategies designed to assertively acquire adequate resources, based on this commitment; emphasis on the importance of voice for oppressed groups; and assessment and interventions strategies that are multi-level. Both traditions stress an integrated practice approach that addresses personal and political aspects of issues. Empowerment strategies utilize consciousness-raising, and the strengths approach stresses storytelling and re-storying.

The following sections of this article briefly describe barriers faced by gerontological social workers and outline the implications of an empowerment/strengths approach for gerontological social work. This discussion is organized by level of practice, However it is important to note that in practice work at different levels of individual and inter-personal practice, and policy practice (organizational and political/economy levels) often occur simultaneously, and are strongly interrelated. This framework is used only to provide the opportunity to emphasize activity that can occur at specific levels of practice.

SOCIAL POLICY/PROGRAMS AND THE EMPOWERMENT/STRENGTHS APPROACH

Estes (1999) and Minkler (2000) provide important insights from the political and moral economy perspectives about the current state of social policy and hence social and health interventions. Estes (1999), for example, states that social policy in the United States tends to reinforce lifelong inequities (e.g., minimal redistribution in late-life income policy and lower incomes of retired persons that decline with age). Continued age discrimination, the treatment of chronic illness with acute medical care rather than rehabilitative and personal support care, framing policy issues as an intergenerational equity debate, lack of resources for long-term-care needs, and a system supportive of exclusion of elders from many aspects of social life, are among many areas of social policy that challenge empowerment and strengths advocates.

Currently, social and health care services for older adults are dominated by the medical model of service. This model is characterized by a high degree of helper-helpee focus (high levels of expertise and assumption of low levels of knowledge and skill by the patient). Problems or challenges for elders in general have been medicalized (Minkler, 2000) resulting in a severe imbalance between medical and mental health and other social services.

Other characteristics of the current system include: (a) extreme complexity in nature of the delivery system (combination of public and private-for-profit and not-for-profit) providers representing different philosophies, values, degree of availability re resources, and eligibility requirements; (b) focus on individual eligibility for services related to income and ability, to the extent that it is difficult to center attention on the common dimensions of problems, for example educational and food services that target only low-income persons in community settings; (c) access issues, including financial availability, ethnic (cultural) sensitivity, sensitivity to older women's issues, limited transportation, values, attitude barriers (for example, the shift from a philosophy of entitlements to one of charity and/or ageism); and (d) lack of mechanisms to assure quality (based in client satisfaction). These characteristics are often deterrents to the development of more comprehensive preventative services. Individually based services also tend not to support collective problem solving efforts of families, informal support networks, and other collectivities.

MOVING BEYOND DOMINANT POLICY AND SERVICE MODELS

Elders themselves have provided clear insights into their needs and the resources they need to address them in community-based long-term care, nursing facility and hospital social work, and hospice care (Cox & Dooley, 1996). They have told us that they prefer to stay in the community as long as possible and to have as much control as possible over their care processes (AARP, 1999; Polivka & Salmon, 2001). The value base of empowerment-practice supports social policy that incorporates a focus on human needs and promotion of social justice including the following components: "(a) a more egalitarian distribution of resources; (b) the elimination of racism, sexism, ageism, discrimination against homosexuals, discrimination against persons with disabilities and a positive approach to diversity; (c) a concern for environmental protection; (d) promoting self-determination (the fullest possible participation in decisions that have an impact on one's life, both personal and political); and (e) fosters self and community-actualization" (Cox & Parsons, 1994, p. 41). The mutual support theme of empowerment is operationalized through increased participation by clients in the policy process, self-help and mutual support activities, various co-op programs, community building work, social action, and related group-based activities as well as client and worker support for policy that assures critical resources. Empowerment models of practice call for the integration of personal and political issues and definitions of need come from clients as they participate in collective consciousness raising and action.

Policies and programs for older adults historically have been developed using a problem-based model. Problems are identified by experts. Policies are then designed based on the professional's definition of the problem. In contrast, policy formulation from a strengths perspective focuses initially on common human needs and barriers to meeting needs rather than on problem definition and analysis. From the strengths perspective needs are the gaps between existing conditions and some desirable condition. When using the strengths perspective, definitions of needs and barriers are viewed as negotiated. Central focus is on valuing the input of people who are disadvantaged in meeting their needs and on searching for resources to help support their efforts. Although many forces besides the needs of clients shape practice, programs, and policies, analysis of their needs and strengths is an appropriate starting place. The complexity of definitions of need is beyond the scope of this paper other than to stress the participation of often voiceless populations in the process of defining needs, strengths assessment, and defining strategies for meeting needs.

The most important differences between the strengths and more traditional approaches lies in the expansion of the role of those who are to be helped and the shift in the role of the helper. When using a strengths approach, the implication is no longer made that there is some expert who provides services, informs the public, and develops policy goals. Rather the role of helper is to give voice to clients perspectives, to help negotiate definitions and goals that include these perspectives, and to continue the focus on client as collaborator. Focusing on strengths does not mean that maladies are ignored. Rather resiliency, resources, promise, and dreams are to be given center stage. After all, if effective programs and policies are to be created, these elements will surely be key building blocks. A central social work task is to support the focus on client as collaborator throughout the process.

Policy makers are urged to focus on uncovering the methods used by the people most affected by the barriers to meeting their needs. It could be expected that the policy or program that builds on these insights will be ones that will be useful in helping other people facing the same barriers to also experience a successful outcome. The focus on searching the environment for opportunities and resources challenges social workers to identify and use informal and formal community resources more imaginatively.

In reflecting on the merits of using a strengths and/or empowerment perspective in policy and program development, it becomes apparent that both offer an antidote to victim blaming. Social workers using a strengths perspective are required to assertively look for strengths and resource in the clients, their families, and their environment. Empowerment-oriented practice on the other hand, stresses a participatory critical analysis (of the personal and political components of their common issues) and collective action to create desired policy. Overall, policy development efforts that build on the strengths approach clearly articulate the necessity of linking client group and policy formulation, point out that clients must be involved throughout the process, and stress the importance of focusing on client outcomes in evaluating effectiveness.

Examples of policy efforts that support participation and social justice related to older adults include: (a) the participatory guidelines that characterize the Older Americans Act (OAA), of 1965; (b) the Nursing Home Reform Law of the Omnibus Budget Reconciliation Act (PL 100-203) of 1986; and (c) multiple policy efforts to assure adequate income, health care, and housing resources as a right of citizenship, such as SSI (a form of guaranteed income). While all these policies fall short of their intended goals, assertive support of policy strategies that provide late life resources and allow opportunity for participation of elders and their families in the design of policy that governs the nature of social and health services, is key to effective practice.

DESIGN OF HEALTH AND SOCIAL SERVICES

At the service design and delivery level, strengths and empowerment-oriented practitioners and other advocates for effective services for older adults have designed programs that attempt to modify the medical model by calling for increased client participation in service design and implementation. Review of current literature suggests the following guidelines for programs to assure quality of service for frail elders: (a) living environments that support independence; (b) consumers determine timing and intensity of services; (c) understanding that disability and care arrangements are transitory; (d) environmental supports for aging in place (social and formal support network members); (e) effective care coordination; (f) ongoing assessments; and (g) monitoring of outcomes (Jenkins, 2000; Marek & Rantz, 2000).

Empowerment-oriented practitioners have suggested program characteristics that: (a) make possible transfer of knowledge and skills useful in self-care to clients, their families, and communities; (b) transfer expertise to clients that will increase their policy and program skills; (c) use intervention strategies that help clients understand their personal problems in a broader perspective as public issues; (d) provide training and motivation for clients to critically analyze their life situation and take part in consciousness-raising experiences; (e) emphasize cooperative and interdependent activities for accomplishment of mutual goals and provide respected societal roles for elders; (f) establish worker/client relationships that essentially represent partnerships, or are egalitarian in nature; (g) enable clients to develop or maintain personal support networks; (h) enable groups to take more active roles in decision making that affects their environment; (i) evaluate service provision in terms of its contributions to empowerment and social justice; and (j) inclusion of clients in the evaluation process (Cox & Parsons, 1994).

Clearly, these program characteristics are reflected in strengths and empowerment-oriented policy development at both the political/economy level and national social policy level as well as service design and delivery level. Current efforts that reflect increased participation as a goal of program design include the self-care movement in the health care arena, such as health education programs, growth of support group strategies among health-oriented programs such as the National Stroke Association and the National Cancer Association; the pilot testing of programs that provide elders and their families with money rather than service packages to enhance their role and range of strategies for providing elder care; and a variety of state and local efforts that require participation of clients in service design, delivery, and evaluation.

Communities are now beginning consider ways to develop "age sensitive community infrastructures" in planning for the coming elder boom. For example, use of universal housing codes that enhance accessibility in residential construction is receiving greater attention. State transportation departments are beginning to test visibility of road sign paint with 65-year-old drivers rather than 25-year-old males. It is clear that policies and programs that support older people's strengths so that they can remain an active and contributing part of the community, rather than narrowly focusing on traditional services, will be an important component of planning for the increasing number of older men and women. In sum, focus on compatibility rather than exclusive focus on risk factors, should be central to design of policy and services.

DIRECT PRACTICE INTERVENTIONS

Direct practice interventions (interventions that focus on work with individuals and small groups) built on empowerment-oriented and strengths-based approaches have been developed to address the needs of elderly care-receivers (Cox, 2001; Fast and Chapin, 2000). Both approaches focus on recognition of the strengths and potential of elders and their families as the struggle to meet the challenges of late life.

Empowerment-oriented practice models have been developed using by a combination of empowerment-practice theory and discovering successful strategies employed by elder care-receivers as they have met the challenges of increased disability. Studies focused on the perspectives of elderly care-receivers have suggested the need to address feelings about increased dependency, use of health and social services, communications with professional and personal caregivers, support networks, and quality of life (see for example, Cox & Dooley, 1996). Social work practitioners applying empowerment-oriented frameworks to work with frail elders have found small-group interventions to be especially effective. Empowerment-oriented small groups are multi-functional and include education, self-help, social support, and social action. These groups often engage older care-receivers in sharing coping strategies, analyzing their situation, including identifying their common struggles, engaging in mutual assistance and change efforts (Cox, 1999, 2001). Small-group empowerment strategies have also been applied to older workers' issues and other areas of concern to elders. One-on-one interventions have also utilized similar focal topics and a strategy of sharing knowledge gained from others in similar circumstances. Linkages to collective effort are also key to individual interventions.

The strengths approach provides techniques and tools to help social workers focus on and identify older adult's strengths and abilities as well as strengths of families, and communities (Fast and Chapin, 2000). Strengths assessment and goal planning is anchored tin the belief that people can survive and perhaps even thrive, despite difficult circumstances. Listening to people's stories, exploring alternative meanings of their stories, and affirming their successes, and future possibilities, is key. The social worker acts as collaborator, supports the elder's choices, and actively works to make sure adequate resources are available for the older adult.

GERONTOLOGICAL SOCIAL WORKERS

Social workers face a most demanding and challenging task as we struggle to develop gerontological practice for future decades. The development of empowerment-oriented and strengths approaches have increased the complexity of this challenge. Work to reframe practice issues so that needs of the older adult are normalized rather that pathologized, is central to this process. Social workers can take the lead in this reframing process.

Gerontological social workers who are following the philosophical, value, and practice directions of these empowerment and strengths approaches are faced with the demanding task of integrating the personal, interpersonal, and political components into their intervention strategies. For social workers who are committed to supporting client autonomy, an approach to policy practice and direct practice that is based on collaborating with consumers of service is critical. New strategies are required in order to achieve more egalitarian client/worker relationships and client participation in policy and program development.

Social workers and their clients must practice critical thinking in scrutinizing benefits and drawbacks of a variety of policy frameworks including ones that integrate a strengths perspective. Every conceptual tool serves to illuminate some aspects of a situation and blind us to others. For example, a primary concern relative to focus on strengths is that when need is downplayed, the sense of urgency may be lost. If we focus exclusively on the bereft older person, policy makers and taxpayers may be more likely to agree that these people are indeed deserving of expenditures of tax dollars, than if client strengths are also portrayed. Social workers and clients must find ways to present needs effectively so that sufficient resources are provided to make it possible to build on strengths.

Our commitment to help shape practice, policies, and programs that can provide resources, supports, and opportunities necessary for our clients is vital. Integration of empowerment strategies and the strengths approach into our practice initiatives can help emphasize our crucial role, and provide concrete guidance in how we should proceed in helping to craft effective policy and services. Efforts to see that client voices are heeded are fundamental to effective social work practice, as are our efforts to help clients to access necessary knowledge/information and skills where necessary. Once social workers begin to recognize that elders and their families can partner with them to craft more effective strategies, they may draw energy from working collaboratively to make whatever headway is possible.

CONCLUSION

In conclusion, empowerment and strengths-based approaches have begun to influence gerontological social work efforts. However, much remains to be done. Gerontological social workers must find ways to advance policy, program models, and direct practice interventions that represent the values of these movements. Resources must be found for advancement of theory and research necessary to demonstrate the value of these approaches.

REFERENCES

AARP. (1999). *A profile of older Americans*. Washington, DC: Author.

Breton, M. (1994). On the meaning of empowerment and empowerment-oriented practice. *Social Work with Groups 17* (3), 23-37.

Chapin, R. (in press). Building on the strengths of older women. In K. J. Peterson & A. Lieberman (Eds.), *Building on women's strengths: An agenda for the 21st century, revised edition*. Binghamton, NY: Haworth.

Cox, E. O. & Parsons, R. (1994). *Empowerment-oriented social work practice with the elderly*. Pacific Grove, CA.: Brooks/Cole Publishing.

Cox, E. O. (1999). Never too old: Empowerment–the concept and practice in work with frail elderly. In W. Shera & L. Wells (Eds.), *Empowerment Practice in Social Work: Developing Richer Conceptual Foundations* (pp. 178-195). Toronto, Canada: Canadian Scholars' Press Inc.

Cox, E. O. (in press). Empowerment-oriented practice applied to long term care. *Social Work in Long Term Care*.

Cox. E. O., & Dooley, A. (1996). Care-receivers' perceptions of their role in the care process. *Journal of Gerontological Social Work, 26* (1/2), 133-139.

Estes, C. (1999). Critical gerontology and the new political economy of aging. In M. Minkler & C. Estes (Eds.), *Critical Gerontology: Perspectives and Political and Moral Economy* (pp. 17-36). Amityville, NY: Baywood Publishing.

Fast, B. & Chapin, R. (1997). The strengths model and critical practice components. In. D. Saleebey (Ed.), *The Strengths Perspective in Social Work Practice*, (2nd ed., pp. 115-131). White Plains, NY: Longman Publishers.

Fast, B., & Chapin, R. (1997). The strengths model with older adults: Critical practice components. In D. Saleebey (Ed.), *The Strengths Perspective in Social Work Practice* (2nd ed., pp. 115-130). New York: Longman.

Fast, B., & Chapin, R. (2000). *Strengths-based case management for older adults*. Baltimore: Health Professions Press.

Lee, J.A.B. (2001). *The Empowerment Approach to Social Work Practice* (2nd ed.). New York: Columbia University Press.

Marek, K., & Ranz, M. (2000) Aging in place: A new model for long term care. *Nursing Administration Quarterly*, 24(3), 1-11.

McInnis-Dittrich, K. (1997). An empowerment-oriented mental health intervention with elderly Appalachian women: The women's club. *Journal of Women and Aging, 9* (1/2), 91-105.

Minkler, M. (2000). New challenges for gerontology. In E. M. Markson & L. A. Hollis-Sawyer (Eds.), *Intersections of Aging: Readings in Social Gerontology* (pp. 451-464). Los Angeles: Roxbury Publishing Company.

Perkins, K., & Tice, C. (1995). A strengths perspective in practice: Older people and mental health challenges. *Journal of Gerontological Social Work, 23* (3/4), 83-98.

Polivka, L., & Salmon, J. (2001). *Consumer-Directed Care: An Ethical, Empirical, and Practical Guide for State Policy Makers.* Florida Policy Exchange Center on Aging.

Saleebey, D. (1997). Introduction: Power in the people. In D. Saleebey (Ed.), *The Strengths Perspective in Social Work Practice* (2nd ed., pp. 3-19). White Plains, NY: Longman Publishers.

Towle, C. (1987). Common human needs. Silver Springs, MD: National Association of Social Workers. (Original work published 1945).

Tran, T.V., & Dhooper, S.S. (1997). Poverty, chronic stress, ethnicity and psychological distress among elderly Hispanics. *Journal of Gerontological Social Work, 27* (4), 3-19.

Weick, A., Rapp, C., Sullivan, W.P., & Kisthardt, W. (1989). A strengths perspective for social work practice. *Social Work, 37,* 350-354.

Weick, A. (1987). Reconceptualizing the philosophical perspective of social work. *Social Service Review, 61,* 218-230.

·Death and Dying
and the Social Work Role

Katharine R. Hobart, PhD, MSW, LCSW

SUMMARY. This article examines social work's expanding role in death and dying discussions with clients. In a variety of settings, particularly within health care, social workers are educating clients about advance directives as well as being involved in end-of-life medical decision making discussions. This article explores some of the issues that have been identified through research as of the part of this complicated process. The aging of our population and the continued advancement of medicine will only intensify the need for end-of-life medical decision making and increase the need for appropriate social work involvement. *[Article copies available for a fee from The Haworth Document Delivery Service: 1-800-HAWORTH. E-mail address: <getinfo@haworthpressinc.com> Website: <http://www.HaworthPress.com> © 2001 by The Haworth Press, Inc. All rights reserved.]*

KEYWORDS. End-of-life medical decision making, advance care planning, social work's expanding role, death and dying

INTRODUCTION

Social workers today, particularly gerontological social workers need to be well versed on issues related to death and dying. In a variety of settings including nursing homes, hospitals, hospices, home health

Katharine R. Hobart is Project Supervisor for the Care Receiver Efficacy Intervention at the Institute of Gerontology at the University of Denver Graduate School of Social Work, 2148 South High Street, Denver, CO 80208-2886.

[Haworth co-indexing entry note]: "Death and Dying and the Social Work Role." Hobart, Katharine R. Co-published simultaneously in *Journal of Gerontological Social Work* (The Haworth Social Work Practice Press, an imprint of The Haworth Press. Inc.) Vol. 36, No. (3/4), 2001, pp. 181-192; and: *Gerontological Social Work Practice: Issues, Challenges, and Potential* (ed: Enid Opal Cox, Elizabeth S. Kelchner, and Rosemary Chapin) The Haworth Social Work Practice Press, an imprint of The Haworth Press, Inc., 2001, pp. 181-192. Single or multiple copies of this article are available for a fee from The Haworth Document Delivery Service [1-800-HAWORTH, 9:00 a.m. - 5:00 p.m. (EST). E-mail address: getinfo@haworthpressinc.com].

care, and residential facilities, our clients are often at points in their lives where death and dying issues are particularly pertinent. As gerontological social workers, we need to be familiar with psychosocial aspects related to death and dying. But psychosocial knowledge cannot stand alone, it needs to be complemented by familiarity with death and dying policy including state and federal laws, as well as service delivery and overall best practice standards. Ultimately as individuals and as professionals, we must engage in self-exploration about what death and dying means to us.

DEATH AND DYING

The need to examine death and dying as social workers and as human beings exists due to dramatic changes in the last century in the way people die. While it is easy to romanticize the notion of dying quickly and at home, there is no going back. Nor would many of us wish to revert to a time when people died not just quickly, but relatively young and often from bacterial infections now controlled by antibiotics. The downside of living longer is living those latter years with chronic illnesses. And the real horror is the possibility of lingering those last days and months while hooked to ventilators, heart monitors, feeding tubes, and intravenous lines. The risk of such a death is high; up to 75% of people spend their last days in a hospital or medical center (NCHS, 1991). Advances in medical technology now challenge us as a nation to define quality end-of-life care and the right to deny heroic life-prolonging interventions.

Throughout history, humans have concerned themselves with what constitutes both a good life and a good death. Many of the world's religions treat dying as something to master as a means of ascension from the material world to a more spiritual realm. Tibetan and Egyptian cultures each have a *Book of the Dead.* Judaism has the mystical teachings of the *Kabbalah* and *Zohar.* Native American, Aborigine, African, and Latin American cultures all have varied shamanistic death rituals. According to Buddhist teachings, dying is another stage of living, a phase that holds the possibility of a worthy conclusion.

Weisman and Hackit introduced the concept of "appropriate death" (Steinberg & Youngner, 1998, p.13). An appropriate death is one in which the person is (1) pain free; (2) operates on as effective a level as possible; (3) recognizes and resolves residual conflicts; (4) satisfies realistically possible wishes; and (5) yields control to trusted others.

Ira Byock (1997) expanded the concept of good death to include growth at the end of life. These tasks of end-of-life growth arise from the stage theory models and include: (1) completing one's worldly affairs; (2) coming to closure in personal and professional relationships; (3) learning the meaning of one's life; (4) loving oneself and others; (5) accepting the finality of life; (6) sensing a new self and surrendering to the unknown. In many ways, the theoretical good death runs counter to our cultural mores. For many Americans, death remains an uncomfortable subject for both contemplation and conversation. Byock (1998) proposed that, since the baby boomers transformed the way Americans gave birth, they extend this effort toward changing the way we die. He writes, "We depathologized the concept of pregnancy and birth, saying it was not a disease but a part of healthy living. Similar things can be said about the end of life; we need not patholgize people in order to acknowledge their mortality. In fact people can become healthy in dying" (p. 69).

ADVANCE DIRECTIVE DOCUMENTS

The first step toward revolutionizing any cultural process is to define the ideal. Weisman, Hackit, and Byock have laid some of the groundwork for the "good death." The next step is to create the public policies that make these ideals reality. That is where advance directives fit in. Their enactment in a variety of different forms since 1976 (when California passed the first piece of living will legislation) gave people a tool for controlling end-of-life medical care. These documents allow patients to remain autonomous and to make medical decisions, even after they become incapacitated.

In the United States today, three types of advance directive documents are in use: living wills, durable powers of attorney for health care, and cardiopulmonary resuscitation directives. All three types of directives are written expressions of a person's wishes regarding medical treatment. These instructions are used only if the patient is unable to make his/her own health care decisions. Advance care planning is a newer concept, which acknowledges conversations, medical record notes, and other less formal forms of communications as being as valid as the more formal advance directive documents. Nationwide there exists much variation in advance directive documents. This is due to each state having their individual laws and different advance directive forms.

The use of advance directives was mandated federally with the passage of the Patient Self-Determination Act in 1991 (P.P. 101-508). The Patient Self-Determination Act (PSDA) had the straightforward purpose of increasing public knowledge about the use of advance directives as one of the means for making health care decisions. The PSDA required all health care institutions receiving any federal funding to educate their patients and the community about advance directives.

DEATH AND DYING LAWS

Although an important piece of our "Right to Die" legislation, the PSDA does not stand alone in regards to the ethos of our time, where as a country we are looking at how people die, end-of-life health care and the role of patient self-determination. These end-of-life decisions run the gamut from voluntary active euthanasia (when the physician administers the lethal dose at the patient's request), to physician-assisted suicide (when the physician prescribes medication that a patient takes to end his\her life), to sedation death (when the physician within the palliative care relationship ensures the patient is out of pain to the point of sedation), and even advance directive usage. The line of distinction between the above is a line between forgoing treatment and actively hastening death. Advance directives can be placed with these end-of-life decisions because although advance directives embody a broad range of possible forms, most advance directives are written to refuse treatment in the case of terminal illness or permanent unconsciousness.

Social workers dealing with clients facing death and dying issues need to be familiar with these different state and federal "Right to Die" laws and their implications. Due to the volatile nature of these laws, they must be reviewed regularly to guarantee the accuracy of information. Several websites are particularly helpful in getting updated information on the status of these laws (see Choice in Dying News, Partnership for Caring).

AFTERMATH OF THE PSDA

Although all of the above laws have effected our professional practice, the PSDA has had unique implications. Social workers in a variety of health care settings are educating clients and their families about advance directives. Therefore, it is appropriate to further analyze how the

PSDA and advance directives in particular have effected how clients approach death and dying.

Following the passage of the PSDA in 1991, the research on advance directives has been prolific. Multiple studies have examined the effectiveness of advance directives (e.g. Danis et al., 1991, Connors et al., 1995, Sansone & Phillips, 1995, and Ditto, Coppola, Klepac, Smucker & Bookwala, 1997). Other studies have examined interventions to increase advance directive understanding and usage (e.g., Hare & Nelson, 1991, Sachs, Stocking, & Miles, 1992, High, 1993, Paterson et al., 1993, Moore et al., 1994, Bailly & DePoy, 1995, and Soskis, 1999). Finally, a handful of studies have examined ethnic variation in advance directive usage (e.g., Carrese & Rhodes, 1995, Blackhall, Murphy, Frank, Michel & Azen, 1995, and Hanson & Rodgman, 1996). The majority of this research has been quasi-experimental, relatively large, and medically based studies.

The synthesis of this research creates a somewhat dismal advance directive picture. The picture is one of people claiming they are interested in advance directive usage (Emanuel et al., 1991) and yet overall patterns of usage remain low (only 10 to 25% of Americans have documented their end-of-life choices, [U.S. General Accounting Office, 1995]). This picture also casts doubt on the usefulness of substituted judgment, since advance directive documents even when present are often not being used to guide medical treatment (e.g., Danis et al., 1991, Connors et al., 1995, and Ditto et al., 1997). The research has also indicated that knowledge of advance directives is associated with race, education, and in some studies even gender (e.g., High, 1993, Paterson et al., 1993, Moore et al., 1994, and Hanson & Rodgman, 1996). The combined multicultural research adds to this picture with the notion that ethnicity has significant impact on patients' choices regarding advance directive usage (e.g., Carrese & Rhodes, 1995, Blackhall et al., 1995, and Hanson & Rodgman, 1996).

AN ETHNOGRAPHIC VIEW

In response to the above research, an ethnographic study was done in which twelve culturally and ethnically mixed older women shared their in-depth perspectives on advance directive usage and end-of-life medical decision making (Hobart, 2001). This study was built on the premise that "Eliciting healthcare wishes is often more art than science . . ."

(Eleazer et al., 1996), and that an ethnography would allow some of the more artful sides of advance directive usage to emerge.

The results of this ethnography indicated that these women did not believe in life extension (i.e., being kept alive on a "machine"), and that they did believe in using advance directive documents. A consensus among a diverse group, albeit small in numbers is important. Some women first heard of advance directives during the interview; some had advance directives for years. Nevertheless, all judged these documents to be important. There were a myriad of factors that defined how these women made end-of-life medical decisions and how they used advance directive documents. These factors included gender, ethnicity, independence, relationships, religion/spirituality, thoughts on death, outside influences, and the political world with its oppressive influences. Visually, these factors along with their subheadings and their relationships are displayed in Figure 1.

These women as indicated in the cognitive map, brought a variety of factors into the end-of-life medical decision-making process. They acknowledged this was not a simple process, in fact there was great complexity and depth in approaching advance directive usage and end-of-life medical decision making. The participants within this study also indicated that there were gaps between the technical legal aspects of the advance directive tools and the emotional issues related to death and dying. Social workers have the potential to play an important role in filling this gap.

SOCIAL WORK ROLE

What many of these women identified as missing were the psychosocial aspects, like being in a safe environment to think about and discuss their own death while not in a moment of health care crisis. They also wanted guidance on how to include family members in discussions about how they hoped to die. As a society, we appear to have ignored the psychosocial aspects of this process, which involve discussing difficult issues like dying by skipping right to the legal aspects of filling out forms. Social workers have the training and expertise to identify these psychosocial aspects and to provide opportunities to address them.

Social workers also bring their expertise regarding empowerment and ownership of issues to this process. The health-care community has yet to embrace the idea that the responsibilities of advance care planning belong to each individual person. There appears to be debate over

FIGURE 1

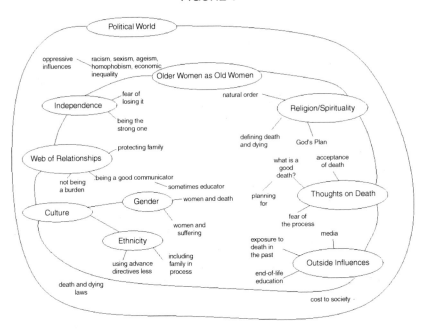

which profession should educate patients about end-of-life medical decision making: physicians, nurses, attorneys, religious leaders, social workers. Each of these professions probably has a role, although social workers have potential to play a unique role by empowering patients to make these decisions for themselves. Social workers should support efforts to provide individuals with culturally appropriate counseling and adequate information to make these advance care planning decisions prior to immediate need for decisions.

Along with addressing the psychosocial gap and empowering clients to make their own end-of-life decisions, social workers have other roles to fill. Our profession should continue to offer academic courses that explore end-of-life issues and provide student placement options that give experience in this area of work. The multidisciplinary role of end-of-life care must also be stressed through our educational process and work opportunities. As researchers, we need to be willing to engage in these multidisciplinary topics and acknowledge our role in this process. We need to critique what we feel is wrong or not working.

Overall, the role of social work in the advance directive discussion is vital, as well as an important fit with social work values and ethics. Our educational and supportive counseling provides an important component of this process. Social workers offer unique skills in an expanded view of advance care planning. As a profession we have the skills to acknowledge advance care planning as a process as well as recognizing the need for people to make these decisions within the context of their lives. Also as individuals and as a profession, we need to be willing to play roles in advance care planning discussions with individuals, families, groups, organizations, and at the policy level.

POTENTIAL SOLUTIONS

Multiple real or potential solutions to improve our current system of end-of-life medical decision making and advance directive usage can be identified. Some of the potential solutions follow.

One way to eliminate the confusion between these different advance directive documents and their cumbersome names is to combine the forms into one document. Some states have already done so. One such state, Minnesota, passed advance directive legislation in 1998, to create one document called a Healthcare Directive, which is divided into two parts. In Part 1, a patient appoints a Healthcare Agent who will make healthcare decisions should the patient become incapacitated. This part also includes a section regarding burial and cremation. Part 2 is called the Healthcare Instructions (formerly referred to as the living will). One component of this part allows patients to discuss their feelings and make statements regarding medical treatments under various specifically listed health care scenarios (*Choice in Dying News,* 2000, pp. 2-4).

Other states are beginning to reassess their piecemeal legislation and to consider alternative ways to make combined and comprehensive statutes that would cover advance directives, surrogate consent, emergency medical services, and even anatomical gifts. The goal of these combined or comprehensive acts is to recognize a single combined advance directive and to simplify the system for consumers. In August 1993, the National Conference of Commissioners on Uniform State Law adopted a comprehensive model act called the Uniform Healthcare Decisions Act, which was endorsed by the American Bar Association in early 1994. Other states that have gone to combined or comprehensive acts include Kentucky, New Jersey, Connecticut, Virginia, Florida, Arizona, and Maryland (*American Bar Association,* 2000, pp. 1-4).

These state trends represent a move in the right direction by reducing the number of documents and simplifying and personalizing the process (e.g., including a discussion of general feelings as a component of the health care directive). Compared to older advance directive forms, which emphasize the legal, business-like aspects of dying, these new Healthcare Directives acknowledge some of the emotional and ethical complexities inherent in this process.

Value histories also acknowledge the emotional and ethical complexities of this process and have been effective among people who have chosen to use them. A variety of different values histories are available, from extended forms to abbreviated one-page formats. All of them allow an individual person to emerge within these discussions rather than simply a set of medical paradigms.

There are many other workbooks and tools designed to assist with advance care planning. All of them acknowledge the personal values inherent within this complicated process. Many of the documents are culturally neutral enough to be used by ethnic group members uncomfortable discussing their own death. Most of these tools try to simplify the process for consumers and make it something that people feel they can handle.

Federal legislation could also play a role in humanizing the advance care planning process. An example of such a bill is the Advance Care Planning and Compassionate Care Act of 1997, a piece of national legislation sponsored by U.S. Senators Jay Rockefeller (D-WV) and Susan Collins (R-ME).

The legislation includes the following provisions:

1. An advance directive valid in one state will be valid in other states, as long as there is no conflict in the laws.
2. Every Medicare beneficiary receiving care under Part A will be entitled to discuss end-of-life issues with a trained professional.
3. A national telephone hotline will be instituted to provide the latest information about where and how to get good end-of-life care.
4. Medical facilities will be required to place any existing directives in the front of a patient's chart so that the doctors and nurses can see them easily.
5. The Secretary of Health and Human Services will be directed to gather information and data and then advise Congress on an approach to end-of-life decision making for Medicare beneficiaries.
6. Medicare's drug benefits will be expanded to include non-intravenous medications for the relief of chronic pain in patients with a life-threatening illness (Choice in Dying News, 2000).

Such a bill has the potential to make the advance care planning process simpler and more useable. The second provision alone, entitling all Medicare beneficiaries to an end-of-life discussion with a trained professional, if done in a culturally and ethnically sensitive manner, could change advance directive usage dramatically within this country. A bill such as this could fill many of the gaps that exist within the current advance care planning process.

Along with the passage of state and federal legislation and the creation of more effective advance directive tools, other potential solutions could include: statewide training projects, television and radio coverage, employee educational projects, individual and group education in the health-care setting, and increased activity of grassroots organizations both nationally and locally. All these measures would serve to heighten the general population's acceptance and awareness of old age, death, and dying, and to increase participation in advance care planning. Taken together, these different elements could change how Americans make end-of-life medical decisions. The majority of these potential solutions have a role for social work, both as direct and in-direct practitioners.

CONCLUSION

The time has come for Americans to acknowledge that end-of-life medical decision making is an important issue and it must be addressed proactively. Ignoring, denying, or avoiding issues related to death and dying will not cause them to go away. The aging of our population and the continued advancement of medicine will only intensify the importance of these medical decisions. The need for an expanding social work role with death and dying issues is evident.

As social workers, we bring multiple skills to these issues. Death remains a challenging subject for many of our clients and their families to discuss. Social workers have the psychosocial skills to assist and facilitate end-of-life care discussions between clients and their families. Social workers also have the ability to help place these end-of-life discussions into the framework of an ongoing process. When advance care planning is viewed as a process, people have the ability to modify and develop their end-of-life care decisions within the context of their changing lives. The concept of educating and empowering clients to make these end-of-life care decisions for themselves prior to moments of medical crisis is a particularly good fit with social work values.

Social workers have other end-of-life care roles as academicians, teachers and researchers. As advocates, social workers have a political role by being involved and encouraging passage of appropriate state and federal legislation as well as grassroots activities. It is time for us as individuals and as social workers to see our current system for what it is.

Perkins (2000) aptly described this system when he wrote, "Patients fear losing their lives to the medical system. They dread being trapped in insensitive medical institutions, tethered to inhumane machines, robbed of personal privacy and subjected to accompanying indignities" (p. 1228). It is possible through education, open discussion, and empowerment that people can reclaim the process of dying as their own.

REFERENCES

American Bar Association. (2000). [On-line]. Available: <www.abnet.org/elderly/psda.html.>

Bailly, D. J., & DePoy, E. (1995). Older people's responses to education about advance directives. *Health and Social Work, 20,* 223-228.

Blackhall, L. J., Murphy, S. T., Frank, G., Michel, V. & Azen, S. (1995). Ethnicity and attitudes toward patient autonomy. *Journal of the American Medical Association, 274,* 820-825.

Byock, I. (1997). *Dying well: Peace and possibilities at the end of life.* New York: Riverhead Books.

Byock, I. (1998, March-April). Mastering the natural art of dying. *Utne Reader,* 68-72.

Carrese, J. A., & Rhodes, L. A. (1995). Western bioethics on the Navajo reservation: Benefit or harm? *Journal of the American Medical Association, 274,* 826-829.

Choice in dying news. (2000). [On-line]. Available: <www.choices.org/notes.htm>.

Connors, A. F., Teno, J. M., Licks, S., Lynn, J., Wenger, N., Phillips, R. S., O'Connor, M. A., Murphy, D. P., Fulkerson, W. J., Desbiens, N., & Knaus, W. A. (for the SUPPORT investigators). (1995). A controlled trial to improve care for seriously ill hospitalized patients: The study to understand prognoses and preferences for outcomes and risks of treatments (SUPPORT). *Journal of the American Medical Association, 274,* 1591-1598.

Danis, M., Southerland, L. I., Garrett, J. M., Smith, J. L., Hielema, F., Pickard, C. G., Egner, D. M., & Patrick, D. L. (1991). A Prospective study of advance directives for life-sustaining care. *New England Journal of Medicine, 324,* 882-888.

Ditto, P. H., Coppola, K. M., Klepac, L. M., Smucker, W. D., & Bookwala, J. (1997, November). *Perceived vs. actual benefits of advance directive completion.* Poster session presented at the annual meeting of the Gerontological Society of America, Cincinnati, OH.

Eleazer, G. P., Hornung, C. A., & Egbert, C. B. (1996). The relationship between ethnicity and advance directives in a frail older population. *Journal of the American Geriatric Society, 44,* 899-903.

Emanuel, L. L., Barry, M. J., Stoeckle, J. D., Ettelson, L. M., & Emanuel, E. J. (1991). Advance directives for medical care–a case for greater use. *The New England Journal of Medicine, 324,* 889-895.

Hanson, L. C., & Rodgman, E. (1996). The use of living wills at the end of life: A national study. *Archives of Internal Medicine, 156:9,* 1018-1022.

Hare, J., & Nelson, C. (1991). Will outpatients complete living wills? *Journal of general internal medicine, 6,* 41-46.

High, D. M. (1993). Advance directives and the elderly: A study of intervention strategies to increase usage. *The Gerontologist, 33,* 342-349.

Hobart, K. R. (2001). Older women's perspectives on end-of-life medical decision making and advance directive usage. (Doctoral dissertation, University of Denver, 2001).

Moore, K. A., Danks, J. H., Ditto, P. H., Druley, J. A., Townsend, A., & Smucker, W. D. (1994). Elderly outpatients' understanding of a physician-initiated advance directive discussion. *Archives of Family Medicine, 3,* 1057-1063.

National Center for Health Statistics (NCHS). (1991). *Vital statistics of the United States, 1988.* Hyattsville, MD.: Public Health Service. II (A): 308.

Partnership for Caring. (2001). [On-line]. Available: www.partnershipforcaring.org

Patient Self-Determination Act of 1990. (1990). Pub. L. No. 101-508, section 4206, 4751 of the Omnibus Reconciliation Act of 1990.

Patterson, S. L., Baker, M., & Maeck, J. P. (1993). Durable powers of attorney: Issues of gender and healthcare decision making. *Journal of Gerontological Social Worker, 21,* 161-177.

Perkins, H. S. (2000). *Chest, 117/5,* 1228-1231.

Sachs, G. A., Stocking, C. B., & Miles, S. H. (1992). Empowerment of the older patient? A randomized, controlled trial to increase discussion and use of advance directives. *Journal of the American Geriatrics Society, 40,* 269-273.

Sansone, P., & Phillips, S. M. (1995). Advance directives for elderly people: Worthwhile cause or wasted effort? *Social Work, 40,* 397-401.

Soskis, C. (1997). End-of-life decisions in the home care setting. *Social Work in Healthcare, 25,* 107-116.

Steinberg, M., & Younger, S. (1998). *End-of-life decisions: A psychosocial perspective.* Washington, D. C.: American Psychiatric Press, Inc.

U.S. General Accounting office. (1995). Patient Self-Determination Act: Providers offer information on advance directives but effectiveness uncertain. Washington, D. C.: U.S. Government Printing Office.

Index

Numbers followed by "f" indicate figures; "t" following a page number indicates tabular material.

193